HOW TO WRITE AN EXCELLENT PERSONAL STATEMENT

An Illustrated Guide

on Writing a University or College Admissions Essay

HOW TO WRITE AN EXCELLENT PERSONAL STATEMENT

An Illustrated Guide

on Writing a University or College Admissions Essay

Written by Quincy Washington

Illustrated by M. W. K. Asror

STORYBUSH BOOKS

StoryBush Books

www.storybush.com
www.placecoach.co.uk

Contents

Contents

Contents

Contents

Contents

Dedicated to those who
seek to harness their potential.

PLACECOACH

About PlaceCoach

PlaceCoach is the trusted leader in university applications and career support. We have helped thousands of students from around the world in their applications to Harvard, Oxford, Cambridge, Yale, MIT, LSE, Princeton and many of the world's top universities.

On one of our flagship packages, we will perfect your personal statement, statement of purpose, motivation letter, recommendation letter, cover letter, CV, resume or other application documents. Having assisted students from around the world, we will help you to secure places at prestigious universities and top companies. We also offer additional services, such as admissions test preparation for university degrees, mock university interviews and mock job interviews, which we can conduct remotely via Zoom or in person. We are dedicated to guiding you along your academic and professional journey. Your success is our top priority and you can rest assured that we will do our best to maximise your chances of securing a place at your dream university or job.

Reach out to us on our various platforms:

Website: www.placecoach.co.uk
E-mail: help@placecoach.co.uk
Instagram: @placecoach
Twitter: @placecoach
Facebook: @placecoach

HOW TO
WRITE
AN EXCELLENT
PERSONAL
STATEMENT

About This Book

How to Write an Excellent Personal Statement is written by Quincy Washington — a law graduate from the London School of Economics and founder of PlaceCoach.

As you read through this book, the advice given will allow you to sharpen your statement regardless of what stage you are at in the writing process. Crafting an excellent personal statement is no mean feat, and this is your chance to showcase yourself in the best light. This process ought to be given your full attention, dedication and care to get it right, once and for all.

HOW TO
WRITE
AN EXCELLENT
PERSONAL
STATEMENT
1x

Audiobook

To listen to the audiobook version of *How to Write an Excellent Personal Statement*, please scan the code below with your mobile device or visit **placecoach.co.uk/audiobook**.

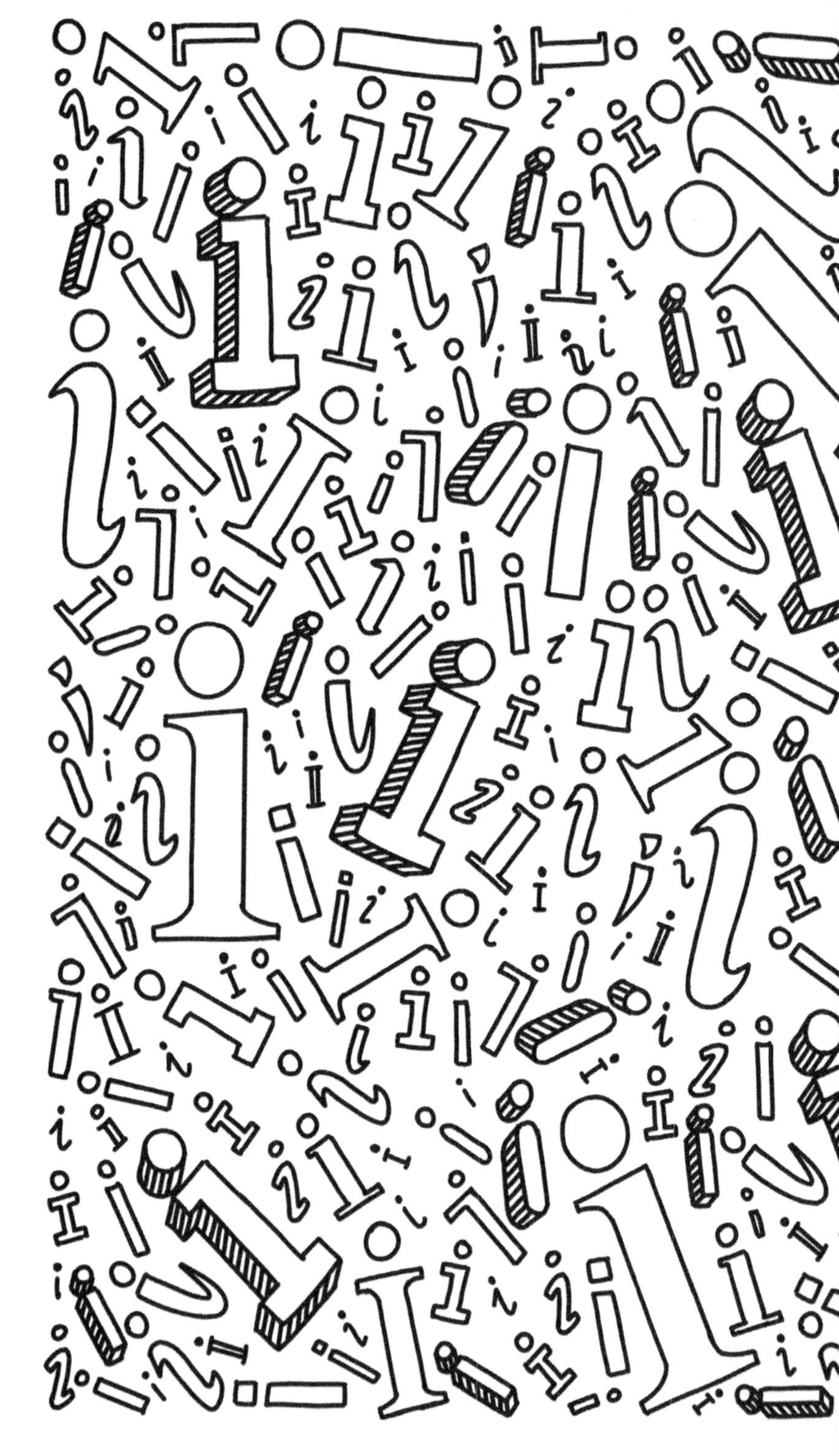

i

Introduction

It is no secret that writing a personal statement is an exercise in self-promotion, and while singing your own praises may not be your forte, you are going to need to write one if you want to bag yourself a spot on the course that you have been dreaming about. If you are going to write it, it may as well be great, right? In this book, you will gain insights into how to do exactly that as I guide you along step-by-step on how to write an excellent personal statement.

What is a Personal Statement?

In the simplest of terms, a personal statement is a short document that gives a university, college or other institution the chance to really get to know who you are — your story, your plans, your challenges, your achievements, your insights and your interests. Practically every university requires one, or something similar or equivalent, such as a statement of purpose, motivation letter, or supplemental essay. So it is pretty clear that this short document can change your life for the better.

Well, that is, if you manage to get it right.

Writing, in and of itself, is a skill, and one that is hard to master, even for the most intelligent and talented of students. This is why it helps to get assistance to fine-tune your writing professionally, so that you are not let down or held back by areas of deficiency in your application that could easily have been ironed out. Equally, you should be mindful of the fact that a personal statement is one of many ingredients that play a role in your application's overall success. Your personal statement, academic record, admissions tests and interview performance are each like eggs, flour, butter and sugar in a cake. Each of them contributes to varying degrees within your entire application.

Just as having too many eggs and no flour would make a pretty awful cake, you should look at your application as a mixture of different components that each serve to make an excellent impression with the ultimate goal of securing your admission to your chosen university. A phenomenal personal statement can save an otherwise mediocre application, but if you really want to seal the deal, it is prudent to put just as much effort into the other areas too — do not forget that.

How to Use This Book

I have divided this book into the ten-step, tried-and-tested process that I have used to help thousands of students apply and gain entry to top universities such as Oxford, Cambridge, Harvard, LSE, MIT, Yale, Imperial and Princeton. This book will serve as a robust framework that you can further flesh out for your personal statement or other college admissions essay. There are various ways to write a personal statement, and this book is designed specifically for those looking to put their ideas into a format that can be further built upon and developed. As you read through this book, the advice given will allow you to sharpen your personal statement regardless of what stage you are at. Feel free to refer back to various chapters of the book that you may need to refresh yourself on from time to time. There are three key stages that you will need to follow when creating a personal statement:

Stage A: Planning

Stage B: Writing

Stage C: Refining

To begin with, I will cover Stage A: Planning, with three chapters:

Chapter One: **Research**

Chapter Two: **Requirements**

Chapter Three: **Narrative**

After that, you will get insights into the writing process in Stage B, where I will cover the following chapters:

Chapter Four: **Structure I**

Chapter Five: **Structure II**

Chapter Six: **Reflection**

Chapter Seven: **Coherence**

Finally, in Stage C, the refining process, I will outline the final checks that you need to make to sharpen your draft in the three remaining chapters:

Chapter Eight: **Feedback**

Chapter Nine: **Diligence**

Chapter Ten: **Completion**

Throughout the book, you will see real-life examples from students anytime that a profile icon appears, such as this:

In addition, whenever you see a squiggly line with a star in the margin, these are 'Author's Highlights,' which are specific points that I deem particularly important. You will also find sections at the end of each chapter where you can contribute your own information to this book, where you see the pencil icon (✏). I am confident that you will benefit enormously from taking this chance to maximise the full scope of your potential in this very important stage of your life, so I hope that you come along for the ride.

Feel free to reach out at **www.placecoach.co.uk**, if you need further assistance — it would be great to hear from you!

And with that said, let's get into the first chapter of this book.

RESEARCH
REQUIREMENTS
NARRATIVE

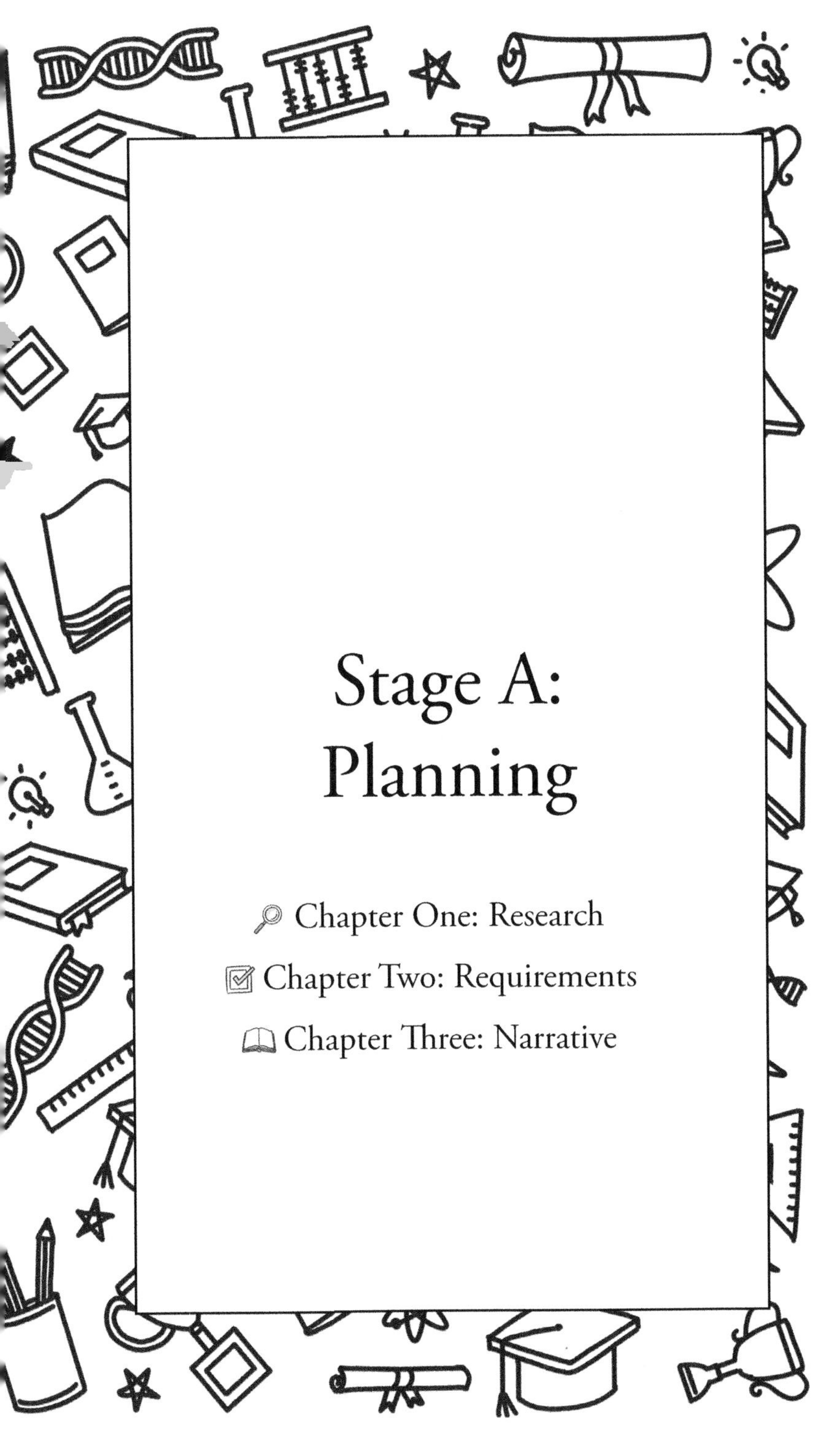

Stage A: Planning

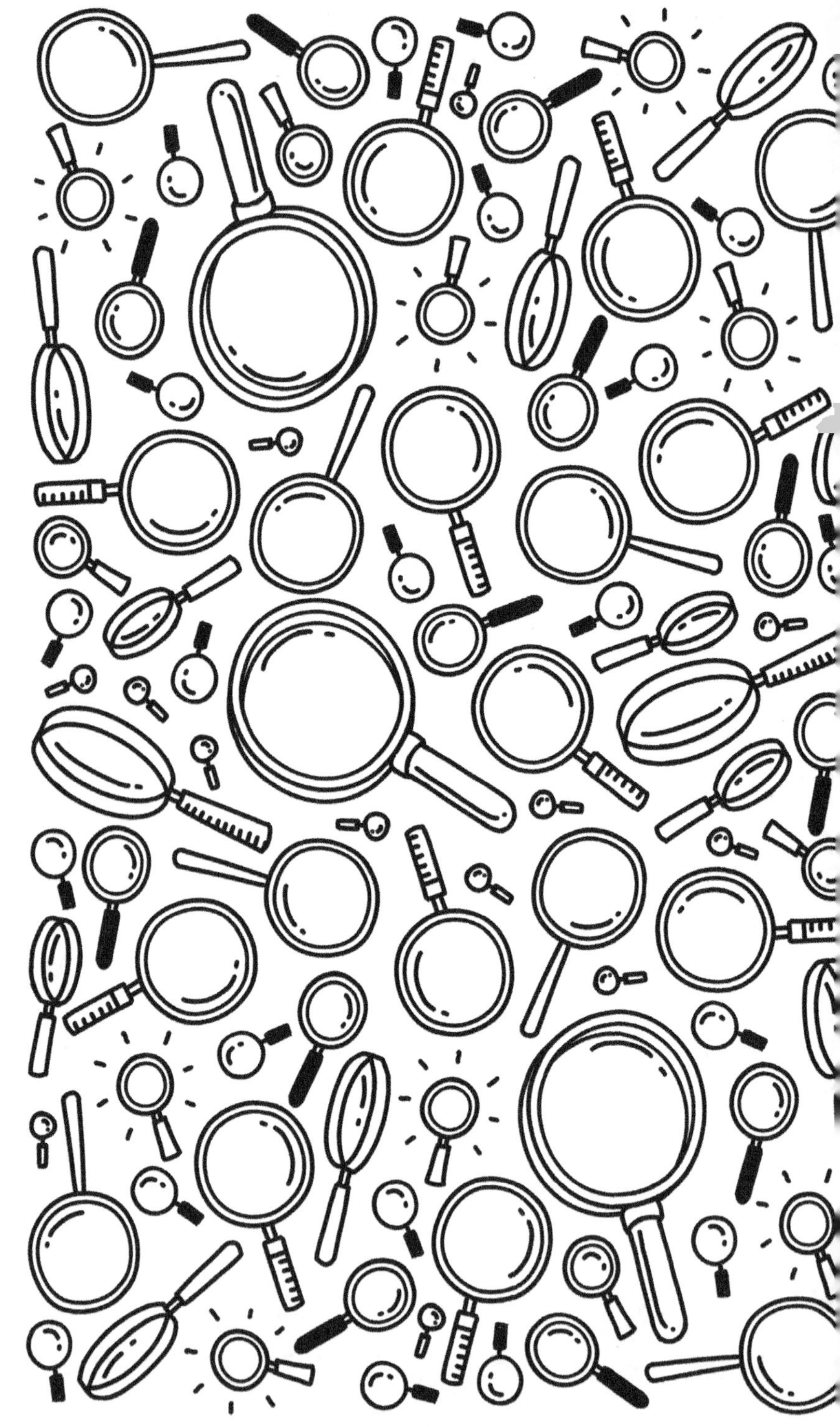

Chapter One: Research

Research. Research. Research. Whatever you do, do not skip this vital step. Looking into the course itself is an essential part of the writing process because it allows you to laser in on the specific elements of the programme that you are interested in. By being aware of any specific aspects of the course that you are applying to, you reduce the chances of getting off on the wrong foot or missing crucial information that you ought to have known. Whether you are applying as an undergraduate or postgraduate student, treat the university's programme page as your road map as you embark on the planning process and the writing process, and continue to refer back to the resources that you find there as you go along.

When it comes to writing a personal statement or college admissions essay, being curious, insightful and reflective is essential in thinking about where to start. You need to carefully consider why you want to study your course, and do so in a manner that goes beyond the generic and clichéd answers of 'wanting to make a difference' or because you believe it is your 'calling.' In essence, you need to be curious about the course in order to learn more about what it involves, but equally curious about yourself, so that you can justify why you would be the ideal student to join the programme. If you are applying to one university in particular, you should start to think about what makes that university so special or ideal for your short-term and long-term goals. The best way to find out what those reasons may be is by taking the time to research the curriculum of your programme, who will be teaching you, and what opportunities would be available to you, were you to be admitted into your chosen programme.

Like most people, admissions tutors respond well to authenticity, and the best way to be authentic is to have a genuine interest in the course that you are applying to. How will you know if you will truly thrive on your chosen course if you have not taken the time to actually learn about what it would entail? Remember, the people on the other end do not know you from Adam. That thought can be scary. You are probably an intelligent and marvellous person to be around, and if they got to know you in person, they would let you in without question. But, sadly, unless you are best friends with those in charge of the college or university admissions process, the best way to convey your abilities and passion will undoubtedly be through your personal statement. So use this as an opportunity to showcase your best self, and critically, to do so authentically by doing your research first.

Remember also that you are trying to be as persuasive as possible, and taking shortcuts will undoubtedly show in your writing. Do not be shy about selling yourself, as this is your opportunity to highlight the defining points of your journey and the key pillars of your character.

It will pay off, in the end, to put in the legwork before you begin writing. By ensuring that you have a full understanding of your course, you can more confidently start writing your personal statement, and it will provide greater context as you go along. Imagine if you were asked to write a review of a movie, but had not bothered to watch it? With great effort, you could probably pull it off, but any seasoned cinema lover would smell a rat, wouldn't they?

Why?

Well, because you would not have much of any real substance to contribute, would you? Your personal statement is no different. Do the research first, before you even put pen to paper, so that you have the right insights and material to use as your arsenal for the writing process.

Your first port of call is your university's programme page, where you will find lots of useful information such as:

- Your programme structure, curriculum and modules.
- The minimum academic entry requirements for your course.
- General admissions statistics.
- Application guidelines.
- Information about deadlines.
- Fees and funding.
- Information about members of the faculty.
- Preliminary reading.

For various reasons, getting to grips with this information is crucial and can save you a lot of hassle further down the line.

Programme Structure

Let's say that you are hoping to study for a master's degree in law at a top university. Before writing your personal statement, it might be really important that you read the programme structure with a fine-toothed comb, as quite often there are predefined specialisms, such as commercial law, criminal law or public law, that can restrain or limit the specific modules that you are allowed to take, or even the number of modules. If you had not taken the time to read the programme structure, you might have erroneously assumed that two modules could be taken, and consequently, write about this in your statement — a big no-no for any admissions tutor.

Academic Entry Requirements

Knowing the academic entry requirements and admissions statistics — both as an undergraduate and postgraduate student — will allow you to gauge where you stand, and what your chances are of actually gaining admission. However, as a little warning, it is equally important not to get too obsessed with these numbers, because you never know whether you will get lucky, even when the odds may seem stacked against you. As the saying goes, 'you'll never know until you try.'

Deadlines

Deadlines are clearly important considerations too, as they will guide and direct the planning, writing and refining process, and you do not want to be left high and dry by handing in an undeniably remarkable personal statement too late. If you have the luxury of time, I strongly recommend that you submit your application in the early round, rather than leaving it till the last minute. In a case where you submit it too late, even if you really are the 'pick of the crop,' if the course is nearly full and there is just one space left, you will have to compete with several other candidates, but for fewer places. So start early.

Fees and Funding

Now, we all know that the cost of educating oneself can often be the sting in the tail of an otherwise worthwhile undertaking.

But remember that education is fundamentally an investment, and one that will hopefully pay off substantially for you in the future. When doing your research, you should also look out for opportunities for scholarships, and be aware that these applications may have different deadlines from the official application and other formats of entry through scholarship-focussed statements.

Faculty Members and Preliminary Reading

Finally, one of the best ways to gain an upper hand during the research stage of your application is to read about members of your faculty. Have a look at any research that your potential teachers and professors have undertaken. Read the books and articles that they have written, and look for media appearances, or any other projects that you find illuminating about them. The reason why doing this extra reading can prove invaluable to your application is because it shows that you have gone the extra mile to learn about the professors who might be teaching you one day. And let's be honest, who doesn't respond well to someone taking an interest in their most cherished intellectual creations? Use that to your advantage and try to imagine yourself at your desired university, and write in such a manner that makes the admissions tutor come on board too. Remember that specificity and having a 'personal touch' makes all of the difference when it comes to personal statements. Admissions tutors are highly experienced at recognising those who genuinely want to be on their programme over those just trying their luck. So do not fall into the trap of skipping the research stage.

The Opportunity of a Lifetime

Always keep in mind that applying to a university is ultimately a competition. While many will apply, not everyone can earn that coveted spot. You may not like to think of it that way, because it can make the task all the more daunting. But it is the truth. Not everyone can get a place, and that is the reason why you are judged on so many parameters. Think about it — if your acceptance was guaranteed, there would be no need for examinations, admissions tests, interviews and personal statements. You would simply sign up and start your course. No fuss. Job done.

But, alas, that is not how it works, is it? And it is certainly not the case for the most rigorous degrees and the most competitive universities. Doing your research helps you to know what you are working with, what you are up against, what you will need to do in order to prepare for your application, and perhaps most importantly, what you bring to the table. This is the opportunity of a lifetime, so give this application 100% of your effort and focus. If and when you get in, the relief and feeling of jubilation that you will gain from achieving your dreams will make all of the effort worth it. So make your personal success your north star, and keep going! You will get there in the end.

That's all for this chapter.

In the next chapter, you will learn about another crucial aspect of the planning stage of '*How to Write an Excellent Personal Statement*, which is knowing your requirements. If you are ready to learn and get this right once and for all, then come along to the next chapter of this book.

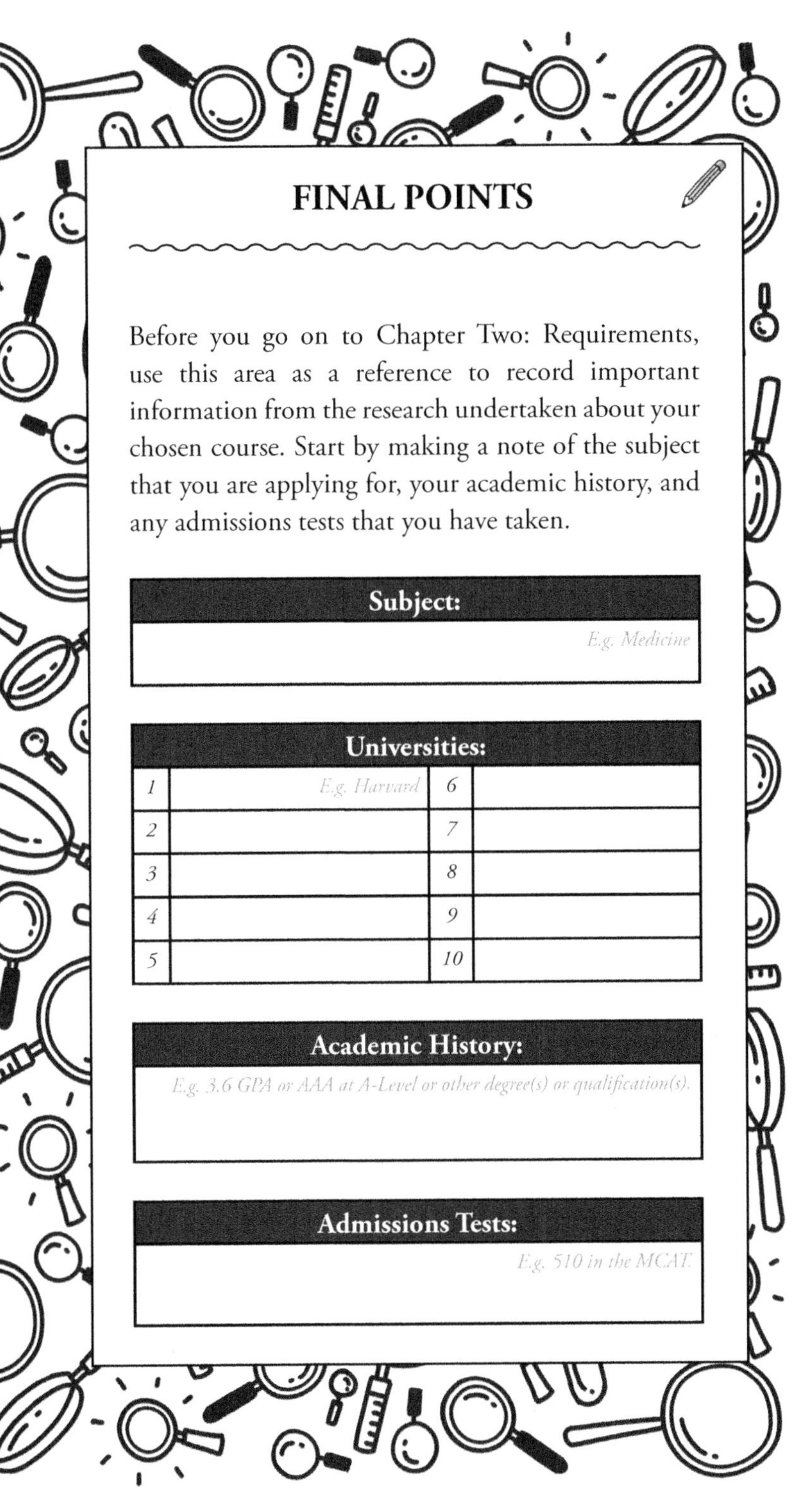

FINAL POINTS

Before you go on to Chapter Two: Requirements, use this area as a reference to record important information from the research undertaken about your chosen course. Start by making a note of the subject that you are applying for, your academic history, and any admissions tests that you have taken.

Subject:
E.g. Medicine

Universities:			
1	*E.g. Harvard*	*6*	
2		*7*	
3		*8*	
4		*9*	
5		*10*	

Academic History:
E.g. 3.6 GPA or AAA at A-Level or other degree(s) or qualification(s).

Admissions Tests:
E.g. 510 in the MCAT.

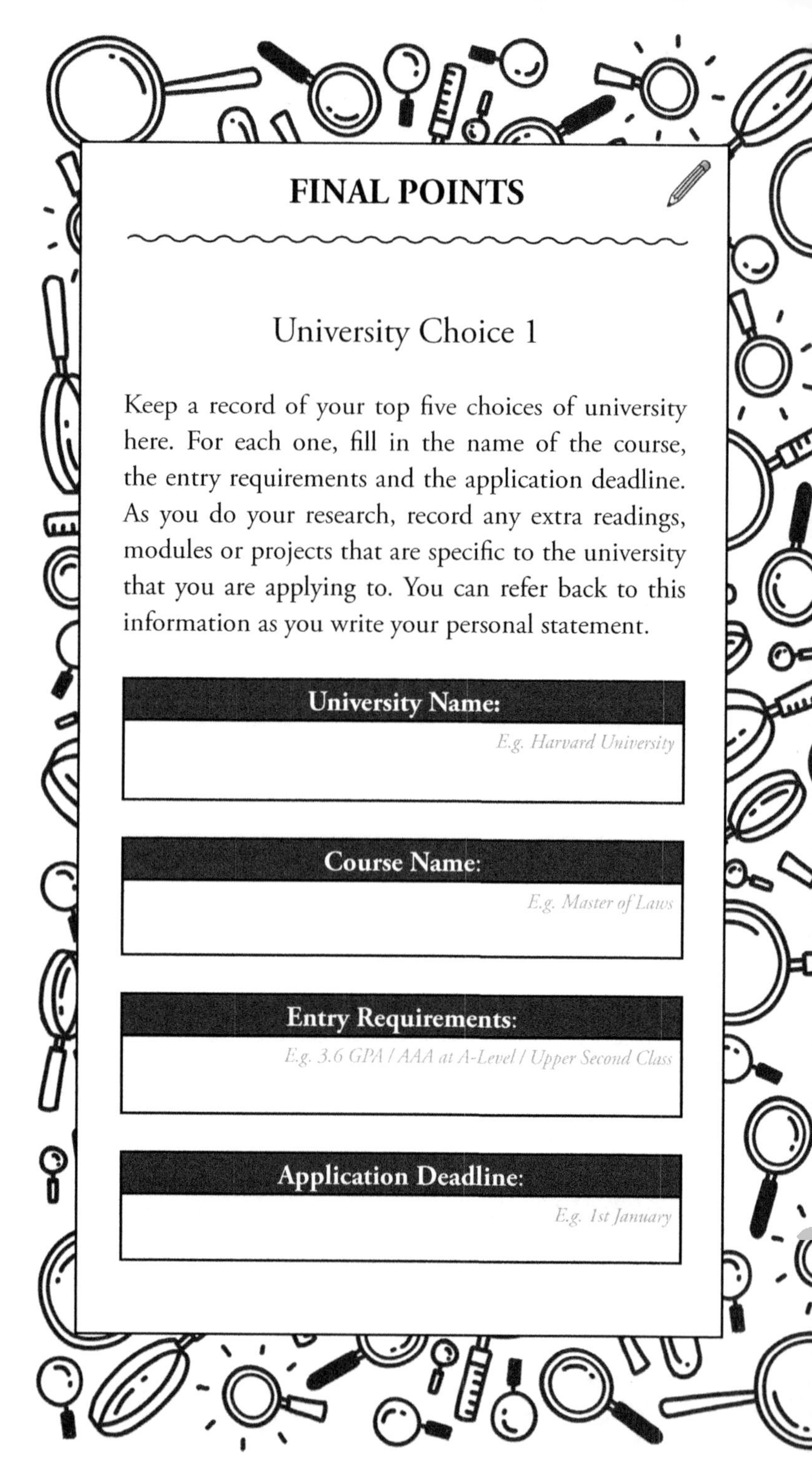

FINAL POINTS

University Choice 1

Keep a record of your top five choices of university here. For each one, fill in the name of the course, the entry requirements and the application deadline. As you do your research, record any extra readings, modules or projects that are specific to the university that you are applying to. You can refer back to this information as you write your personal statement.

University Name:

E.g. Harvard University

Course Name:

E.g. Master of Laws

Entry Requirements:

E.g. 3.6 GPA / AAA at A-Level / Upper Second Class

Application Deadline:

E.g. 1st January

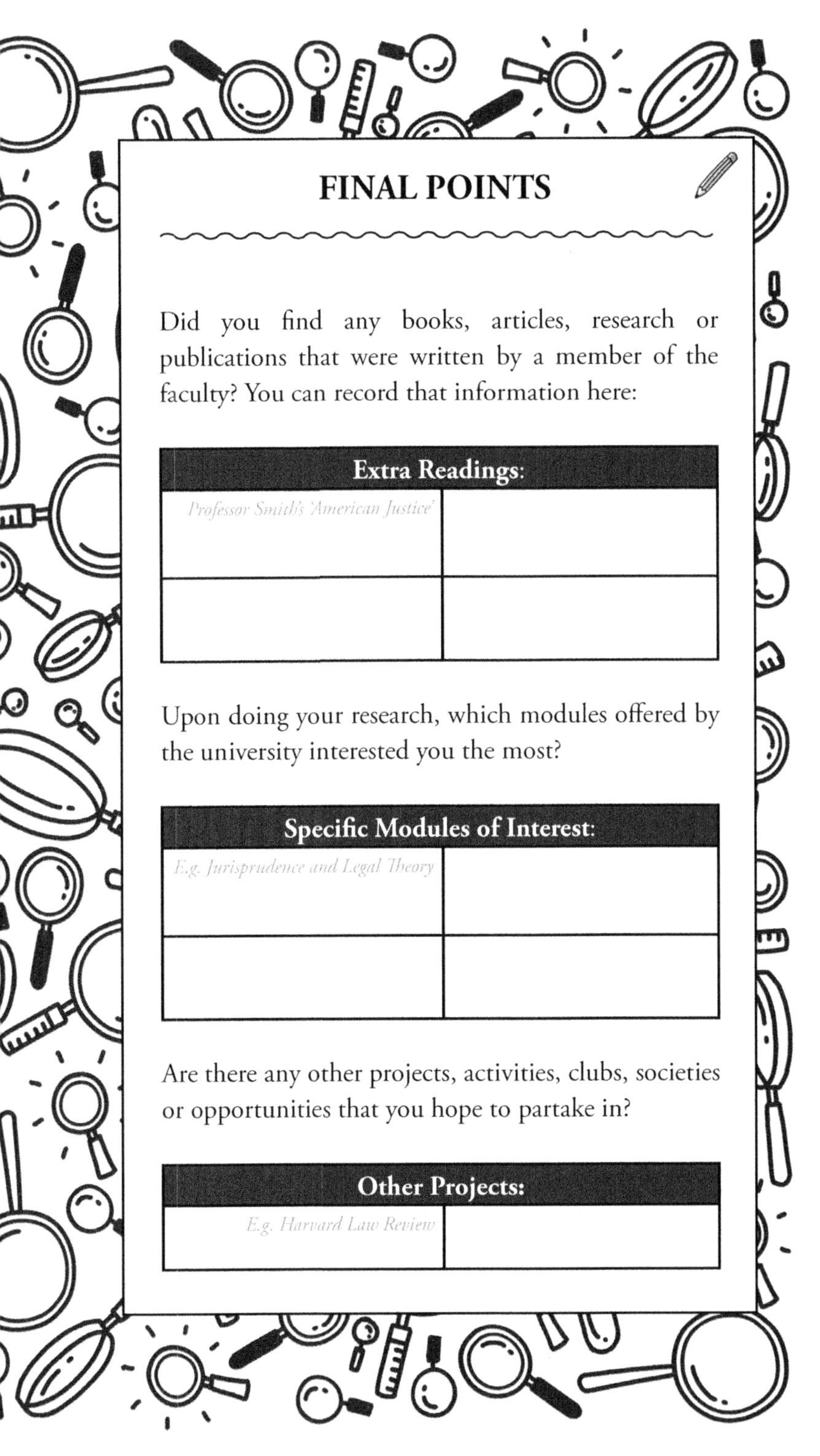

FINAL POINTS

Did you find any books, articles, research or publications that were written by a member of the faculty? You can record that information here:

Extra Readings:	
Professor Smith's 'American Justice'	

Upon doing your research, which modules offered by the university interested you the most?

Specific Modules of Interest:	
E.g. Jurisprudence and Legal Theory	

Are there any other projects, activities, clubs, societies or opportunities that you hope to partake in?

Other Projects:	
E.g. Harvard Law Review	

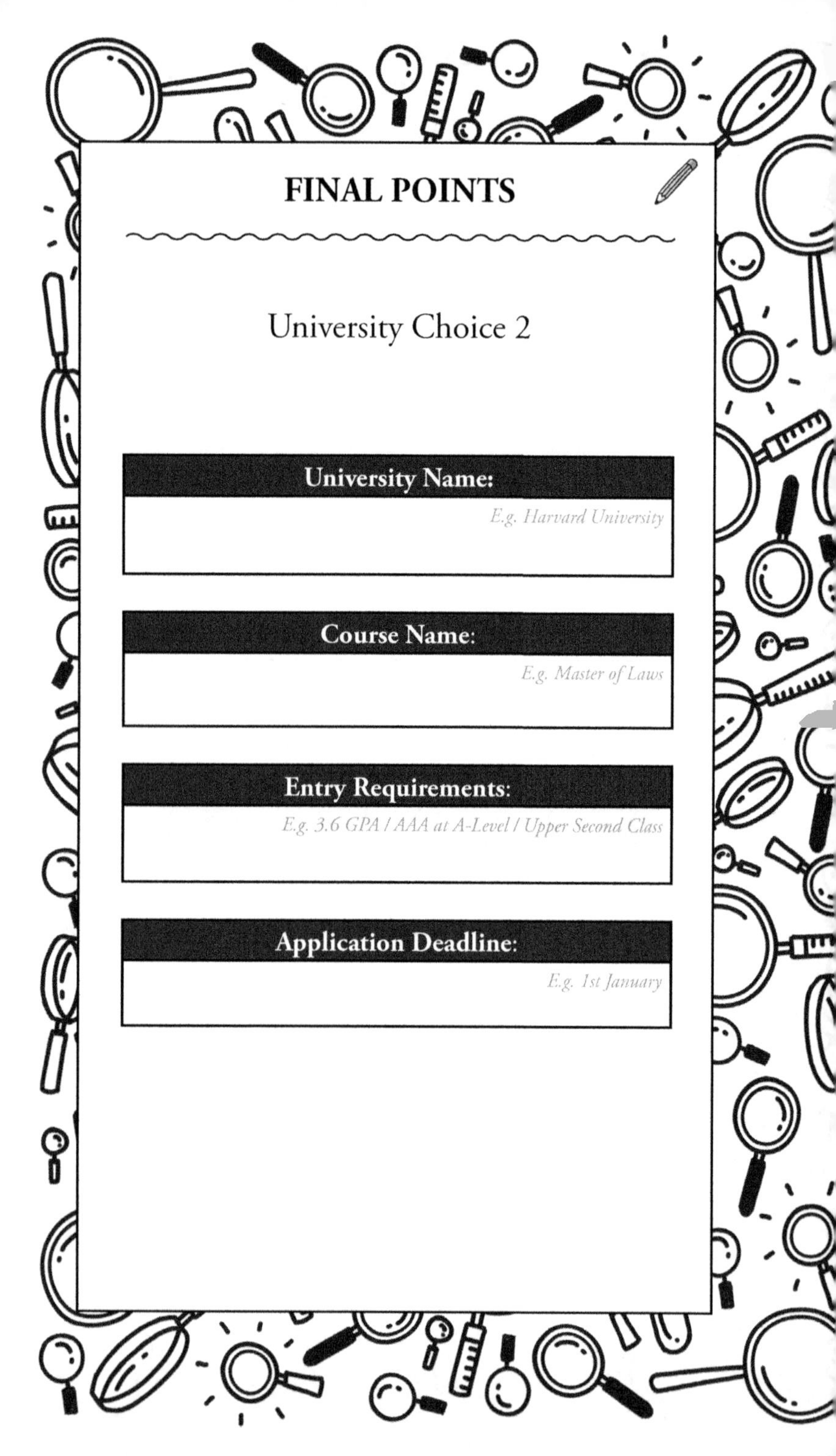

FINAL POINTS

University Choice 2

University Name:

E.g. Harvard University

Course Name:

E.g. Master of Laws

Entry Requirements:

E.g. 3.6 GPA / AAA at A-Level / Upper Second Class

Application Deadline:

E.g. 1st January

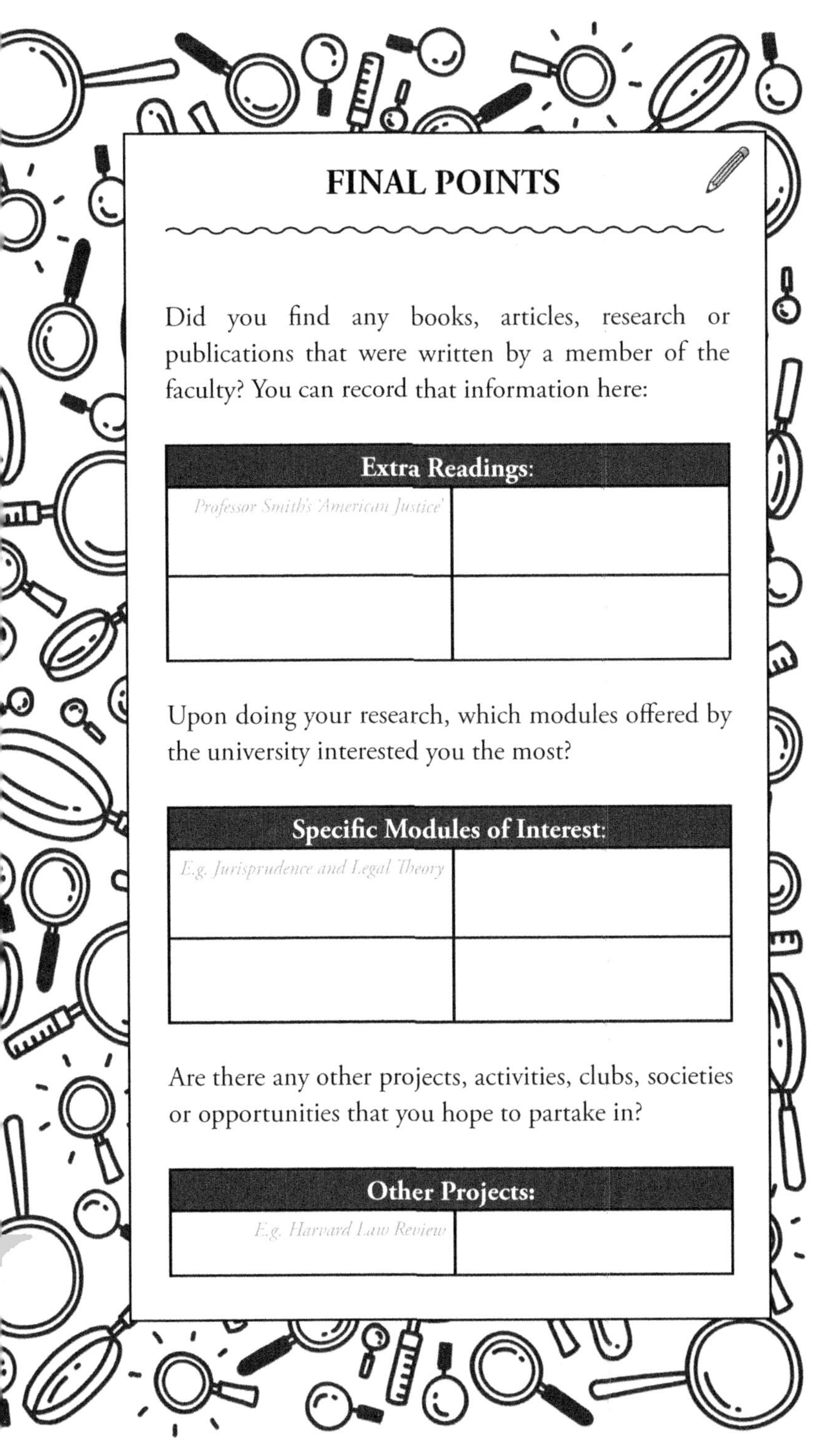

FINAL POINTS

Did you find any books, articles, research or publications that were written by a member of the faculty? You can record that information here:

Extra Readings:	
Professor Smith's 'American Justice'	

Upon doing your research, which modules offered by the university interested you the most?

Specific Modules of Interest:	
E.g. Jurisprudence and Legal Theory	

Are there any other projects, activities, clubs, societies or opportunities that you hope to partake in?

Other Projects:	
E.g. Harvard Law Review	

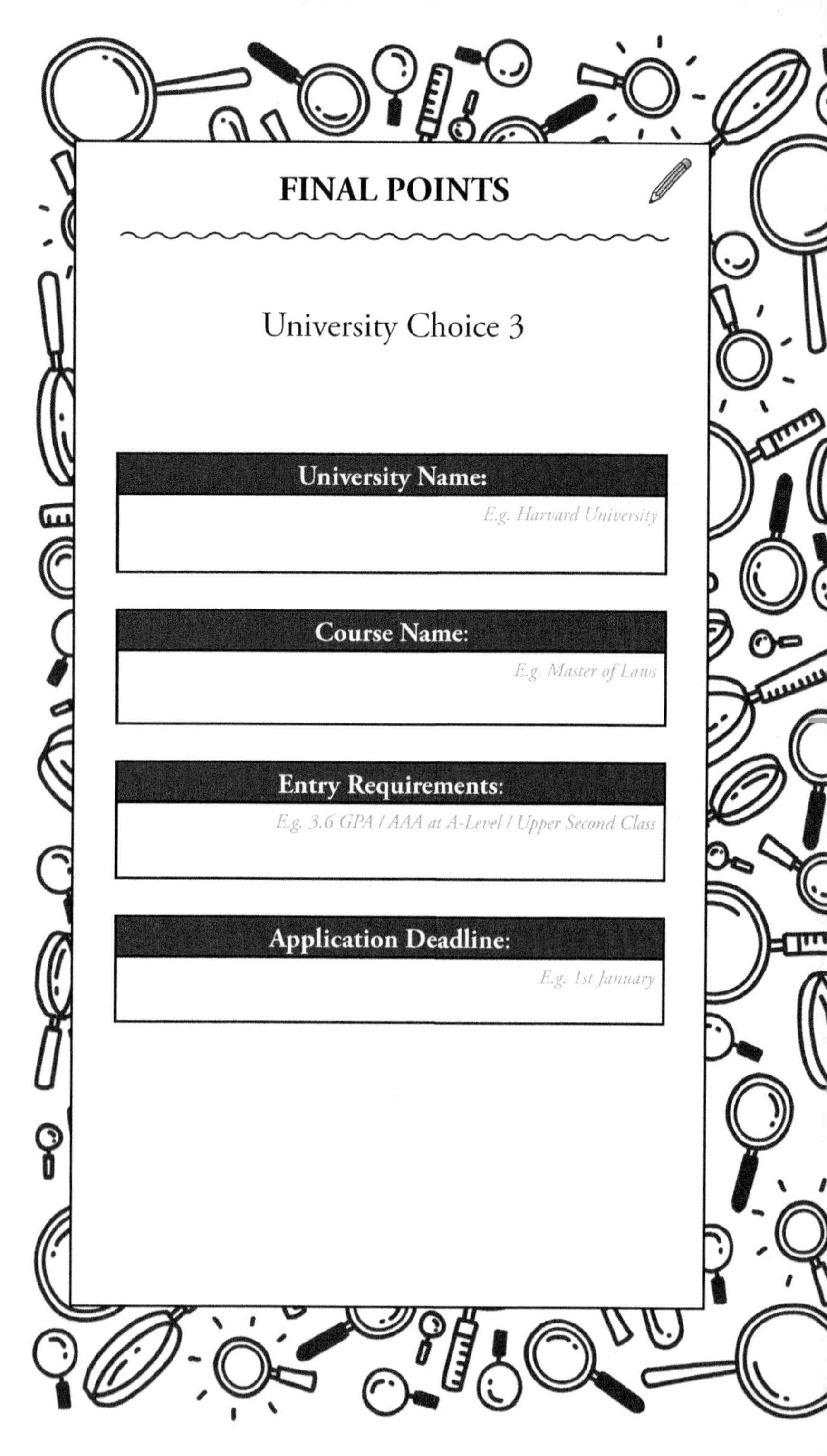

FINAL POINTS

University Choice 3

University Name:

E.g. Harvard University

Course Name:

E.g. Master of Laws

Entry Requirements:

E.g. 3.6 GPA / AAA at A-Level / Upper Second Class

Application Deadline:

E.g. 1st January

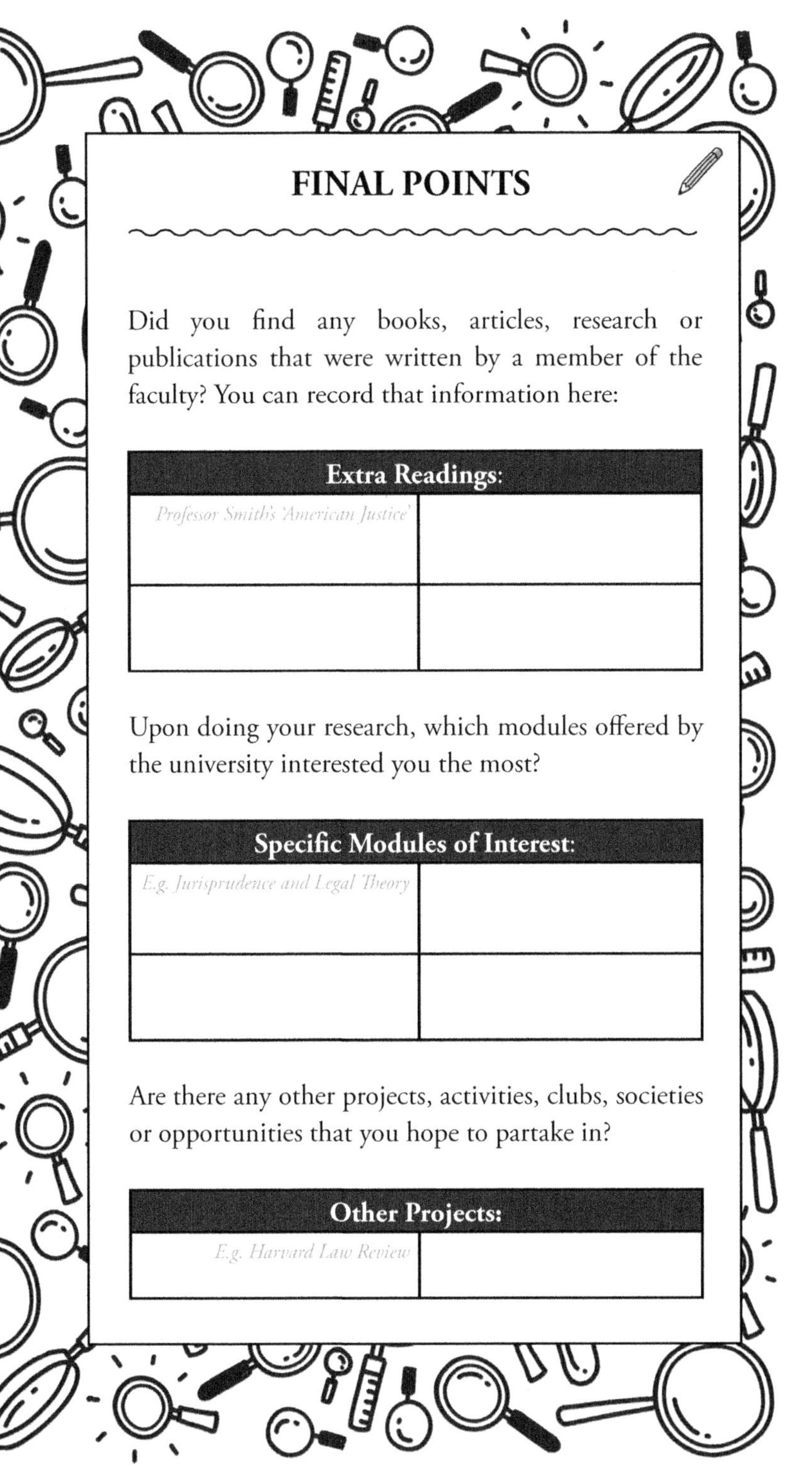

FINAL POINTS

Did you find any books, articles, research or publications that were written by a member of the faculty? You can record that information here:

Extra Readings:	
Professor Smith's 'American Justice'	

Upon doing your research, which modules offered by the university interested you the most?

Specific Modules of Interest:	
E.g. Jurisprudence and Legal Theory	

Are there any other projects, activities, clubs, societies or opportunities that you hope to partake in?

Other Projects:	
E.g. Harvard Law Review	

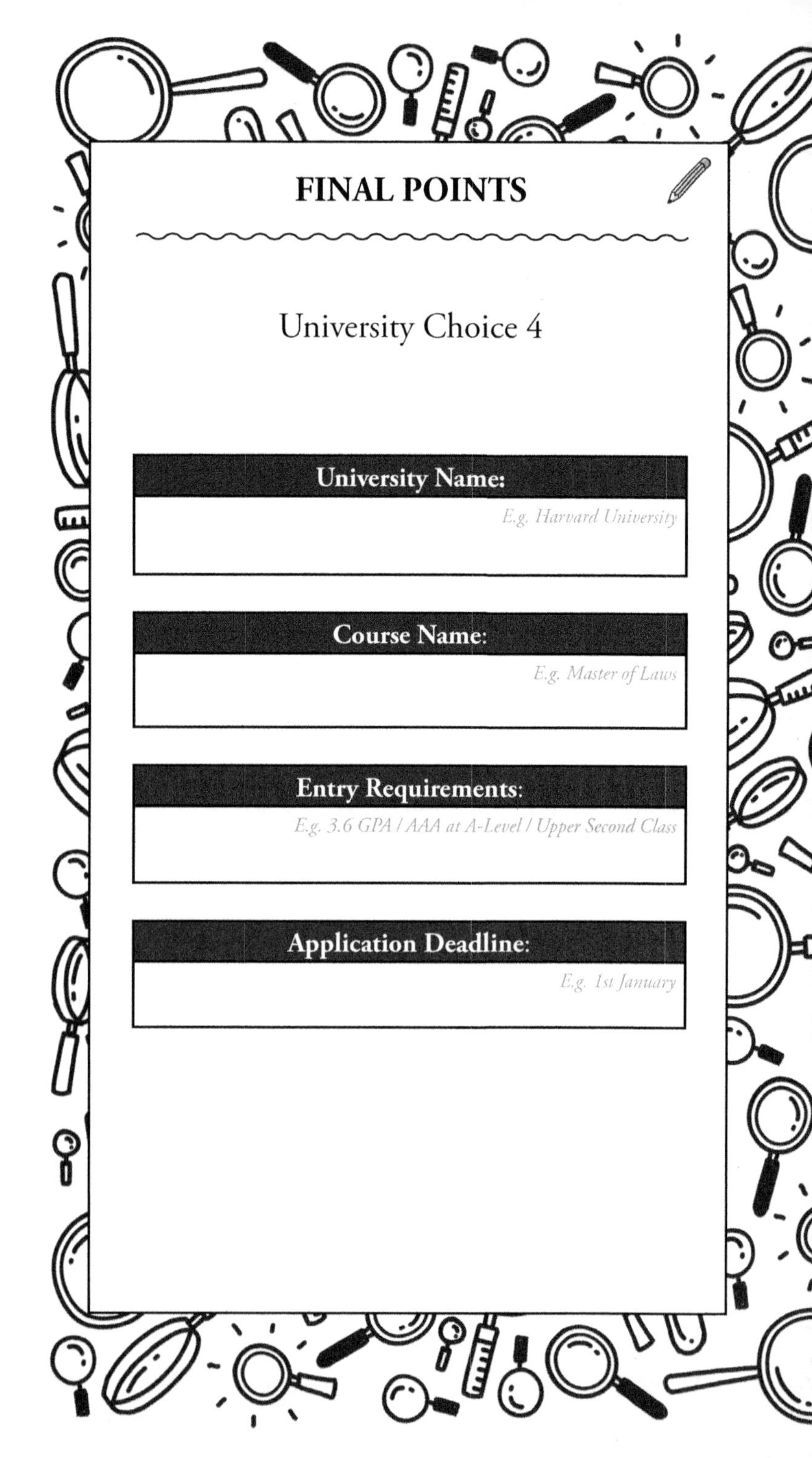

FINAL POINTS

University Choice 4

University Name:

E.g. Harvard University

Course Name:

E.g. Master of Laws

Entry Requirements:

E.g. 3.6 GPA / AAA at A-Level / Upper Second Class

Application Deadline:

E.g. 1st January

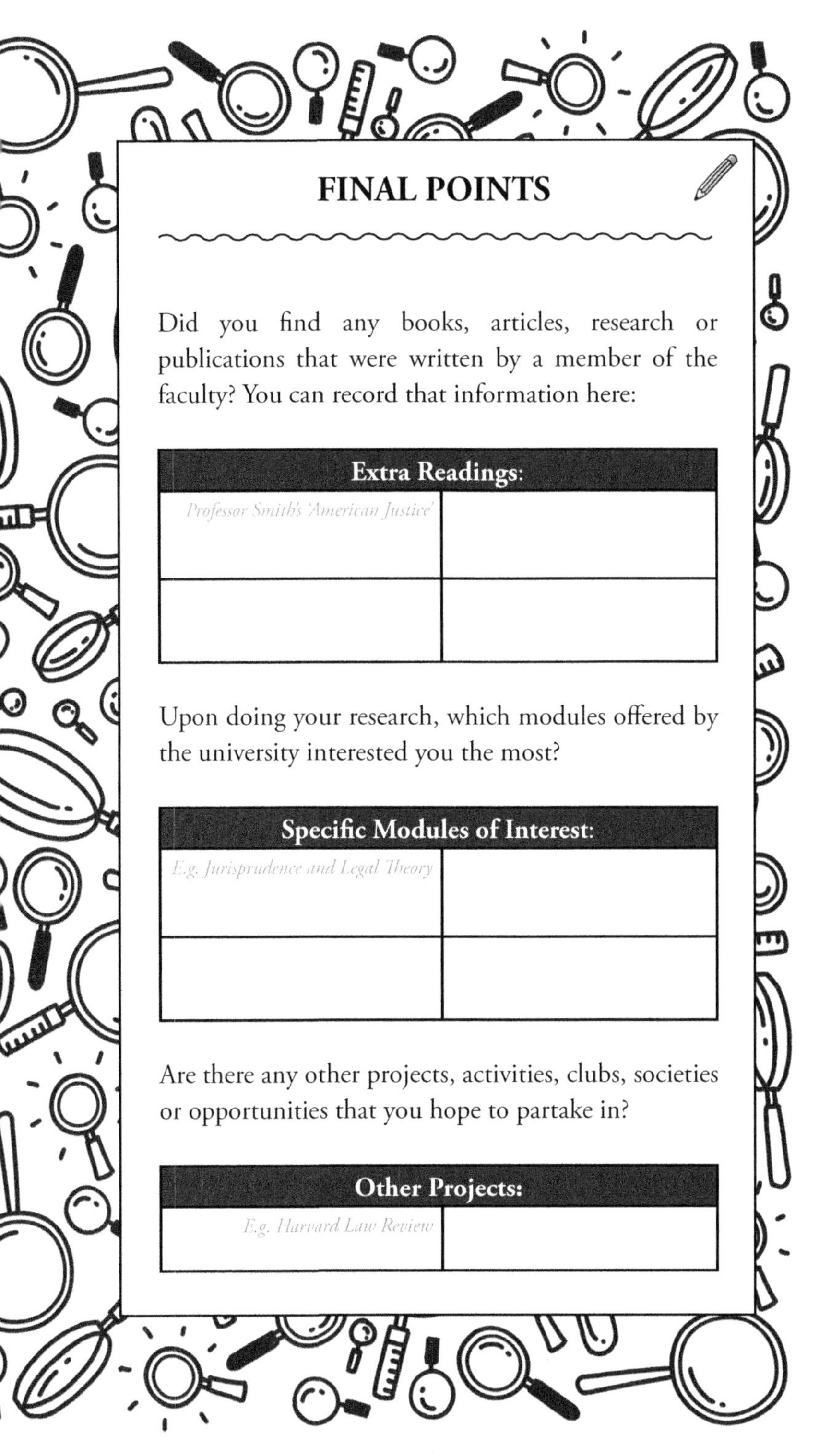

FINAL POINTS

Did you find any books, articles, research or publications that were written by a member of the faculty? You can record that information here:

Extra Readings:	
Professor Smith's 'American Justice'	

Upon doing your research, which modules offered by the university interested you the most?

Specific Modules of Interest:	
E.g. Jurisprudence and Legal Theory	

Are there any other projects, activities, clubs, societies or opportunities that you hope to partake in?

Other Projects:	
E.g. Harvard Law Review	

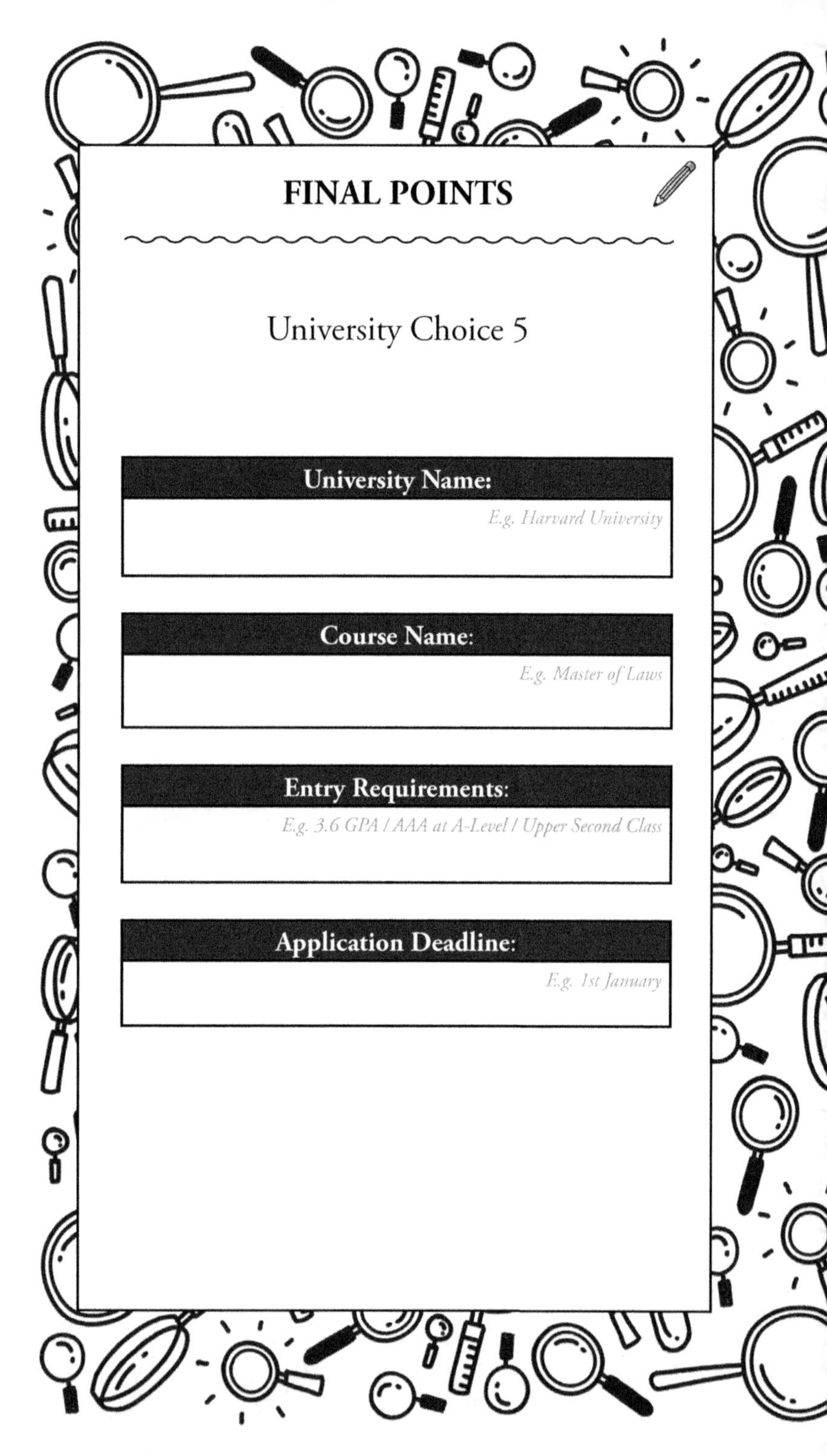

FINAL POINTS

University Choice 5

University Name:

E.g. Harvard University

Course Name:

E.g. Master of Laws

Entry Requirements:

E.g. 3.6 GPA / AAA at A-Level / Upper Second Class

Application Deadline:

E.g. 1st January

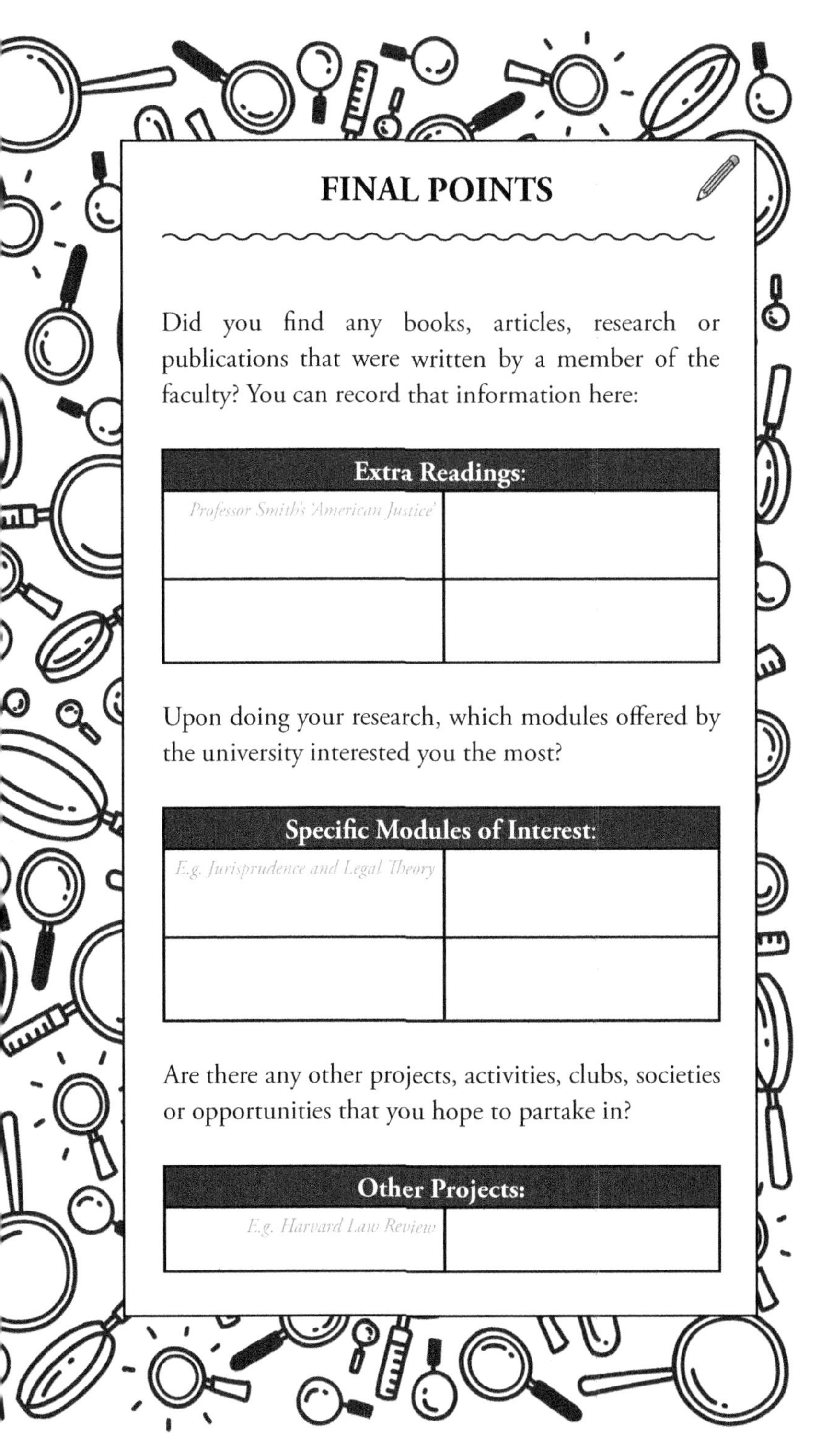

FINAL POINTS

Did you find any books, articles, research or publications that were written by a member of the faculty? You can record that information here:

Extra Readings:	
Professor Smith's 'American Justice'	

Upon doing your research, which modules offered by the university interested you the most?

Specific Modules of Interest:	
E.g. Jurisprudence and Legal Theory	

Are there any other projects, activities, clubs, societies or opportunities that you hope to partake in?

Other Projects:	
E.g. Harvard Law Review	

Chapter Two: Requirements

Well done for deciding to stay the course and learn more about how to meander through the often perilous and much-dreaded process of crafting a personal statement. In the previous chapter, I explored the importance of doing your due diligence with regard to conducting research on your chosen course. In this chapter, I will be going through the preparations that you will need to make sure that you have in place before you fully get started.

So what exactly do I mean by 'requirements?'

Anytime that you begin the process of writing any application document for a course — whether that is a personal statement, statement of purpose, supplemental essay, diversity statement or motivation letter — you need to be aware of a few important factors that will serve as guidelines throughout the subsequent writing process.

The most common of these are:

- Requirement One: *Word and Character Limits*
- Requirement Two: *Page Formatting*
- Requirement Three: *Essay Type*
- Requirement Four: *Specific Questions or Instructions*
- Requirement Five: *Tone*

So let's deal with the first:

1. Word and Character Limits

No matter what anyone tells you, it is never a good idea to go over a word or character limit. Do not think that you will be the exception, or that the admissions tutors will let it go. They most likely will not. Keeping to this requirement is a very simple instruction, and it ensures that every person is judged fairly. Before you put pen to paper, be mindful of how much space you have, so that you do not need to spend extra time removing copious amounts of text due to having overshot your word count, or conversely, inserting filler words for a body of text that is slimmer than you would have originally hoped. I will get into how to structure your personal statement in chapters four and five, but for now, just be mindful of your word and character count.

In most cases, it is a safe bet to get as close to the stipulated word or character count as possible, but not above it. This usually indicates that you have fully taken advantage of the chance to showcase yourself in the best light while observing the rules. On the other hand, if you have only used up 300 words for a personal statement that has a limit of 1000 words, while it is not the end of the world, you run the risk of giving the impression that you do not have that much to say. It is not a hard-and-fast rule, but you cannot go wrong with sticking as closely to the word and character count as possible. So that is what I recommend.

2. Page Formatting

The second requirement is pretty simple, but perhaps surprisingly, a fair few candidates fall foul of not following these clear instructions. Universities will often stipulate formatting requirements for your document. Once again, this is designed to ensure that you are being judged on the substance and not merely the 'style' of your writing. For example, most universities will request that you send your document in a standard font, such as Times New Roman at size 12, with one-inch margins (which is 2.54 centimetres). They may also ask that you leave your lines either single-spaced or double-spaced. Observing these requirements from the start will save you a huge amount of stress down the line. For example, imagine that you are a few hours away from your submission deadline, and you have written the most beautiful personal statement in font size 11 and single-spacing. Let's suppose that you now learn that the university needs your font size to be 12, and double-spaced.

Oops!

You would have massively overshot your limit, and would now have to remove big chunks of text, not to mention, with very little time to do so. Sounds like a pain, right? It really is. So save yourself the hassle and check all of the requirements before you start. As an added tip, only include information, such as your full name, page numbers, or even the words 'Personal Statement' or 'Statement of Purpose' or similar titles in the header or footer if it has been expressly stated by the university that you ought to do so. If in doubt, just leave it blank, so that you are not needlessly penalised for including extra text that was not actually asked for.

3. Essay Type

You will need to pay close attention to what kind of document you are writing, as there are various permutations and formats of an application essay that go beyond a personal statement. As you know, a personal statement is a document that allows an admissions tutor to get to know your background, experiences, achievements, and your future goals in a concise and compelling manner. However, you may be asked to submit one of the following:

- Statement of purpose
- Motivation letter
- Common App essay
- Supplemental essay

Many students conflate a personal statement with a statement of purpose, so let's start by outlining the key distinctions between them.

	Personal Statement	**Statement of Purpose**
Direction	Focuses on your personal experiences, values and character.	Focuses on your educational and career goals.
Content	Uses personal anecdotes, reflections, stories and experiences that provide an insight into your journey, your motivations and what has influenced you.	Expounds upon your academic background, research interests, and career objectives, and is typically tailored to one institution.
Use	More commonly used in university and college applications and scholarship applications.	More commonly used in graduate school applications and research fellowships.

A motivation letter is similar to a personal statement insofar as its goal of shedding light on what has influenced and guided your academic career so far, and why you would like to study your chosen course. A motivation letter can be formatted as a formal letter, whereas the text for your personal statement will usually be a standard text on an A4 page, as discussed earlier on. A Common App essay is a staple of university applications across hundreds of select universities and colleges in the United States. In addition, you might be asked to submit a supplemental essay, which admissions tutors use to glean more insights and information about specific areas of your character and the extent of your personal development. While Common App essays are shared across many universities, a supplemental essay will be specific to the university that you are applying to. The primary characteristic of Common App essays and supplemental essays is that they start with a prompt, which is a specific question, statement or topic that is designed to elicit a response that allows admissions tutors to know more about you. Have a look at a few examples of supplemental essay questions:

"Why are you interested in attending our university? How do our specific programs and resources align with your academic and career goals?"

"Describe a time when you faced a significant challenge or setback and how you overcame it. What did you learn from this experience?"

"How have your extracurricular activities, community involvement, or work experiences shaped your personal growth and influenced your aspirations?"

"Share a story or an experience that illustrates your commitment to diversity, equity, and inclusion.

How do you envision contributing to a diverse and inclusive campus community?"

"Explain why you have chosen your major or field of study. What sparked your interest, and how do you see it fitting into your future plans?"

The following are examples of common app essay prompts:

"The lessons we take from obstacles we encounter can be fundamental to later success. Recount a time when you faced a challenge, setback, or failure. How did it affect you, and what did you learn from the experience?"

"Reflect on a time when you questioned or challenged a belief or idea. What prompted your thinking? What was the outcome?"

"Reflect on something that someone has done for you that has made you happy or thankful in a surprising way. How has this gratitude affected or motivated you?"

"Discuss an accomplishment, event, or realization that sparked a period of personal growth and a new understanding of yourself or others."

"Describe a topic, idea, or concept you find so

engaging that it makes you lose all track of time. Why does it captivate you? What or who do you turn to when you want to learn more?"

You will notice that parts of the questions are highlighted. These are keywords, which I will explain in the next point.

4. Specific Questions or Instructions

The fourth requirement is one of the most important to follow, and please be in no doubt that it will make or break your personal statement. It is to simply answer the question and observe the specific instructions given by the university. For example, here is a set of instructions for an MBA application to Harvard Business School.

"As we review your application, what more would you like us to know as we consider your candidacy for the Harvard Business School MBA program? Word limit: 800. Single-spaced."

Before you even think about answering the question, the first signals that should be firing in your mind are the requirements:

- 800 words.

- Single-spaced.
- What question is being asked?

Luckily, in this case, Harvard has asked for something rather broad, as they say, 'What more would you like us to know as we consider your candidacy?' This question is open-ended and it likely would have come as part of a series of supplemental essays or similar documents for the application. On this occasion, a generic answer might suffice. But let's try one that is a little different.

Have a read of another example. This is from a candidate who applied to study for a master's degree in strategic marketing at Imperial College London. In the application, Imperial says:

"What would you contribute to the cohort and to the Imperial Community? Please do not exceed 1500 characters."

Once again, upon seeing this, you should be thinking about your requirements, just like I have advised. From this question, you know that one of the requirements is to stick to 1500 characters. However, Imperial has not specified the line spacing or other formatting. So, in this case, I recommend that you use a standard font, such as Times New Roman at size 12 with either single- or double-spacing with one-inch margins. In terms of what is actually being asked for this question, Imperial has been specific about what they want to hear from you, and it is something that you need to take notice of. A common mistake that students make is answering a question they wish were being asked, rather than the one that is written in front of them. To prevent any deviations from the question, and to ensure that you stay on track, I strongly recommend that you highlight the key points of the question before answering — perhaps in different colours.

In this case, you would highlight the words 'contribute' and 'to the Imperial Community.'

For example:

"What would you contribute to the cohort and to the Imperial Community? Please do not exceed 1500 characters."

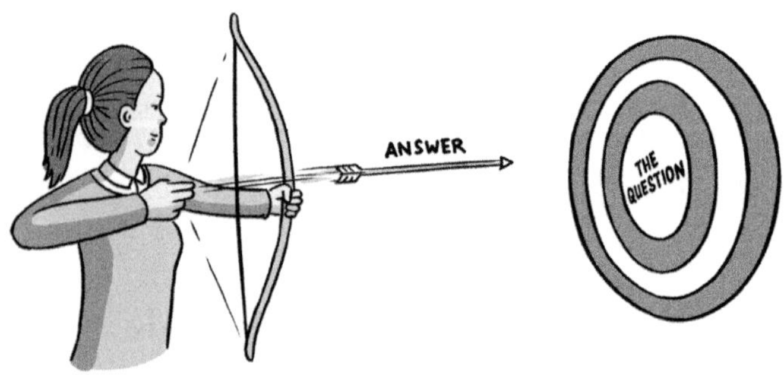

Those are the keywords here. The question is not asking what you have done in the past — which you might be tempted to write about. Rather, it is asking you how you can 'contribute' to the Imperial community. And there's a key distinction here too. The question is not asking you how you can contribute within your field, and upon graduation, but rather how you can contribute directly to the cohort and the Imperial community. Be careful to spot these subtle differences that others may overlook. This is why you should highlight the keywords and phrases: 'contribute' and 'to the

Imperial Community.' The ability to focus on the question being asked is a great skill to have because it means that, as you begin writing your response, you will not be doing so from a false premise. Coupled with the research that you do on your course, as I discussed in the previous chapter, adhering to these requirements is important. It means that you get off to a good start, and this way, you can ensure that you are heading in the right direction.

Let's try one more before you go on to the next chapter. This candidate is applying to study for a master's degree in accounting from the University of Michigan, and their application reads:

"Michigan deeply values student engagement beyond the classroom. Please describe two or three meaningful ways in which you have engaged in your communities. 200 words minimum. Content beyond 300 words will not be reviewed."

With this example, you should be thinking about the requirements once again. They clearly state a minimum of 200 words. They have warned that any content beyond 300 words will not be reviewed. As usual, you will want to keep the font at the standard Times New Roman, size 12. For the question itself, there are at least two parts that you need to pay attention to and highlight. Any guesses?

It would be wise to highlight the phrase 'two or three meaningful ways,' and the phrase 'engaged in your communities,' like this:

"Michigan deeply values student engagement beyond the classroom. Please describe two or three

meaningful ways in which you have engaged in your communities. 200 words minimum. Content beyond 300 words will not be reviewed."

Because in this case, Michigan wants to know how you have engaged in your community, and they have asked that you describe two or three examples of this.

It seems simple enough, right? But if you go on to write about ten ways that you have engaged in the community, even if it is true, and genuinely impressive, you would not have answered the question. They asked for two or three ways, not ten. Similarly, if you were to write about two or three aspirations that you have for your future career, you would not be answering the question, because Michigan is asking about how you have engaged with communities in the past. These points really cannot be stressed enough. If you are given instructions for your personal statement or other application essay, do not write from the perspective of what you would hope is being asked. No. Just answer the question as 'tightly' as possible. And by 'tightly,' I mean that you make it clear right from the start, and occasionally throughout the essay, that you are answering the question. You need to reassure the reader that you understand what is being asked. Do not leave even a whiff of suspicion that you do not understand the question, or that you are shooting off on a tangent and departing from what the question is really asking. In essence, you want to give the reader the full confidence that you 'get the message' and that you are sticking to it. Hopefully, I have made this point abundantly clear.

5. Tone

When it comes to speech, you will be familiar with the term 'watch your tone,' and in writing a personal statement or other college admissions essay or document, the same principle applies. The dictionary defines 'tone' as:

"The mood implied by an author's word choice and the way that the text can make a reader feel."

The reason why you should pay attention to your tone is because writing a personal statement is not a one-size-fits-all endeavour, and creating a 'cookie-cutter' piece of writing is less likely to lead to favourable results than taking the time to actually get to know what your university is specifically looking for. For example, if you compare the university applications of the United Kingdom with the United States, you will find that UK universities tend to place greater emphasis on demonstrating academic exploration than their counterparts across the pond. On the other hand, while US personal statements value academic exploration, many US colleges place a great degree of importance on storytelling, personality, flair and originality. In addition to this, some universities have specific styles of writing that they discourage or even forbid. For example, some institutions will impose strict guidelines about topics that you should not mention. Once again, this is why undertaking research is important. If you have a sound understanding of the tone that is required in your writing, you increase your chances of delivering your message in a way that admissions tutors will positively respond to.

Now that you have gotten Research and Requirements out of the way, it is time that you get into the real nitty-gritty of bringing a personal statement to life. As you go along, try to think of each chapter of this book as a layer of bricks that, ultimately, will make a house. You should strive to get every single layer as perfect as can be in order to ensure the stability, integrity and beauty of that whole house. So take it step by step, and if you need to return to a previous chapter for a quick refresh, that is absolutely fine too.

In the next chapter, Narrative, I will explore the final, but very important stage, of planning a personal statement, which is deciding on the storyline, theme, approach and angle that you will opt for as you begin writing. You are doing a fantastic job by investing in your future, and I really appreciate you reading this book. Let's take this up a notch, and head on over to Chapter Three.

FINAL POINTS

Before you go on to Chapter Three: Narrative, double-check that you are adhering to all of the requirements stipulated by your chosen university. Tick each box as you go through the list and provide any relevant information on the right-hand side.

Complete the following information:		
	Word or Character Limit	*E.g. 1000 words*
	Page Limit	*E.g. Two pages*
	Font	*E.g. Times New Roman*
	Font Size	*E.g. 12*
	Line Spacing	*E.g. Double-spaced*
	Margin Spacing	*E.g. 2.54 cm or 1 inch*
	Document Type	*E.g. Personal Statement*
	Tone	*E.g. Formal*
	Are you following the instructions clearly?	
	Are you answering the question directly?	
	Other Requirements:	

Chapter Three: Narrative

In the previous two chapters, you learned about the benefits of undertaking research in preparation for your course and adhering to the requirements stipulated by your university in writing your personal statement. In this chapter, I will be exploring one of the most important aspects of your writing. It is what turns words into a story, and a wall of text into a masterpiece. Yes — your narrative. But, before you go any further, let's start by defining what a narrative actually is.

A 'narrative' is:

"A story or a description of a series of events, and a particular way of explaining or understanding events."

In knowing how to write effectively, if words are akin to bricks, then the narrative is the mortar. In the simplest terms, a narrative is how you connect the events of a story in a way that converges into a theme or style that represents who you are.

For example, your narrative might be a story of triumph after having overcome adversity, and how this has motivated you to study for your chosen degree. Your narrative could also be a personal or unique observation about changes unfolding in your chosen field, and how you hope to contribute to this in your future profession. Your narrative could be a commentary on an aspect of your subject that you find illuminating or surprising, and why this motivates you to pursue the subject as a degree. It could also be a bold vision or idea that you hope to bring to fruition through studying your course, or even a poignant moment that had a palpable impact on you.

Narratives are incredibly important because they give your reader a foundation to know who you are, where you are coming from and why studying your chosen course matters so much to you. Without a strong narrative, your writing misses out on the chance of making a really strong impact, and it is likely to sound verbose and vague, and perhaps lack direction. Conversely, a strong narrative provides multiple benefits. It will help to improve the structure, consistency and flow of your writing. It gives the reader an idea of what to expect, which eases the reading experience. A narrative also provides a baseline that you can return to from the first paragraph to the last, thereby creating a 'storyline' that interweaves in between your writing and keeps it coherent, which encourages your reader to stay interested. In creative writing, when you connect the start of your story to the end by making each part mirror the other, it is called 'bookending', which is a powerful and effective technique that you can also use. A strong narrative helps to make your writing more authentic, original and compelling — which is always a good thing. If you can craft a narrative that is highly specific and personal to you and your experiences, this is another plus that will keep your reader hooked right till the end. Fundamentally, a narrative is the 'skeleton' of your writing, and as you draw from your own experiences, you 'add meat to the bones' and make the writing your own.

But without a strong narrative, you run the risk of making your writing disjointed, unintelligible or incoherent. It is all about a storyline, but not in the sense of writing 'once upon a time' or fairy tales. No. A personal statement is about using your lived experiences — such as your academic accomplishments, work experience, extracurricular projects, additional readings and other insights — to illustrate where you have come from, and where you are going. That is what creates your 'story.'

Writing with Evidence

A cardinal rule of writing is:

"Show, don't tell."

★ For academic writing, the rule of 'show, don't tell' most definitely applies too. So, for example, let's say that you want to apply to study nursing, and you want to prove to the admissions department that you are calm under pressure and have empathy. Rather than merely saying the words, *'I am calm under pressure and have empathy'* — which is not very convincing on its own — why not tell us a story about how you exhibited these characteristics in your life? Perhaps it could be that time when you worked as a waiter at a restaurant and had to handle the complaints from disgruntled customers, or a placement at a care home, where you patiently attended to the needs of elderly residents. Stories of lived experiences will support your statements far better than you trying to convince the reader without concrete evidence and examples. So make sure that you use them, as they carry a lot of weight.

Let's explore a few more narratives.

If you are interested in studying medicine, your narrative could revolve around a poignant moment that occurred in your personal life, such as witnessing a family member going through a health-related struggle. Alternatively, if you have undertaken work experience, you might want to talk about an experience that you had with a patient and how this influenced your decision to pursue a career in medicine. While narratives of this nature are not new, you should not shy away from them on the grounds that they are not entirely unique. This is because what makes a narrative special are your personal perspectives and reflections. So the more specific you make your narrative, the more you take ownership of it, and the more compelling you will sound.

Equally, it is important to note that you do not always need to have a gripping, Oscar-worthy story of your life as your narrative if you do not actually have one. It is always best to tell the truth and not inflate or embellish your experiences. Finding real-life examples to build up your narrative can be tricky, especially if you are applying straight out of secondary school or high school and have not had much work experience yet. But, just write from the heart, work with what you have got and be yourself. Your reflections on events, and your genuine ideas, are just as powerful as a fantastic story. So do not worry too much about it. If you are struggling to come up with a 'story,' you can be equally as engaging by invoking my previous point of talking about your personal and theoretical observations, or wise reflections that you have made about your field of study and other insights that you hold.

Setting the Pace

A narrative 'sets the pace' as you write, but other tangible achievements and experiences will invariably take centre stage as you get further into your personal statement. In this way, a narrative tends to be most important for the first paragraphs of a personal statement. But afterwards, it is usually acceptable to find yourself referring less to the overall narrative until you reach the conclusion, which ties it all together and reiterates your original points. Try to think of your narrative as the 'fire that lights the match,' and stays burning throughout the statement. Your narrative is that spark in the first paragraph of the statement, as it establishes your context, theme, background and direction. But afterwards, once the reader has understood your narrative, you do not need to emphasise it as much, as the examples that you incorporate into your writing will help to corroborate this theme.

What you must not do, however, is introduce a new narrative in the penultimate or final paragraph of your writing. This tends to be distracting, and as your space is limited, you ought to spend your time reinforcing your original narrative where you can, and reaffirming the specific qualities that you hope to display, rather than hopping from one narrative to another, in a desperate bid to cover as many bases as possible. Such a strategy makes it a cumbersome affair for you to write your personal statement, as there are far too many points to consider and then interweave. But equally, it will be a bit of a nightmare for an admissions tutor to have to read a disjointed patchwork of narratives. If you indulge in 'narrative hoarding,' any reader will be longing to be put out of their misery by swiftly moving on to another student's personal statement that is written more succinctly than yours, and you will miss out in the long run — so it's a lose-lose situation.

Instead, spend some time brainstorming, and ask yourself:

- What is my 'why?'
- Why do I *really* want to study this course?
- What is my context, and what examples should I use to build up my writing and explain this to the reader?
- What qualities are required for my chosen programme, and how can I display them in my writing?
- What value do I bring to the table?
- Was there a standout moment that made me decide on my chosen degree, or have I wanted to pursue it for a long time?
- Do I have aspirations of what I hope to do after graduation, and if so, what?
- How will this degree help me to reach my goals?
- How will this university help me to reach my goals?

When you ask yourself these questions, stick to one narrative, and aim to explore that theme deeply, rather than superficially and sparsely. With each point that you make, try to focus on demonstrating depth in your thoughts, insights and perspectives, rather than merely showing breadth in the variety of narratives, experiences and ideas that you have. As I pointed out earlier, the best way to get your ideas across is by deciding on your narrative, and then using your stories, experiences, insights and lessons from problems that you have faced to build upon this basic framework. Finding a suitable narrative is the first part, so if you manage to do this, you have laid down a strong foundation that you can more confidently flesh out. Later on in this book, I will explain how to write about your experiences in a way that is reflective, compelling, engaging and memorable, but for now, focus on building a strong foundation for your writing.

A good place to begin is to talk to your friends, family and teachers. They can help you to figure out what your greatest skills are, and they can remind you of challenges that you have faced, which you can use to build your narrative in your personal statement. It is also wise to pay attention to the specific qualities that the university is looking for in your course — such as leadership, compassion, and creative problem-solving — and try to infuse these into your writing. In addition, reading articles, listening to podcasts, or even watching documentaries can help to get you into the mindset of writing about your chosen field.

All of these steps, from 'Research,' as I covered in Chapter One, to adhering to the 'Requirements' in Chapter Two, and deciding on your narrative, form your Planning Stage. By taking these necessary steps in the key areas that you are intending to write about, you are making sure that you leave no stone unturned. In addition, engaging in all of this reading and planning will help you to get the juices flowing, so to speak, and avoid writer's block, as you will have the right vocabulary, themes, references and ideas at your fingertips.

Write What You Know

Writer's block happens to the best of us, so if you are stumped as to what to write, do not feel too bad about it — just write what you know. Please bear in mind that the best way to start writing is to simply… start writing. Write about the subjects, interests, challenges and opportunities that you are genuinely invested in. It will come a lot easier when you write about what you are familiar with. Remember that you cannot edit a blank page, so it is better to just write something, and then change it later.

Once you have gotten some ideas down on paper, you can then go about changing them, which is better than having nothing to work with at all. The longer you stare at a blank screen or a blank sheet of paper, the harder it can be to actually get started.

If you are struggling with writing your first draft, another good tip is to write as you would speak to a friend. Start from there and just be yourself so that you can get some bullet points and phrases down to begin with. You can even record yourself talking about your subject and play it back to brainstorm ideas. It does not need to be perfect from the start, and as long as you have enough time before your deadline, you can always come back to it later, change it and improve it. So be yourself, and write from the heart.

And with that, you have now completed the Planning Stage of crafting a personal statement, and it is now time to get stuck into the writing part. So make yourself a cup of tea, grab a few nibbles, and find a comfy and quiet place to write the document that might just change your life.

It is time to begin writing.

Join me in the next chapter as you do exactly that.

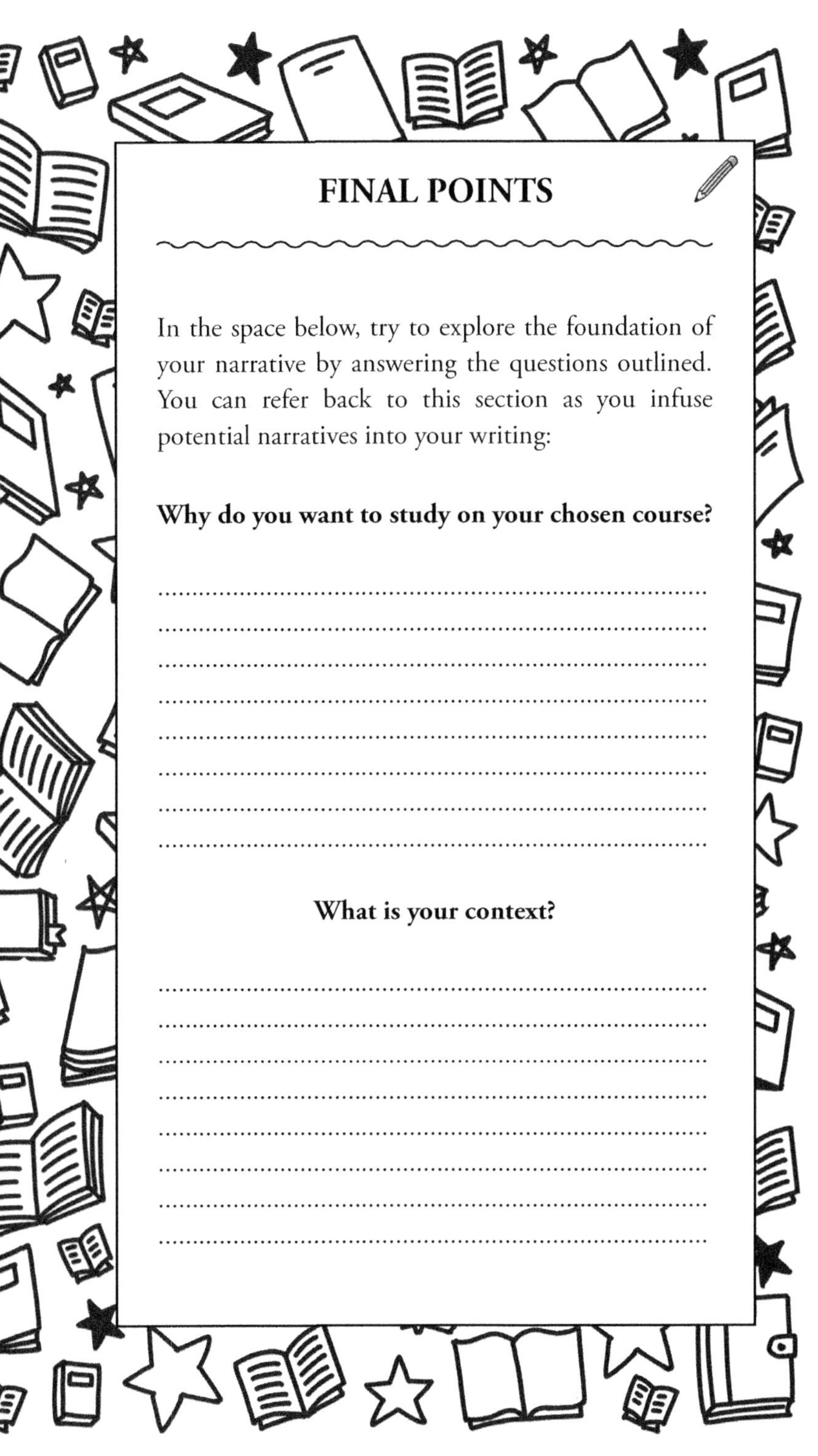

FINAL POINTS

In the space below, try to explore the foundation of your narrative by answering the questions outlined. You can refer back to this section as you infuse potential narratives into your writing:

Why do you want to study on your chosen course?

....

....

....

....

....

....

....

....

What is your context?

....

....

....

....

....

....

....

....

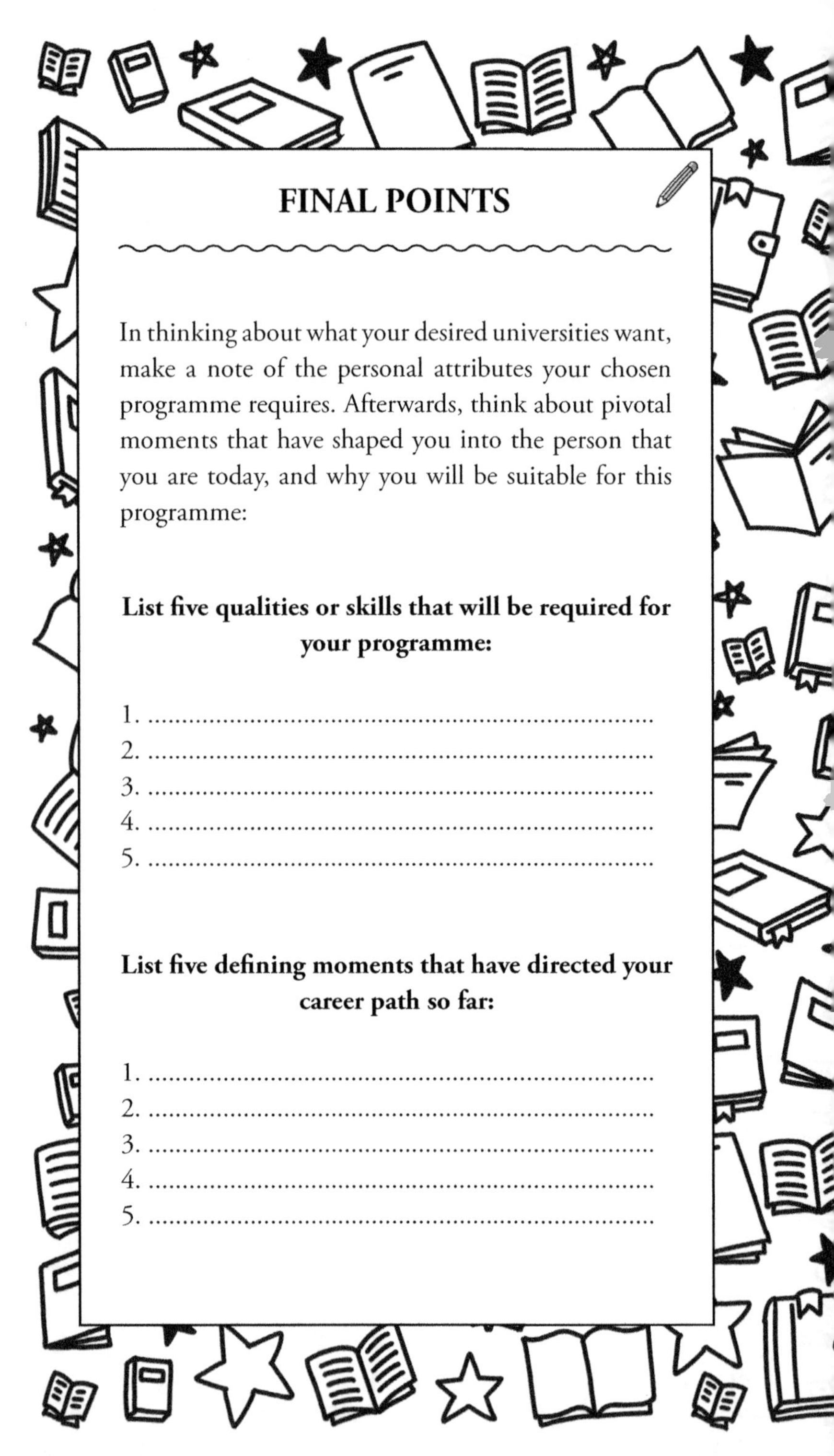

FINAL POINTS

In thinking about what your desired universities want, make a note of the personal attributes your chosen programme requires. Afterwards, think about pivotal moments that have shaped you into the person that you are today, and why you will be suitable for this programme:

List five qualities or skills that will be required for your programme:

1. ....
2. ....
3. ....
4. ....
5. ....

List five defining moments that have directed your career path so far:

1. ....
2. ....
3. ....
4. ....
5. ....

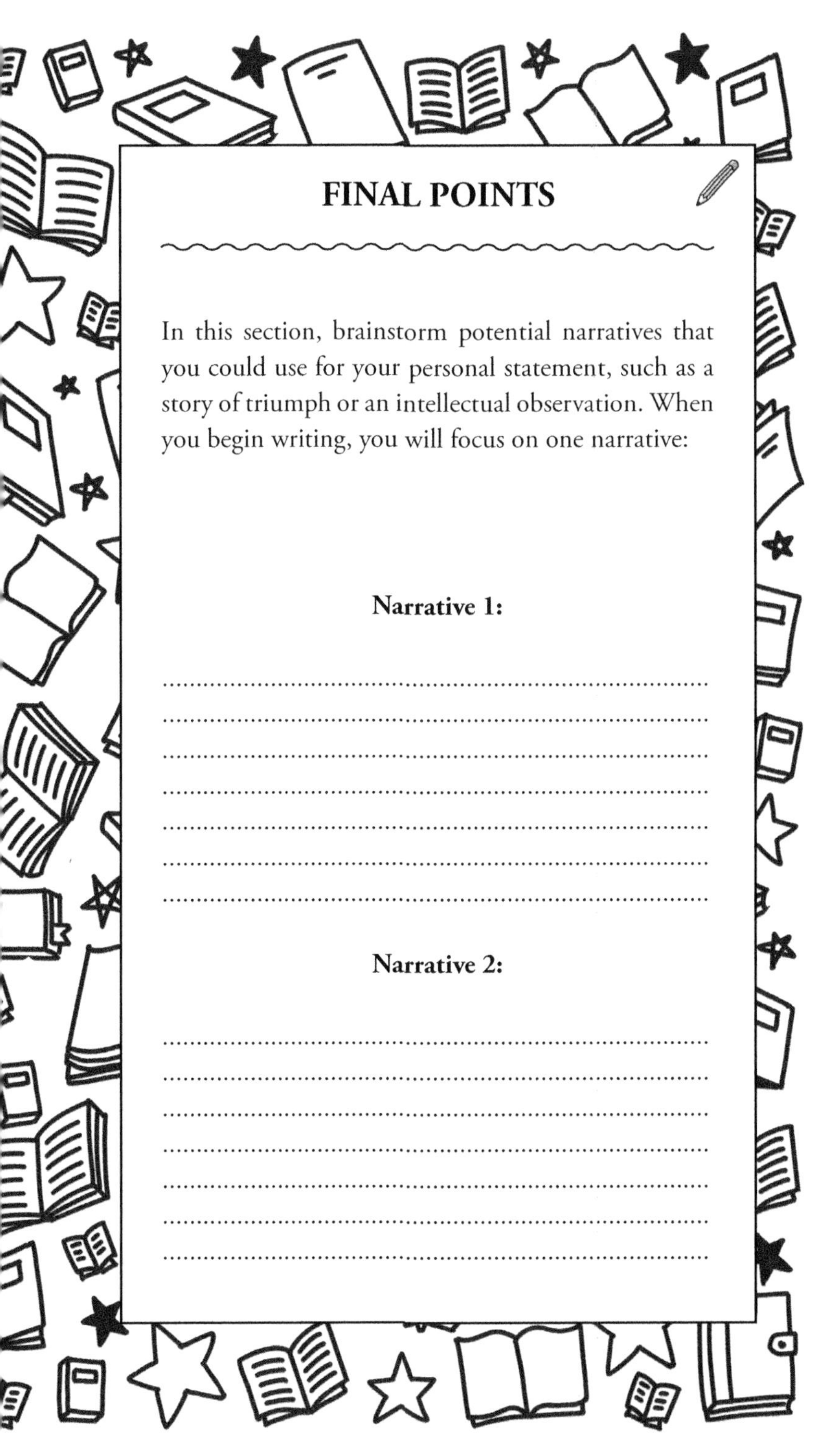

FINAL POINTS

In this section, brainstorm potential narratives that you could use for your personal statement, such as a story of triumph or an intellectual observation. When you begin writing, you will focus on one narrative:

Narrative 1:

....

....

....

....

....

....

....

Narrative 2:

....

....

....

....

....

....

....

FINAL POINTS

Narrative 3:

....
....
....
....
....
....
....
....
....
....
....

Narrative 4:

....
....
....
....
....
....
....
....
....
....

FINAL POINTS

Narrative 5:

....
....
....
....
....
....
....
....
....
....
....

Narrative 6:

....
....
....
....
....
....
....
....
....
....

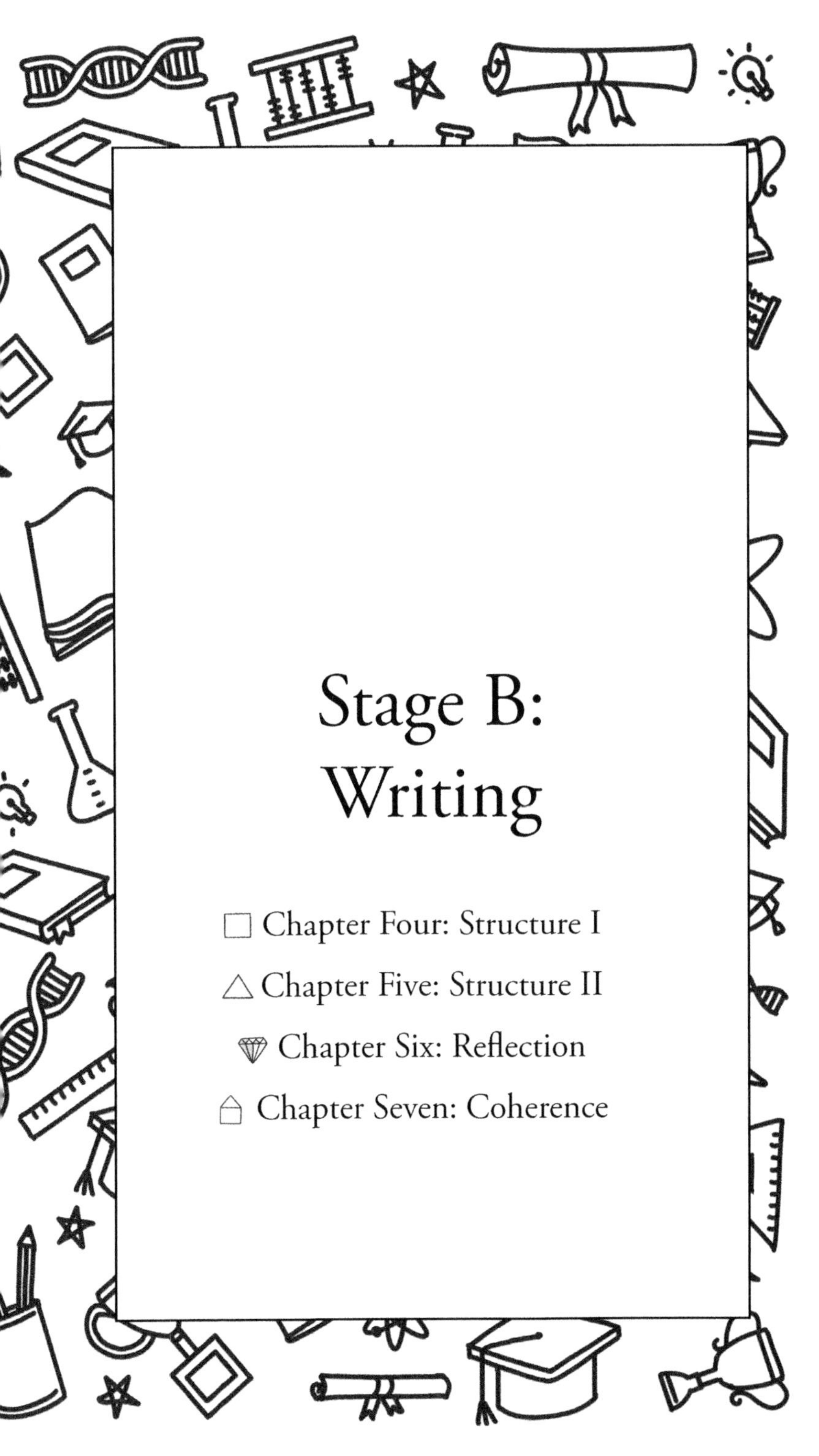

Stage B: Writing

Chapter Four: Structure I

In the previous three chapters — Research, Requirements, and Narrative — you learned all about the planning process of crafting a personal statement. Admittedly, planning your personal statement before you write it can feel like a boring exercise, but it will pay off in spades further down the line. As you begin the writing phase of your personal statement, I recommend that you use a word processor, such as Microsoft Word, Google Docs or Apple Pages. If you prefer to write by hand, you can do that instead, but be sure to make clear any corrections and edits that you will need to refer to later on. In addition, make a note of the deadline of your application, as well as the word and character limits and page formatting, and calibrate your page so that you are ready to begin writing. Then open up a web browser with your university's programme page displayed and start to think about potential narratives, as I explained in the previous chapter.

You want to be asking yourself what your 'why' is, what your context is, what value you bring to the table, what your aspirations are, and how the specific course that you are applying for at your chosen university will be of great benefit to your academic life and professional career. Depending on which university you are applying to, some will prefer that you focus on demonstrating intellectual curiosity more than professional ambition — which is more common for undergraduate courses. However, other universities value a student who has a passion for the vocational and professional aspects of their career, and thus, in this case, your writing should be more forward-looking, rather than academic. Once again, by doing your research, as I outlined in Chapter One, you will know which one applies to you, and can better navigate how to frame your writing. Once you can confidently build up your narrative, and have fully explored the research and requirements from the first three chapters, you have the ingredients to begin writing.

So, let's not hang about any longer.

In this chapter, Structure I, you will start to lay the groundwork for your personal statement, using your lived experiences, insights, achievements and challenges to bring your narrative to life. There are, indeed, various ways to write a personal statement, and numerous structures that 'work.' But for the purposes of this book, I will be focussing on a tried-and-tested structure that can be further built upon and made unique to you. No matter what anyone says, all good writers know that a sound structure and plan is an essential part of formulating any written piece in a way that is coherent, consistent and easy to follow. At the end of the day, producing written work that the reader can actually understand is a key objective. What use is it to write something that, while brilliant in your eyes, is too obscure, convoluted or complex for the average person to understand?

One of the crucial factors of a personal statement's structure is that each individual paragraph should make its own point, but equally reflect the overall narrative and theme that you are trying to convey. In essence, your personal statement is like a six-course meal, where the starter is your first paragraph and the dessert is your conclusion. On its own, each meal has to be great in its own right, but when taken together with other meals, also needs to make sense. This is like your narrative — with all of the parts 'fitting' together in a coherent and consistent form.

To better understand the flow of writing, you can start by planning your paragraphs — ideally, from paragraph one, the introduction, to paragraph five or six, which will be your conclusion, depending on how much space you have. Outlining a structure will be much easier once you have worked out your narrative and the main points that you want to get across. This is because having a strong narrative will point you in the right direction and allow you to carve out a logical path forward, moving between each topic that you want to cover in each paragraph.

The Classic Structure

There are multiple ways to convey your thoughts within a personal statement and this should not be a 'one-size-fits-all' approach, but as a good starting point, you may want to look at the following structure that I can attest provides a robust framework which you can build upon. As you go through this structure, it may help you to make bullet points of the topics that you plan on covering in each paragraph, which you can do in the Final Points section of this chapter.

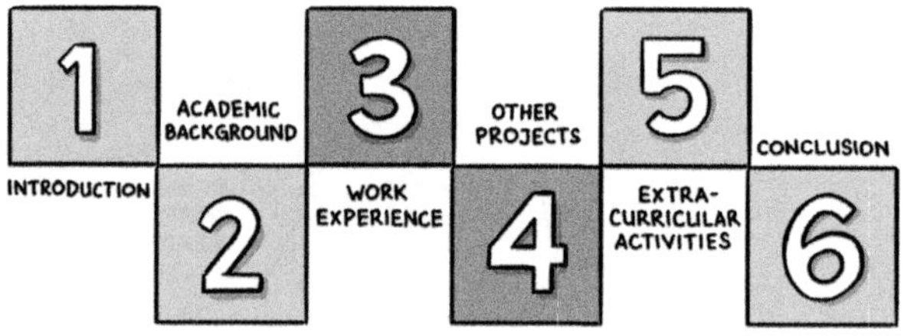

Paragraph One: **Introduction**

This is your opener, where you make your first impression. It sets the scene and introduces your narrative.

Paragraph Two: **Academic Background/Insights**

This is where I recommend that you discuss your educational history and intellectual perspectives — being careful to not merely list your accomplishments like a CV.

Paragraph Three: **Work Experience**

In this paragraph, you should talk about your work experience, internships or other professional history and experiences that demonstrate how you approach practical tasks in a real-life setting.

Paragraph Four: **Projects and Super-Curricular Work**

In this paragraph, you may wish to discuss other related projects, insights, achievements and interests that go beyond your school work. However, you can also play it by ear and write about a separate work experience placement here. Or for example, if you have decided to change majors or careers, you can provide further clarity as to how your path has evolved over time in this paragraph. Remember — it is okay to use this structure as a starting point and then flesh it out in a novel or more inventive way later on.

Paragraph Five: **Extra-Curricular Activities (Optional)**

In your penultimate paragraph, you might want to include information about your extra-curricular activities. You may also opt to talk about books, articles or research that you have read about in preparation for your course. This is also a great space to discuss any mitigating circumstances surrounding your application — that is if you have not been given a separate form within which to do so.

Paragraph Six: **Conclusion**

This is your final paragraph, where you tie all of your points together.

A Good Introduction

Let's start with perfecting your introduction. For this, I will use an example from a student whose applications was successful. The following is from a student, Dan, who went on to study law at the University of Oxford.

Dan writes in his introduction:

> "In conducting research into the legal profession, I found the arguments against the lack of adequate human rights particularly absorbing. My initial view that the legal system constantly adapted for the better was challenged by Helena Kennedy's *Just Law*, which suggested that civil liberties have actually been lost in recent legislation. I began to appreciate the challenges of maintaining personal freedoms during a climate of fear, and gained a broader understanding of the issues surrounding human rights as a part of law."

After reading that, if you had to pinpoint the narrative that Dan was going for, hopefully, you can see that it is not based on an elaborate or otherworldly story. It is simply an intellectual observation about the challenges of maintaining personal freedoms and civil liberties. Dan also mentioned that his views were challenged, which suggests that he is genuinely invested in and concerned about the issues surrounding the erosion of civil liberties. Remember what I said about 'show, don't tell' earlier on? What Dan has done particularly well here is portray highly sought-after qualities about himself — such as intellectual curiosity, open-mindedness, an analytical mind, and a desire to make a difference — without ever uttering those words himself. This introduction is not flowery, verbose or elaborate, but it tells us a great deal about Dan in an effortless and elegant way.

As you can hopefully gather by now, making an excellent first impression is crucial. There are various ways to do this well, and equally, there are ways to do it badly. Starting off with the latter, I strongly advise you to stay away from using quotes, clichéd phrases, being overly descriptive or talking excessively about other people, such as your parents. But a quick caveat here. If you have to use a quote, make sure that it actually refers directly to your narrative, and that you offer your own insights, rather than plucking somebody else's wisdom from thin air, thinking that it will make you look good. It, in fact, does the opposite. If you have to talk about your parents, keep it brief, and try not to be sycophantic. While it would be inspiring to hear that your father had to struggle for years in order to become an optician, what does it say about you?

The keyword is 'you.'

The personal statement is about you, not your parents. Also, be careful with sob stories — which, if you did not know, are stories or information about a struggle that you have gone through that are predominantly designed to evoke sympathy rather than simply state the facts. If you choose to mention something of this nature, try to make sure that it showcases laudable skills about you — such as the perseverance, determination and grit that you had to summon from deep inside yourself to get through your struggle. Focussing on those strengths allows you to write in a manner that turns a negative into a positive. Remember that you will not impress the admission tutor by riding a 'pity wave,' particularly if another student has unquestionably excellent qualities too.

The Dos and Don'ts of the Introduction

It is a good move to avoid generic or banal phrases, and instead, try to focus on being reflective, insightful, succinct, and perhaps clever in your introduction. Whatever angle you employ in your introduction, always remember to connect your writing back to yourself, and ideally, the university course itself. Write your motivations for studying the course. This could be anything from a recent discovery within your chosen field, a unique or illuminating perspective on contemporary issues, such as Dan's example on civil liberties, or simply stating clearly why attaining the degree that you are applying to will be of benefit to your long-term career. Particularly in the case of statements of purpose, you may also write what you hope to achieve upon graduation.

Fundamentally, always bear in mind that excellent writing comes in various forms, but if you know one that works, then it is prudent to invest your time and energy in following through on that method, in the absence of another option. Writing a personal statement is like cooking an egg: there are many ways to do it, but some are far wackier and riskier than others. Unless you have an ingenious alternative, getting the basics right is always a great start.

A Bad Introduction

Now that you have an idea of what constitutes a good introduction, have a read of what I consider a poor introduction for a personal statement by Timothy — who wanted to study history at the University of Cambridge.

Timothy writes in his introduction:

> "'Those who don't know history are doomed to repeat it.' These words were spoken by the highly esteemed and notable Anglo-Irish statesman, economist and philosopher, Edmund Burke in the 18th century. I have always dreamed of studying history since I was a little child, and honestly, for as long as I can remember, it has always been my dream to study at Cambridge, because of your incredible faculty, and because you rank as number one on lots of league tables, and because your city has so much culture. I studied three A-levels at college. One in History, which I got an A in, one in English, which I got an A in, and one in Geography, which I got an A in too. And I feel that I would honestly be a great Cambridge student. I am fascinated by medieval history, because it is honestly so interesting, and I know Cambridge will help me to achieve my dream of becoming a historian."

This is a 'neither here nor there' style of introduction, and you might be surprised to know how often candidates write in this way. Let's start right from the beginning with the quote:

"Those who don't know history are doomed to repeat it."

Quotes are not the death knell to your personal statement, but this does not get Timothy off to a flying start.

Why?

Because this quote is so overused. Most of us have heard it before, and it reeks of cliché and banality right from the very beginning.

But more importantly, why is that quote even there?

What purpose does it actually serve?

How does it enhance the writing?

The ensuing sentences do not follow logically after the quote, and it reads as though Timothy has simply typed into Google 'quotes about history' and picked the first one that sounded alright.

In addition, phrases such as 'for as long as I can remember,' 'I have always dreamed,' and 'since I was a child' are nothing unique, unfortunately. They are somewhat empty and vague, and fail to make any true impact that says something special or interesting about him. After this, Timothy starts to write somewhat ingratiatingly about the University of Cambridge's 'incredible faculty,' mentioning that they 'rank number one on lots of league tables.' While this may indeed be true, does including this information make Timothy look more like an ideal candidate for this history programme?

No. It serves no purpose at all, and gives the impression that Timothy does not have enough personal insights or interesting perspectives of his own to offer, so much so that he is desperately looking to curry favour with the admissions tutor. This does not work, so please do not try to use this approach.

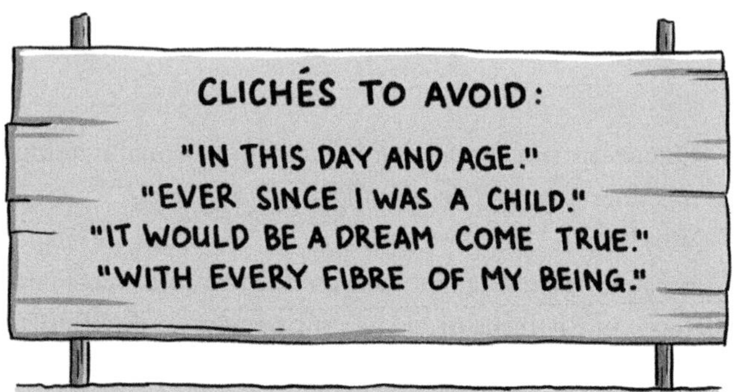

Timothy's statement also suffers from a severe lack of specificity, as illustrated by statements such as 'because your city has so much culture.' It is rather repetitive and tedious to read too. He uses the words 'dream' and 'honestly' three times in that first paragraph alone, and 'always' is used twice. You may want to avoid using words such as 'honestly' or 'truly,' because if you have made your point strongly enough, those words will not be needed. They are 'filler words,' which dilute the quality of your writing. It is presupposed that you are being honest when writing a personal statement, so emphasising this with the adverb 'honestly' is superfluous.

Timothy also mentions his A-level grades in a long-winded fashion, needlessly repeating what can easily be found on his academic transcript, and the only glimmer of specificity that arises when Timothy mentions medieval history is quickly doused, as he merely describes it as 'honestly so interesting,' without explaining anything in particular about why he deems it so.

Overall, this introduction is poor, even though Timothy does not actually make many glaring grammatical errors or spelling mistakes — which is commendable. Timothy's introduction is poor because it is superficial and does not show any evidence of personal insights or wider engagement within the subject of history. At the end of reading that introduction, the admissions tutors know nothing more about Timothy other than him wanting to study at Cambridge. And that is not enough to gain admission, sadly.

Hopefully, you can understand why this style of introduction simply does not work, and that, compared with Dan's successful application to law at Oxford, Timothy's statement is unremarkable due to its lack of depth and specificity. As you saw with Dan's example, he made a good impression by sharing his genuine insights on a specific area of law. The reason why this works better than Timothy's ramble is because we actually learn something about Dan. Dan's curiosity and queries about civil liberties are exactly what an admissions tutor wants to see because this is the kind of mindset that will be required of him as an Oxford student.

Introduction Styles

Crafting a solid introduction for your personal statement may end up being the most time-consuming part of the entire writing process. This is because a great amount of brainstorming and a dash of creativity is usually needed in order to really produce something that will have the kind of impact that will get you noticed for the right reasons. Notwithstanding this fact, most introductions tend to adopt common formats that, while similar in style, are differentiated by their content. Try to think of it like the multiple genres of music: pop, rock, metal, hip hop, country, electronic, classical, reggae and jazz. While two pop songs might have wildly different lyrics, different singers and different melodies, they both belong to the same genre. This principle also applies to introductions. The more you read through introductions to personal statements, the easier it will be to notice the most frequently used styles that students tend to adopt, and perhaps follow a similar format while putting your own spin on it to make it your own. The following are the most common styles that I have found students using in their personal statements:

- Intellectual Exploration
- Honest Critique
- Micro Musings
- General Observations
- Introspective Commentary
- A Defining Moment
- Creative Imagery

Intellectual Exploration

Dan's previous example for his successful application to study law at Oxford was an example of intellectual exploration, as he expounded upon the difficulties of upholding civil liberties and how his beliefs had been challenged. The advantage of demonstrating intellectual exploration in your introduction is that it gives an admissions tutor a chance to instantly get an idea of how you think. As a student about to embark on further study at university, you are not expected to be an expert within the field that you are pursuing. However, if you can demonstrate depth and clarity of thought about what you hope to study, this gives an admissions tutor a better chance of seeing you as the kind of student who will adjust well to a higher level of learning.

Maebh was given an offer by the University of Oxford, where she went on to study English language and literature. Her introduction followed a style that displayed intellectual exploration particularly well. Have a read of what she wrote.

Maebh writes in her introduction:

> "Literature is a limitless source of human knowledge; one that is a personal experience to each reader and forever changing as we look back into the past with our own experiences. Looking at Charlotte Brontë's *Jane Eyre* with a focus on mental health and post-colonialism introduced me to the idea of reading older texts with the value of hindsight and a modern outlook. Jean Rhys' novel *Wide Sargasso Sea* seemed to offer one solution to Bertha's silence within Jane Eyre and I found the idea of writing about silenced characters within literature compelling in both its imagination and necessity."

Maebh's introduction is short, but impactful. While she cited a commonly read literary work, Charlotte Brontë's *Jane Eyre*, she lasered in on an aspect of literature that was highly specific, as she focussed on the contemporary issues of mental health and post-colonialism. Reading older texts with the 'value of hindsight and a modern outlook' is an interesting perspective within English literature, and it demonstrates Maebh's strong analytical skills.

Dan's and Maebh's introductions both show intellectual exploration; however, the evidence that they use is external to their own experiences. In Dan's case, he cited Helena Kennedy's book, *Just Law*, and Maebh mentioned Charlotte Brontë's and Jean Rhys' novels. It is an equally effective strategy to demonstrate intellectual exploration while shedding light on your own experiences. This tends to work well because you make your writing personal to you, while simultaneously impressing the admissions tutor with your intellectual commentary.

Gresa, who secured an offer to study politics and international relations at University College London, did this rather well when she expounded upon her family's experiences during the Kosovo War.

Gresa writes in her introduction:

> "Studying history is an insight into how our modern-day institutions, customs, and values have evolved to be what they are today. I grew up listening to my family's experiences during the Kosovo War and hearing the newest developments surrounding the struggle for statehood. My personal understanding of the conflict has been enriched by watching the

> documentary, 'Lufta ne Kosove,' which argued that the war was an inevitable reaction to the pre-existing ethnic tensions in the region of Kosovo, escalated by the Yugoslav Wars in the 90s. I found the documentary's arguments were validated by the book written by Serbian human rights activist, S. Biserko, in *Yugoslavia's Implosion*. This issue remains prevalent today; the 2021 Human Rights Helsinki Report found that there was explicit racism toward Albanians in the north of Serbia. Linking historical conflicts to modern-day political issues is a key reason why I want to study these subjects together."

While Gresa starts off her introduction with a broad statement about what history is, she does not wait to let us know about the stories she heard about the Kosovo War during her childhood and the steps that she took to further educate herself on the matter through the documentary and book. I strongly recommend that you strive to strike the right balance between demonstrating intellectual exploration while also providing personal evidence to make your narrative all the more compelling. Throughout your personal statement, the two parts that carry the most weight will always be how you think and the evidence that you use to provide credibility and legitimacy to your writing. It is not enough to merely regurgitate information from a book that you have read, because that does not reveal anything noteworthy or impressive about you. So please remember that it is a mixture of your insights and experiences that will make you come across well. If you manage to display both of these qualities strongly, you are on the right track.

Honest Critique

Another common style of introduction that students use in their personal statements involves writing in a manner that criticises, scrutinises and evaluates established principles, social norms, beliefs or other issues worthy of debate. This style of writing is a compelling way to make a bold statement to the admissions tutor about your opinions and ideas, and you will often see this in humanities subjects, such as history, philosophy and politics. To write your introduction as a form of 'honest critique,' you are more likely to make an impact on the reader if you do not sit on the fence. This carries a degree of risk, particularly when discussing divisive or contentious issues, but it will certainly get you noticed. It also allows you to radiate passion and purpose, which can often be hard to achieve if you are not genuinely invested in or deeply care about the issues at hand. I would advise that if you opt for an honest critique in your introduction, make sure that your arguments are sound and logical, and that your facts are accurate. The goal is to demonstrate powerful insights, not just powerful words and bellicose language. Always bear that in mind with this style of introduction.

Have a read of this example from Anna, who managed to strike the right balance with her introduction, securing entry to study philosophy, politics and economics at the University of Oxford.

Anna writes in her introduction:

> "They all act selfishly: corrupt politicians, vulture funds, and the average voter. Although this may be an allegation, it is undeniable that temporal comfort is more often than not chosen over the possibility to provide a better future. I see this in abundance in politics and not seldom economic intentions are behind it. I want to understand such processes by studying how economics and politics influence each other. Are economics the cause for political actions or is it the other way around?"

The first line of Anna's introduction is attention-grabbing, as she opens with a forthright statement, and she does not sit on the fence.

Despite this introduction taking the form of an honest critique, Anna also provides intellectual exploration here, as she explains that economic intentions are the root cause of the 'selfishness' that she initially referred to. Interestingly, her ideas about the relationship between economics and politics is an example of the causality dilemma, also known as the 'chicken or the egg question,' as it questions 'which came first?' Perspectives such as these are highly valuable in your introduction because they demonstrate nuance and carefully considered thought about the issues at play. While not sitting on the fence makes your argument more compelling, the ability to think critically in areas that are not clear-cut is a hallmark of an intelligent student.

Esther, a student who went on to study modern history and economics at the University of Manchester was also vocal about the state of the education system in the United Kingdom, as well as her perspectives on British history, colonialism and other topical issues.

Have a read of what Esther wrote.

Esther writes in her introduction:

> "The current curriculum is not inclusive. It fails to depict all the sides of British history, the good and the deplorable. During lockdown, I founded a campaign called 'Black History Matters' on social media, which educated people on key overlooked Black British figures such as Harold

> Moody. I was invited by Warwick University to be a keynote speaker for a webinar called 'The UK Curriculum: Our Fight for Education Equality,' where I spoke about the importance of the inclusion of different perspectives and narratives in the UK curriculum and the small steps that can be taken to ensure this. For a few years, I have been investing in looking beyond the perspectives presented to me in my curriculum and unearthing different viewpoints. Studying economics and history would allow me to explore the symbiotic relationship between the two, giving me the knowledge to analyse past events and use economic theories and concepts to infer about the future. I am particularly interested in the rise of the British Empire and the impact of colonialism and imperialism on the African economies and policies used to combat postcolonial issues. In order to maintain a favourable macroeconomic environment in this situation, investments in agriculture and technology may prove essential to promote longer-term growth."

Similar to Anna's introduction, Esther's first line is attention-grabbing. Esther goes a step further in her introduction by providing evidence of the steps that she took to raise awareness about Black British figures, which demonstrates specificity and dedication to an important issue. In your introduction, the deeper and more personal you make your writing, the greater the space you create to distinguish yourself from other students. I advise that if you choose to write about an important issue, you do not mention it in passing to tick a box, and then skip to another topic. Rather, it is more effective that you continue to explore that topic and shed light on your perspectives, opinions, realisations and experiences that relate to that issue, just as Esther has done. Similar to Anna, Esther does not merely make a statement to get attention and end it abruptly. She goes on to explore the symbiotic relationship between economics and history — a perspective that also resembles Anna's stance on economics and politics. Despite exploring a contentious and sensitive issue, Esther demonstrates a forward-looking approach as she evokes passion for her subject.

Micro Musings

If you had to stand at the front of a room of 100 people and give a riveting 10-minute speech about garden peas, could you do it? What would you talk about and which angle would you choose? Most likely, if you simply stated the facts about what garden peas are and their various uses, you would find your listeners dozing off within the first minute. However, if you used garden peas as a metaphor, motif or passageway into a wider topic or observation, you might still be able to sustain the reader's attention. Where personal statements are concerned, the notion of taking something seemingly small or insignificant and finding a way to expand it into written work that still captivates the reader's attention is what I call 'micro musings.' It is a skill that is very hard to achieve in an introduction because there are many ways to lose the reader's interest. But, when it is done well, it really makes a strong impression because you will stand out from the crowd, and the courage to write about something so obscure will make the topic that you are writing about that much more interesting.

Have a read of this example from Barnaby, a student who was successful in his application to a top university, where he studied theology.

Barnaby writes in his introduction:

> "The thought of pretzels leading to a world-class education might appear preposterous at first, and yet it is thanks to an unassuming pretzel that I find myself on the cusp of studying theology at a leading institution. Taken at face value, pretzels are rather unremarkable to the average person, and while I do not claim to be an expert in these baked delights, I know that there is so much more to them than meets the eye. It was while sitting on a bench in a local park that I spotted a perfectly normal, unbitten pretzel right next to me. It had clearly been left by someone else, and I had no plans of consuming it. However, as I stared at its interweaving arms — the signature 'knot' design that we are all familiar with — it occurred to me that someone, somewhere, at some point, must have conceived the idea of this design that bakers around the world continue to use. That day, I became unexpectedly contemplative as I considered that lone pretzel on the bench as a microcosm of our existence. In the same way that a pretzel has such a distinct shape that was clearly

designed by someone, is it logical to think that something as complex as the universe could have simply appeared out of nowhere? Upon further research, I learned that the pretzel was apparently invented in 610 A.D by an Italian monk who wanted the pretzel to resemble the crossed arms of praying children. He gave the name, 'pretiola,' to his baked creations, which translates to 'little rewards,' as he had used what would later become known as the 'pretzel' to reward children for learning their prayers. Today, I admit that I find myself brooding on existential thoughts, but it is my hope that studying theology will provide a pathway for illumination and enlightenment, even if the true answers will forever remain hidden."

Barnaby's introduction is a stellar example of micro musings in action. He uses his thoughts about a simple pretzel as a gateway to a much larger, philosophical question about our existence as human beings. This is clever, and it makes his introduction captivating to read. Admittedly, Barnaby leaves the reader in suspense in this introduction, it is not until the fourth sentence that we understand the point that Barnaby is making. However, the profundity of Barnaby's ideas and the juxtaposition between a simple pretzel and the magnitude of his existential thoughts make the wait worth it. If you choose to use micro musings in your introduction, just as Barnaby has done, it is vital that you are confident that the point that you are making is well-reasoned and eloquently articulated. You do not want to frustrate the reader with endless rambles about something banal, only to leave a sour taste in their mouths from having reached an underwhelming conclusion.

Introspective Commentary

If you are an introspective person, you are someone who privately considers, reflects upon and evaluates your thoughts, emotions, actions and ideas. Being introspective is an excellent skill to portray within a personal statement, particularly in your introduction, as this is where you need to establish your narrative and your context. Writing an introduction in the style of introspective commentary is most effective when you find a way to write about your reflections in a way that logically connects you studying on your chosen course as the solution to your thirst for answers. For example, upon reflecting on your past introspectively, you might discover a part of your character or your story that compels you to study a specific subject or pursue a career in your chosen field. This is your 'raison d'être' — your 'reason for being,' and if you can communicate whatever this may uniquely be for you in a manner that is persuasive and compelling, you will make a strong impression on the reader.

Once again, it is best that you have a read of what this looks like with a real-life example. This introduction is from a student, Harry, who secured an offer to study medicine at Imperial College London.

Harry writes in his introduction:

> "Throughout my teenage years, I was eager to grow older and develop a sense of self. Now at eighteen, I cannot help but feel overwhelmed by multiple responsibilities and ever-present obstacles. I wanted to help people but could not fathom an answer to the question: how? I was made aware that the sense of purpose I sought comes from the service to others, by observing doctors around me. This idea of service is what medicine represents to me. Service is prevalent in all health professions, but with medicine, this act of service is an attempt to balance the ability to heal and the capacity to cause harm. I vehemently believe life in medicine will offer me a sense of fulfilment but not without difficulties. Hard work and resilience serve as sacrifices to uphold medicine's raison d'etre, saving lives."

As you can hopefully see, Harry's personal quest to 'grow older and develop a sense of self' is his raison d'être. He cogently explains that the way in which this can be achieved in his case is by being of service to others. As I pointed out, the goal is to not merely indulge in introspective commentary, but to make your chosen course 'the solution to your thirst for answers,' which will provide clarity, wisdom or purpose within your career.

General Observations

An introduction does not always have to be profound. In this case, making a general observation or commentary about your subject is a perfectly reasonable way to articulate your ideas and insights within your subject. One of the risks with making general observations in your introduction, however, is that you must strive to also keep your writing personal and reflective, and not just descriptive. The admissions tutors still need to know about what you actually think, so make sure that you include your own contributions too.

Henry was offered a place at the University of Cambridge, where he studied veterinary medicine. Have a read of what he wrote.

Henry writes in his introduction:

"'Man's best friend' is a commonly used

> phrase that sums up much of our history and relationships with animals. These relationships, including those between other species, fascinate me greatly and it is by becoming a vet that I wish to contribute further towards the care and study of our animal companions. We value them as we value our family, therefore I wish to protect my clients' emotional well-being by providing essential care for their pets. I have seen some of the qualities vets must possess in order to carry out the multitude of tasks that benefit animals and indirectly their human companions. Determination and tenacity coupled with the belief that their actions are beneficial are vital to one's success as a vet."

This is a somewhat light-hearted introduction, but it is easy to read and makes Henry come across as a caring and pleasant person. You should also bear in mind that different subjects require their own unique blend of skills. In this case, Henry evoking compassion, care and kindness is appropriate because he wants to become a vet — a profession that would benefit from these character traits. Similarly, Harry, from earlier on, demonstrated a desire to make a difference by helping others, which aligns with the skills that will support his aspirations of becoming a medical doctor one day. Barnaby was contemplative and philosophical about his existence, which is appropriate for theology. Esther and Anna stated their views with passion, and considering their ambitions to respectively study politics, philosophy and economics, and modern history and economics, it makes sense that these traits were portrayed. A key point here is that each subject has its own desired skills that you ought to display. As I mentioned in Chapter One: Research, it helps to fully understand your subject and the course itself so that you can deliver a bespoke piece of writing that matches the requirements, but also exceeds expectations when an admissions tutor reads your personal statement.

A Defining Moment

The human experience is punctuated by moments of revelation, discovery, change, failure, success, self-doubt, betrayal, fear and enlightenment. Each of these events may not be the easiest to go through, however, they are usually moments that lead to a development of your character or some kind of personal metamorphosis, depending on how you react to the changes that come your way. In a personal statement introduction, writing about 'defining moments' of this nature can be very compelling, as you invite the reader to follow your personal journey of growth. Writing about a defining moment achieves the aim of conveying your introduction in a personal way, and if you manage to write something of magnitude or importance that captivates the reader, you will have made a strong impression.

Have a read of Sanjeev's introduction for his application for a master's degree in mental health sciences.

Sanjeev writes in his introduction:

> "Tomorrow is always a day away — until it isn't. We live each day with the expectation that the mundane but perfectly normal lives that we know will always look the same. Having lost both of my legs in an automobile accident, I can attest to the fragility of life and the mental strain of going through a tragedy. Prior to the accident, I was due to take the reins of my father's agricultural business in India, but that all changed on one fateful day. The trajectory of my life completely shifted, my priorities changed and, in more ways than one, I was suddenly a different person. Every day of my life, I am reminded of what I lost; but over time, I have strived to develop patterns of thinking that focus on what I can do, rather than what I cannot do. It has not been an easy journey, but today, I feel a sense of purpose by empowering others through their own hardship, and I believe that understanding mental health from a multi-disciplinary perspective, drawing from biological, psychological and social foundations, will allow me to more adequately help others."

Sanjeev's story is an example of a truly defining moment. The reader can not help but feel empathy for him, but also a great amount of admiration, as he is focused on turning a tragedy into a triumph, by helping other people with their mental health. In literature, stories such as Sanjeev's are examples of 'peripeteia,' which is when a person has to contend with a sudden reversal of fortune or change of circumstances. For a personal statement, stories that demonstrate peripeteia are compelling reads, particularly when students show perseverance, purpose and grit in spite of their diversity. Whatever your 'defining moment' may be, you may want to consider including this in your introduction, provided that you are comfortable sharing that information. A defining moment does not need to be negative either. As long as an event had an impact on you and your path, it might be worth writing about.

Creative Imagery

Finally, another style of writing that students tend to employ in their introduction is the use of creative imagery. While writing infused with imagery can be pleasant to read, you should also be mindful of the fact that too much of it can be distracting. Before you incorporate any imagery, you ought to make sure that you are contributing something of real substance, and not just flowery and overly descriptive language. Remember that while your personal statement should demonstrate excellent word choices, tone, coherence, spelling and grammar, these are the most basic of requirements. You will not score extra points by writing a Pulitzer Prize-winning piece if the basic pillars of what makes an excellent personal statement are not met.

Bill received an offer to study engineering at the University of Leicester. Have a read of what he wrote:

Bill writes in his introduction:

"One's first flight is often a very memorable moment: the growl of the engine as the plane hurls down a runway and rises above the clouds — likewise, my passion for engineering flew high. The marvel of flight and the computational systems used in aiding its possibility reveals to me the ways in which, through engineering, the impossible can become possible. I believe I will be able to make a consequential impact in future innovations that take the world to new heights. From the motors in a small hand-held fan to the massive GE90 Engine, engineering has been woven into the fabrics of our everyday lives and the genius of inventors and innovators before us inspires me to seek higher education, and to be among those who make our world an easier place to live in."

"The growl of the engine."

"The plane hurls down a runway and rises above the clouds."

"The impossible can become possible."

"Take the world to new heights."

"Engineering has been woven into the fabrics of our everyday lives."

Everything about Bill's introduction appears carefully constructed to reinforce the theme of 'one's first flight,' and he uses imagery as a literary device to create a vivid picture in our minds, as readers. While imagery and descriptive language can be risky when overused, Bill strikes the right balance with this introduction as an admissions tutor gets a real sense of how passionate he is about studying engineering, and in the end, his passion is inspiring.

Making an Impression

One of the common concerns that students have is wondering how they can make their introduction 'stand out.' Being flashy and over-the-top in your introduction can make your writing come across as contrived and gimmicky, so just as I said about imagery with Bill's example, it is a good idea to proceed with caution. However, if you are looking for ways to grab the reader's attention from the first line, you may want to look to two tried-and-tested methods. The first method is known as a paraprosdokian.

Paraprosdokians

A paraprosdokian is a figure of speech wherein a sentence or phrase follows a path with an unexpected twist, leading to a surprising and often humorous ending. Paraprosdokians employ the element of surprise to upend audience expectations in order to create a dramatic outcome.

Here are a few examples of paraprosdokians from the first lines of personal statements:

"It has been said that democracy is the worst form of government except all those other forms that have been tried."

"The difference between fiction and reality is that fiction has to make sense."

"Growing old is tough; not growing old is worse."

"Laughter is the best medicine... if you don't have insurance."

You can be very creative with paraprosdokians as a means to start off with a bang, but just remember to reel it in from the second sentence onwards. That is really important. Once you have made your mark, let it simmer with the reader, and then move on to writing about something of real substance in the ensuing lines. If you want to be bold, witty and inventive, that is fine. But remember to only do it in moderation.

Have a read of this example from Kyle, a candidate who was successful in his application to study for his degree in nutrition:

Kyle writes in his introduction:

> "If 'change is inevitable,' the vending machines in the school canteen have clearly bucked the trend.

> In fact, it was in my frustration of having to rely on the stale junk food from the old vending machines every lunchtime that I started to think deeply about what I was actually putting inside my body. Until then, I mindlessly consumed whatever food was available to me without stopping to think about what was actually good for my body. I vowed to never order from the vending machines again, and focussed my attention on becoming educated on nutrition, which I now hope to study at a higher level."

As you can see, Kyle's first line about the 'change' from the vending machines is attention-grabbing and humorous in nature. After a bold start, he then expounds upon his reasons for wanting to study nutrition.

In Medias Res

The second method for grabbing a reader's attention in the introduction uses the literary device 'in medias res,' which, translated from Latin, means 'in the midst of things.' This is the practice of beginning an epic story or other narrative by plunging straight into a crucial situation that is part of a related chain of events. It is common to see this with students applying to study courses such as medicine, who will often describe a gripping or character-defining moment that ignited their passion to become a doctor. This method can be really effective in pulling the reader right into the action without much need for exposition or 'setting the scene.' This allows you to make your point quicker and to satisfy the reader with the highlight and apotheosis of your story within a few lines, and subsequently write reflectively as you evaluate and ruminate on your experiences.

Have a read of this example from Nancy, a candidate who was successful in her application to study for her master's degree in sports science:

Nancy writes in her introduction:

> "As I stared down at the Earth thousands of feet beneath me, it occurred to me that this was the first time in my life that I felt completely weightless. Jumping from a plane and hurtling down towards the ground at over 100 miles per hour is a sensation that cannot accurately be described until you do it for yourself. Once the parachute opened, all I saw was the most exquisite blend of green and blue — a spectacular marriage between the luscious green fields below me and the ethereal blue sky from a perspective that was simply unmatched. My first thought when we glided down towards the ground was how paralysing fear can be up until the point that it is overcome. Skydiving has been on my bucket list for years, and up until that jump, I was riddled with fear, but equally, an inexplicable desire to go ahead anyway. As I look to further my career, it is the irresistible allure of performing during highly pressurised moments

that motivates me to study sports science. As a self-confessed thrill-seeker, I am excited to use my knowledge of biology and my passion for sport to help other athletes perform at their best."

Nancy's introduction leverages the power of 'in medias res' by pulling the reader right into the decisive moment of her story — one which would fill many people with trepidation: jumping out of a moving plane. This is highly effective in grabbing the reader's attention. In addition, Nancy's ability to connect her skydive with how she hopes to help athletes is very apt, as she knows what it means to face one's fear and perform under pressure.

When it comes to grabbing the reader's attention, paraprosdokians and in medias res both have their uses. But please remember that 'attention' is not the vital currency here, ★ and its value decreases over time. The strongest currencies in a personal statement are your insights and the evidence that you use to back them up. If you manage to strike the right balance between sustaining the reader's attention, sharing your insights and providing clear evidence, you are well on your way to writing an excellent personal statement.

Paragraph Two: Academic Background

In your second paragraph, I recommend that you write about your academic background and how your intellectual perspectives have developed over time. In essence, you want to impress upon the admissions tutor why and how your academic background has prepared you for further study, and what you can contribute to the university intellectually if admitted. If you are applying as an undergraduate student, you will most likely write about your A-levels or other similar qualifications that you obtained in secondary school or high school. If you are applying as a postgraduate student, you might write about your undergraduate degree or research that you have undertaken. But be careful not to repeat too many details that the admission tutor can find on your resume or transcript. The goal is to be reflective and offer your own personal perspectives and insights about specific parts of your chosen field, rather than regurgitate a comprehensive list of your achievements. You might also question a widely accepted aspect of your subject, or write about a topic that you explored within your subject that you found surprising, revelatory or illuminating. The goal is to evoke passion, curiosity, enthusiasm, specificity and dedication to your chosen course.

Have a read of this example from Amy, a student who was successful in her application to study for her undergraduate degree in pharmacy.

Amy writes in paragraph two:

> "Studying biology allowed me to expand my understanding of areas of personal interest to me, such as stem cell research through the use of pluripotent stem cells to produce glucose-responding cells that mimic the role of beta cells. This topic resonated with me as my cousin has leukaemia, and I know of the struggle of finding a viable bone marrow transplant donor for this treatment. The ground-breaking work that is currently being carried out in clinical trials for drugs and treatments that we may all benefit from in the future underscores the sheer magnitude of the work being undertaken in this field."

Amy does an excellent job by not only mentioning her academic background, but doing so in a manner that feels somewhat more personal and revelatory than the average student. She offers personal insights about how stem cell research has impacted a close family member of hers, and goes on to offer her opinions about the groundbreaking work being done in this area. The value in this paragraph lies in the fact that we learn more about Amy, beyond simply knowing that she studied biology at A-level. This is what you want to emulate. You need to build upon your academic transcript 

and offer insights and perspectives that allow the admissions tutors to really get to know how you think. Writing about your academic background should not be an overly complex task, provided that you tell the truth and do so reflectively. So make sure that you do exactly that.

Now have a read of this example from Oscar, a student who was successful in his application to study law at the University of Cambridge.

Oscar writes in paragraph two:

> "Attempting to deepen my knowledge, I read *The Concept of Law* by H. L. A Hart. Hart argues that there is no necessary connection between law and morality. This argument was convincing as I believe that the law does not hold any such moral authority as unjust laws are possible and there are ethical areas where the law does not have a standpoint. This reflects my experience of living in Afghanistan where the laws enforcing gender discrimination were immoral under a liberal egalitarian moral framework. This led me to the conclusion that a law being identified as law derives from people believing they are obligated to follow it rather than it being inherently moral. I analysed other arguments regarding the connection between law and morality which led me to read *The Controversy*

> *Between Professor Hart and Professor Fuller* by G. Breckenridge. Fuller argues that the purpose of the legal system is to uphold 'the inner morality of law,' which I also found to be a compelling argument. The arguments put forward by both Hart and Fuller enhanced my understanding of the controversy surrounding what the purpose of the law is, which is a central topic I would like to further explore."

Oscar's analysis about where law derives its authority is a classic, but highly relevant topic to discuss as a budding law student. Oscar goes a step further by not only sharing his intellectual insights, but also linking back to his own experiences of living in Afghanistan and making his writing personal to him. This paragraph is strengthened by Oscar's ability to not only state the findings or discoveries from books he has read, but also implant his own opinions and reflections.

Have a read of some of the phrases that Oscar uses:

"I believe that the law does not hold any such moral authority..."

"This reflects my experience of living in Afghanistan..."

"This led me to the conclusion..."

"I analysed other arguments..."

"I also found..."

Do you notice how each of these phrases show evidence of Oscar's own contributions, responses and reflections regarding his academic interests? This is what you should strive for in this paragraph. Do not rely on simply referencing what someone else has said or the academic material that you have read, as this does not reveal anything about you.

Have a read of another second paragraph from a personal statement. This one is from Chloe, who received her offer to study human sciences at the University of Oxford.

Chloe writes in paragraph two:

> "To expand my knowledge of what DNA reveals, I read Rutherford's book: *A Brief History of Everyone Who Ever Lived.* He mentions the discovery of Homo floresiensis remains in 2003, explaining how skeletal remains provide evidence for evolution and how we categorise our ancestors into different species. It led me to do further reading to learn why the discovery caused controversy. The bones found were small in skull size and stature. One theory suggests this was a helpful adaptation for island living; others suggest it is evidence of a pathological condition, like microcephaly. Multiple fossils of similar size were found, and it is improbable that they all suffered from microcephaly, hence why the island dwarfism theory is more compelling to me.

> Before reading this, I had never considered how we understood so much about our ancestors and their existence. It demonstrated the complexity of human evolution and how we evolved from our ancestors. It also showed the importance of an interdisciplinary approach; combining biology, geography and anthropology to link the fossils and the environment to explain the findings. Independent exploration into this discovery was riveting and gave me a real insight into evolution, and I am eager to broaden my understanding of this topic."

You will hopefully notice how Chloe manages to also interweave her own personal perspectives into this paragraph. She does not fall into the trap of simply listing her academic insights as though she is reading from a textbook. Instead, she demonstrates reflection with the following phrases:

"It led me to do further reading to learn..."

"Before reading this, I had never considered..."

"Gave me a real insight into..."

"I am eager to broaden my understanding..."

These phrases provide evidence of Chloe's genuine interest in human sciences, and this makes her second paragraph a pleasant read. Another point to bear in mind in your second paragraph is that universities place varying degrees of importance on demonstrating academic or intellectual insights. As Chloe applied to Oxford, this style of writing is precisely what admissions tutors are looking for. Depending on the university that you are applying to, you should do your research to write in the manner that is most suitable.

Now have a read of this second paragraph from Alec, who received an offer to study history and economics at the University of Cambridge:

Alec writes in paragraph two:

> "I completed an independent research project on the role of Anthony Eden in the Suez Crisis following Nasser's nationalisation of the canal. This event was unique in its significance not only in the context of Britain's colonial demise, but also in the wider context of the Cold War. My study of Eden's correspondence with Eisenhower revealed Eden's increasingly paranoid thinking and exposed a critical breakdown in communication during the height of the crisis. The Suez crisis can broadly be viewed as a clash between the new, post-war, world order and the pre-war generation running the country. However, I concluded that the assertion that the crisis was the fault of Eden's paranoia alone was unfounded; factors such as Nasser's provocative belligerence should also be taken into account. This project also shed light on Britain's current

> global position and helped to explain her foreign policy."

Once again, we can see that in sharing his academic insights, Alec has not merely read from the textbook. He has actually contributed his own ideas — particularly with this statement:

> *"I concluded that the assertion that the crisis was the fault of Eden's paranoia alone was unfounded; factors such as Nasser's provocative belligerence should also be taken into account."*

It's a bold move to assert your opinion in this way, but it reads really well in Alec's case because he writes as though he is already studying history and economics at Cambridge. This makes it easier for an admissions tutor to see him as having the right qualities to receive an offer. You should strive to do the same. As I have said before, if you need to adjust your style of writing to suit the style of the university that you are applying to, then that is fine too. Essentially, you want to strike the right balance between being authentic to who you are and being quietly aware of the standards, styles and expectations of the university that you are applying to. It is good to have a bit of both. Be yourself, but be somewhat aware of how your writing will be perceived by the admissions tutor. Alec strikes the right balance and writes excellently. He is very much the kind of student who will excel at Cambridge.

Finally, have a read of this second paragraph from Thea, who received an offer to study Spanish & French at King's College London.

Thea writes in paragraph two:

> "I have recently become especially interested in French Law. I have thoroughly enjoyed researching and learning about the role of the French feminist and lawyer Gisèle Halimi in the legalisation of abortion in France. Her fight for equality began at the age of 12 when she starved herself for eight days in order to achieve the right to be able to choose to read. This desire to choose never faltered throughout her life and in 1971, she cofounded the movement, 'Choisir,' alongside Simone de Beauvoir. Over the course of the next few years, Halimi fought for the rights of women all over France to choose, and represented a 16-year-old girl in court when she was charged for an illegal abortion after being raped. The young girl was acquitted and this trial, known famously as the Bobigny trial, changed the perspectives of people all over France. In my opinion, if it weren't for Halimi winning this trial then the legalisation of abortion in France would have happened much later than 1975 as Halimi forced people to consider that if women didn't have the right to choose what happens to their own bodies then there was no way that they could have any real social standing. My interest

> in French Law led to choosing it as the topic for my A-Level Independent Research Project, developing my critical analysis, evaluation and academic research skills."

At this point, you will hopefully have noticed that each of these students has not only recited text from their respective subjects, but also contributed their own insights, which is vital. Thea sheds light on her own views rather well:

"In my opinion, if it weren't for Halimi winning this trial then the legalisation of abortion in France would have happened much later than 1975."

Thea's insights about a significant legal, social and ideological change in France are insightful and interesting to read. She actually shares her opinions about the French feminist and lawyer Gisèle Halimi and focuses on depth and critical analysis.

And now, with a strong introduction and second paragraph, you are paving the path to producing an excellent personal statement. There is a lot that goes into how you start a personal statement, but just remember to try, try and try again. The hardest part can often be just getting something down on paper, but it does not have to be perfect on your first go, so just start. Join me in the next chapter, Structure II, where you will learn about what to do in the next four paragraphs of your personal statement.

FINAL POINTS

For your first paragraph, answer the following questions to brainstorm ideas that can be incorporated as your introduction. You can always come back to this section when writing your next paragraphs.

Brainstorming for Your Introduction:

What interesting perspectives do you have on your chosen subject?

....
....
....
....
....
....
....
....
....
....
....
....
....
....
....
....
....

FINAL POINTS

Did any moment inspire you to study your chosen subject?

....

....

....

....

....

....

....

....

....

....

What aspect of your subject has challenged you?

....

....

....

....

....

....

....

....

....

....

FINAL POINTS

In the space below, make notes on ideas, stories, observations or remarks that you may want to include in your introduction.

Paragraph 1: Introduction

....

....

....

....

....

....

....

....

....

....

....

....

....

....

....

....

....

....

....

....

FINAL POINTS

Use this space to make notes on what you may want to include in your second paragraph.

Paragraph 2: Academic Background

....
....
....
....
....
....
....
....
....
....
....
....
....
....
....
....
....
....
....
....

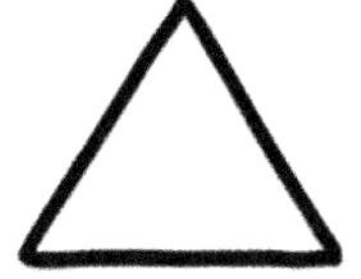

Chapter Five: Structure II

In this chapter, I will be covering what you should write in paragraphs three, four, five and six of your personal statement. So, to avoid further delay, let's get right back into it, shall we?

Paragraph Three: Work Experience

If your introduction sets the narrative, pace and tone of your writing, and paragraph two provides insights into your intellectual background and perspectives, then paragraph three is where you seal the deal by demonstrating real-life applications of your skills in action. Yes — paragraph three is where you will write about your work experience or other similar projects that go beyond the theory. This is another excellent chance to show concrete evidence that demonstrates the value that you will bring to your chosen course.

Have a read of this excerpt from Preston — a student whose application to a postgraduate degree in international relations at a top university proved successful:

Preston writes in paragraph three:

> "Having studied politics at Georgetown University, I have established a robust foundation of knowledge in the topics that I hope to build upon at your institution. In the spring semester of my third year, I pursued an off-campus internship at the New York State Assembly and was delighted to be assigned to work with local government politicians, as well as our senator. As part of the internship, I was required to analyse bills, report my findings to representatives, and submit bi-weekly reports to my supervising professor. At the culmination of this internship, I wrote a 30-page report detailing my findings, of which I received widespread commendation from senior colleagues. Working at the upper echelons of state-level politics was illuminating, and with the experience gained at a local level, I sought to broaden my horizons and global perspectives. As a result, I travelled to Cuba, followed by Haiti, where I am currently undertaking charity work with orphans living in poverty. Both countries intrigue me because they exist in the shadow of

> recently troubled histories — clear evidence of their resilience. In light of their blighted pasts, the humanitarian efforts made to restore order and peace are shining examples of what can be achieved through international cooperation, and this continues to motivate me to pursue a career in international relations."

Hopefully, you can glean some inspiration from Preston's third paragraph in the way that he describes his work experience. He was incredibly fortunate to have worked with local government politicians and his senator, but he was equally reflective and insightful about his own experiences. We get a clear idea of Preston, through his narrative, as a person who seeks to be of service to the community. As he has undertaken voluntary work with orphans in Cuba and Haiti, it is also apparent that Preston has a genuine desire to make a difference. Preston's third paragraph of his personal statement ticks multiple boxes because his work experience is solid and his reflections on those experiences are insightful. This is the goal when writing about your work experiences.

A student named Ethan received an offer to study medicine at the University of Glasgow. He wrote about his work experience in paragraph two, rather than paragraph three.

Ethan writes in his paragraph about work experience:

"Shadowing a plastic surgeon for a week in a secondary care position provided an insight into the demands and challenges facing NHS workers, such as long hours and staff shortages. Whilst observing a consultation with a patient who underwent a rhinectomy due to substance abuse, I witnessed the qualities required to succeed as a doctor along with the importance of a multi-disciplinary approach to care. The consultant emphasised the importance of being non-judgemental as a doctor whilst showing empathy and following an ethical code. I have developed such skills whilst working for Relationships Scotland as I am often the first contact for many clients who find it difficult to discuss their situation and may become emotional. Such a role has also improved my organisational skills and ability to work as part of a multi-disciplinary team. Dialogue with medical students gave me an insight into the challenges that may arise during patient care. Volunteering with Citizens Advice gave me experience facing many of these challenges, such as language barriers, intoxication or anger towards oneself, making me an ideal candidate for a career in medicine. Helping vulnerable members of society has taught me how to approach delicate subjects with empathy, whilst teaching music at a sensory impairment school allowed me to appreciate the importance of individualised care and the personal reward of helping someone reach their goal."

Ethan does an excellent job of demonstrating multiple insights that he gained from his work experience. In fact, if you take the time to extract all of the qualities that Ethan has either witnessed in action on his work experience placements or demonstrated himself, you will see just how many insights Ethan has managed to include in one paragraph.

- The demands and challenges facing NHS workers.
- The importance of a multi-disciplinary approach to health care.
- The importance of being non-judgemental.
- Showing empathy and following an ethical code.
- Organisational skills.
- Working as part of a multi-disciplinary team.
- Facing issues such as language barriers, intoxication and anger towards oneself.
- Handling delicate subjects.
- The importance of individualised care.
- The value and reward of helping others reach their goals.

In total, Ethan infuses ten qualities into his paragraph about work experience, and yet, as you read through, it does not come across like he is simply listing experiences from his CV. There are two crucial reasons why this is the case. Firstly, he sticks to two key experiences and focuses on deeply exploring the various roles within each experience, rather than picking multiple experiences and only exploring them lightly. Secondly, for each experience, Ethan's statements remain reflective and diverse. He leaves the admissions tutor in no doubt about whether he is suited for a career in medicine, as he clearly has derived multiple insights from his work experience placements. He has 'been there,' and he has proof.

I strongly recommend that you opt for Ethan's approach of using a few work experience placements to impress upon the admissions tutor the insights or lessons that you gained. Focus on depth, and be sure that by the end of this paragraph, the admissions tutor knows a lot more about what you learned from your experiences, and not just what you did or who you shadowed. Even if you shadowed a leader in your chosen field, that person is not the one who will be attending the university that you are applying to — you are. So always bear that in mind. If you are lucky enough to get hands-on work experience within your chosen field, then make sure that you write reflectively about your responsibilities, challenges and achievements. But equally, if you only witnessed another professional in action, you can also share your insights about what you learned. The most important factor in all of the experiences and insights that you share is that you focus on doing so reflectively. In the next chapter, Reflection, I will go through exactly how to do that with an 'R Funnel.'

Transferable Skills

Please remember that while your academic background is one way of appraising your intellectual might, your work experience is equally valuable because it shows your conduct, reflections, lessons and professional progression in a real-life setting. This is why it is so important. If you are applying to study law, you might write about a crucial lesson that you learned during your work placement at a law firm or through observing court proceedings. Generally speaking, having work experience that aligns directly with your chosen degree is advantageous. However, if you worked at a local supermarket or for your family business, you can also infuse these experiences into your personal statement by drawing on the transferable skills that you gained there. For example, being a cashier at your supermarket may have taught you how to work effectively with numbers and how to coordinate with a team — both of which are skills that would prove useful if you wanted to be an accountant. Equally, working at your family business may have provided opportunities for you to demonstrate leadership, assertiveness and organisational skills, each of which may complement the skills you would need to take on an MBA.

Whether you have a lot of work experience or very little, with each sentence that you write, try to be aware of how each experience resonates with a skill that your university may be looking for. It pays to be aware of certain keywords and qualities that you can strategically display in how you describe your experiences, without being too robotic. For example, if you know that being able to cope well under pressure is a key skill for a doctor, you may want to focus more on exhibiting this specific quality when writing about your work experiences, projects or other opportunities. Or, if you know that manual dexterity and precision are important skills for a dentist, you might place extra emphasis on portraying these attributes in your application to study dentistry.

Ultimately, when it comes to writing about your experiences, you need to work with what you have got. Do not be tempted to make anything up or embellish your stories or experiences. It is not the right thing to do, and admissions tutors may figure out that you are not telling the whole truth. And in the event that you are invited to an interview, you may find yourself in a bit of a pickle if you cannot talk about those elaborate, but made-up stories. So save yourself the hassle and write honestly, authentically and reflectively.

Paragraph Four: Other Projects

In writing any personal statement, there are various ways to organise your paragraphs. However, it is often more intuitive to write about your motivations, your academic background and your professional background in the first three paragraphs as a foundation. Once you have this baseline, you can always rearrange your paragraphs to bring them to life or inject a creative spin where you deem appropriate. Paragraph four is the place where you can usually be the most flexible. This section of your personal statement can be used to build upon your work experience, but it is also used to share insights that directly support your chosen degree, such as a competition, activity, research or project that you have taken part in beyond the classroom. These are referred to as 'super-curricular' activities and work, as they demonstrate your commitments, engagements and projects that go beyond your typical classwork, but still remain relevant to your academic and professional development.

By this point in your essay, you will hopefully have made a strong impression with your introduction in paragraph one, your intellectual insights in paragraph two, and your application of skills through work experience in paragraph three. Impressing the reader in your first three paragraphs means that if you decide to talk about a further project that is a little unconventional in paragraph four, it is less of a risk because you covered the basics and laid the essential groundwork first. Perhaps the best way to see what this looks like is to read a real-life example.

This paragraph is from a student called Ming, who successfully gained admission to study economics at a leading university.

Ming writes in paragraph four:

> "The passion that I have for economics is largely a result of witnessing the responses to ballooning inflation in the midst of a cost-of-living crisis over the past few years. I realised that economics is a field that, while academic, affects each of us in personal and palpable ways, and thus, I feel that it is a subject worth studying at a higher level. To further supplement my learning, I have attended lectures at the Institute of International Monetary Research, one of which was by

> Professor Delaney, on the origins of inflation. He argued that despite it being relatively difficult to predict inflation, there is a strong correlation between the expected inflation made by the Bank of England and it transpiring to be so in reality, thereby demonstrating the accuracy of their forecasts. Professor Delaney's arguments made me particularly keen to read his article on 'The Microeconomic and Macroeconomic Consequences on Disruptive Events,' such as pandemics. His article proved illuminating insofar as the socio-economic impact that unexpected events can have on the larger economy, and I hope to explore this further in your optional module on 'Economic Epidemiology.'"

Ming's fourth paragraph has a lot to offer beyond his academic background and work experience, as it is clear that he has cultivated a genuine interest in economics, such that he has gone out of his way to attend lectures at the Institute of International Monetary Research. He also makes some interesting observations on what he learned in these lectures and the articles that he read, rather than just stating that he read those articles and attended those lectures. This makes his writing reflective, and it is useful to the reader because we are keen to know about him and his state of mind, and not just the people whose intellectual works are already celebrated all around the world. As Ming's example shows, the fourth paragraph is a great opportunity to demonstrate your dedication to your chosen field beyond your normal studies or work. You could also write about a book, publication or set of articles that shed light on an issue that you are interested in, if you so choose.

You will notice that Ming wrote briefly about a specific module in economic epidemiology. This is a great idea, particularly if you are tailoring your application to one university. Mentioning specific modules, projects, clubs or opportunities that you are interested in can make you stand out for all the right reasons, as well as referring to other members of the faculty who you are looking forward to engaging with. By writing in a manner that is specific to your chosen university, the admissions tutor is more inclined to see you as being the 'right fit.' So use this to your advantage where you can.

Let's have a look at one more example. This excerpt is from Chloe, a human sciences student at Oxford whose second paragraph you may remember from the previous chapter.

Chloe writes in paragraph four:

> "During the summer, I participated in several summer schools. The Sutton Trust Summer School involved subject lectures in biology and psychology. In a practical microbiology session, we learnt about culturing bacteria, using different agar to culture different bacteria. These lectures were a good insight into researching in microbiology and an exciting opportunity to develop my knowledge of practical methods. Another involved lectures on social and cultural anthropology, specifically on research in the

> field and reflecting on how public spaces are used by the community. This introduction to anthropological research methods and how ethnographers work showed me how research varies and how knowledge is gained in different disciplines. A further biology summer school involved conducting a virtual investigation with cell culture models to investigate potential anti-cancer drugs and conclude which should be recommended for clinical trials. Writing a lab report on the methods and results was a chance to develop analytical and research skills. I also wrote a discussion paper, learned how to cite references, and reflected on what I could improve after comparison to other research papers."

This paragraph from Chloe is effective in that it provides further evidence of her activities and projects. As you reach the end of the fourth paragraph, the reader has already gotten an idea of who you are, so it is generally advised to not introduce a new narrative — as I mentioned earlier. Try to write in such a manner that allows each paragraph to build upon and complement the one before it. Were you to introduce a new or random story at this point, it would run the risk of being too much of a distraction and too disruptive. Instead, you should be confidently gliding towards a conclusion with a focus on simply sealing the deal and finishing in style.

Paragraph Five: Extracurricular Activities

After paragraph four, you will either go straight to a conclusion or, if you have the space in your word count, a fifth paragraph. This is typically quite a short paragraph about extracurricular activities, and its length will depend on various factors, such as the subject that you are studying, whether you are an undergraduate or postgraduate student, and what style or specific requirements the university has. It is generally accepted that the more advanced and more technical your course is, the less space you will have to write about extracurricular activities that are not directly related to your course. This differs from one university to another, which is why doing your research, as I mentioned in Chapter One, is important. On occasion, paragraph five can also prove useful in mentioning mitigating circumstances that may have affected your academic performance, such as an adverse event that you faced that disrupted your coursework or examinations. As a general tip, when mentioning anything that may have negatively affected your progress, it is always good to demonstrate how you have overcome the difficulty that you faced, and present your experience as one of perseverance, tenacity and triumph — rather than being down in the doldrums, indulging in a 'pity party.' While any person with a pure heart may empathise with your plight, you do not want to give your admissions tutor the chance to confuse the reality of your struggle with pessimism, excessive self-deprecation or a lack of dedication. Remember that adversity can work to your advantage if you are able to use your experiences as a lever to propel you forward. Universities can be very understanding about making provisions for extenuating circumstances, so do not feel like your application is damaged because of them.

Have a read of Ashley's penultimate paragraph for her

successful application to study medicine.

Ashley writes in paragraph five:

> "Beyond the classroom, I am an avid writer and creative person. In fact, I created a biology resources website to help other students access key learning resources during the examination period. I also enjoy reading articles in the British Medical Journal, which allows me to stay abreast with current affairs within the medical field — for example, the controversy surrounding the extremely long waiting times in Accident & Emergency Departments across the country. This motivated me to produce an article for my school's scientific magazine exploring this issue further. While balancing my time between my head prefect roles, practising karate, and attending medical societies, I have found that partaking in the hobby of pastry-making has helped to improve my patience, while also providing a much-needed outlet during stressful periods. If fortunate enough to study at your university, I hope to establish my own pastry-making society, and I very much look forward to interacting with other like-minded, creative medics."

Ashley's penultimate paragraph is slightly longer than average, but she does a great job of talking about her commitments, activities and projects beyond the classroom. She has been strategic by mentioning activities that reinforce qualities that present her as a highly capable future doctor. For example, rather than just mentioning that she enjoys writing, her experiences are specific to medicine as she has put together a biology resources website. Her reading of the British Medical Journal provides further support and indication of her commitment to medicine, and even though the similarities between pastry-making and medicine are practically nonexistent, she manages to interweave this hobby into her personal statement by drawing on some of the skills that a capable doctor will need, such as patience and the ability to pursue a therapeutic outlet during stressful periods. Finally, it is fantastic that Ashley mentions that she would like to establish a pastry-making society at university, if given an offer, because this suggests that she would be a highly involved, engaging and active medical student. Overall, Ashley has done paragraph five justice, and she presents herself very compellingly.

While Ashley's paragraph on extracurricular activities was on the longer end, Demi, a student applying to study economics and statistics at the University of Toronto, opted to focus on how his involvement in his school's conservation club opened his mind to the dangers of climate change. Have a read of what he wrote:

Demi writes in paragraph five:

> "The growing awareness and the increasing amount of information regarding the changing of the Earth's climate and the natural environment persuaded me to join the local conservation club. The club activities involved reinvigorating a seemingly wasted space of land; the main aim was to create new habitats for local wilderness in order to enhance the ecosystem. We also wanted to change the visual aesthetics of the area to make it more attractive for the students and staff of the school. We tried to involve the local community by holding fundraisers where we could sell hand-made products such as birdhouses and bird feeders, sourced from local materials acquired in the ecology area, which proved to be a success with the locals. The money raised was used in reducing our school's carbon footprint."

In this example, Demi provides strong evidence of his genuine concern for the environment, as he has taken proactive steps to address issues in his school community. While Demi's extracurricular activities do not directly support his degree in economics and statistics, they give us insights into his interests in other areas, which is useful.

Writing about your extracurricular activities is an excellent opportunity for you to portray your achievements and other qualities that will impress an admissions tutor. Do not be afraid to write enthusiastically about your projects or activities, as this is your time to shine. Eddie, who received an offer to study mathematics at the University of Surrey wrote about his achievements particularly well.

Eddie writes in paragraph five:

> "Despite devoting a large amount of time to pursuing academic achievements, I have always been a keen sportsman; representing both my secondary school and various local football clubs. I am proud of my achievement of making my debut for the under 18's semi-professional team, Hornchurch, in the FA Youth Cup at the age of 15. Throughout my sporting career, I have been praised and awarded with various accolades; the most prestigious of these being the 'Best All Round Sportsman' over a five-year period at secondary school, and my 'Manager's Player' trophies awarded every year in the course of my football career. I would be delighted to continue my obsession of competing in sports at university level in not only football, but in a range of sports."

By applying to study mathematics at the University of Surrey, the main value that Eddie brings to the table is his intellect. However, an admissions tutor reading Eddie's personal statement would also be impressed by his extracurricular activities. Eddie clearly has a lot of accolades and impressive experiences outside of his academic work. Eddie is not only a formidable mathematician, he is a talented footballer who wants to continue competing in the sport at university. This makes him come across as well-rounded and proactive.

Have a look at another example from Tahmid, who received an offer to study geography at University College London.

Tahmid writes in paragraph five:

> "As a content creator with a following of over 170,000 followers, I have worked with Public Health England on a campaign to promote welfare for students during exam season by providing tips on managing stress. This helped me to develop critical thinking skills to deliver my message successfully. I have also gained ambassador status from Collins through content creation which has let me build my self-assurance and leadership abilities. My desire to study geography is absolute and I take pleasure in widening my knowledge of human geography."

Tahmid does not shy away from sharing his extraordinary achievement of reaching 170,000 followers as a content creator. He also goes a step further with the concerted efforts that he has made by working with Public Health England to promote the welfare of students. By mentioning the critical thinking skills that he gained from his experiences, he reminds the admissions tutor that his activities are not merely excursions from his chosen subject, geography. Rather, the admissions tutor is reminded of the transferable value that critical thinking skills will have while Tahmid is studying for his degree.

Have a look at one more example. This paragraph is from Xin, who received an offer to study medicine at the University of Glasgow.

Xin writes in paragraph five:

> "In secondary school, I was a member of the Red Crescent Society. I acquired techniques and experiences which allowed me to aid the sick or injured. I was also the first-aider in charge during my senior year in camp. My familiarity with public duties has taught me to be alert to unexpected events, and to prioritise patient care above all. I also served on the prefectorial board. During the prefect's annual gathering, I was the planner in charge. This gave me the opportunity to exercise my planning skills and to learn to foresee problems that may arise and find solutions to mitigate them. Working with my group of prefects has also helped me to improve my communication skills."

Xin's paragraph about her extra-curricular activities is effective in the way that she still manages to write about experiences that display desirable qualities for a doctor, such as being alert, responding to unexpected events, planning ahead, leadership and communication. As you write about your activities beyond the classroom, be mindful about using the space you have to demonstrate your best traits.

Mitigating Circumstances

Earlier on, I mentioned that paragraph five can also be used as a space to shed light on mitigating and extenuating circumstances. The reason why I recommend that this is reserved for the penultimate paragraph is that when you want to discuss a potentially negative topic, good timing and the right tone will make all of the difference. For example, if you focus on mitigating circumstances right from the start, this carries a degree of risk, because it might cast a dark shadow over your entire essay, which can be hard to recover from. On the other hand, if you have already made a stellar impression in your first four paragraphs, an admissions tutor may respond more favourably to you factually providing insights about your mitigating circumstances towards the end of your personal statement. You should do so by demonstrating a forward-thinking, reflective and constructive attitude towards the adversity that you faced. In this way, you can usually turn a negative into a positive, and continue to impress the reader.

Mariah, a physiotherapy student applying to a postgraduate programme at the University of Birmingham managed to do this rather successfully, as she described the challenges that she faced while studying abroad.

Mariah writes in paragraph five:

> "The year abroad also helped me succeed in my final year after transferring universities. My

> grades declined as I adjusted to the new teaching approach and environment, and I struggled with some family issues. I felt that I was okay to sit the exam within days of experiencing this issue, but I was not. The style of teaching in America placed pressure on me to become even more productive with my free time. When returning from my study abroad year, I carried over the consistent productivity to boost my expected degree classification."

Mariah is transparent about the challenges that she faced, as she mentions family issues that she encountered and the difficulties of adjusting to a new style of teaching. She also acknowledges that she may have misjudged her readiness for her examinations. This is normal, and it shows self-awareness. Considering that an admissions tutor will see her academic transcript anyway, it is prudent that she address any areas of deficiency in her application herself, rather than allow them to be discovered later on, and not have the chance to explain what happened. Mariah concludes her paragraph with a positive and forward-looking statement about carrying over her productive approach to studying in order to boost her degree classification. This is encouraging, as it shows that Mariah has a positive outlook and the capacity to overcome adversity in a constructive and pragmatic manner.

Not all circumstances are considered 'mitigating,' but if you would like to write about a part of your character or journey that is not an overt advantage, then do not be afraid to do so.

Have a look at another example from Mia, who received an offer to study English literature at the University of Bristol.

Mia writes in paragraph five:

> "As a dyslexic, I always struggled to read but I found ways around my difficulties, so I could still harness the wonders of the literature. To access these stories that I struggled to read fluently, I spent hundreds of hours listening to audiobooks and practised reading every night with my parents. Dyslexia has helped me to think about literature in different ways to other students and I now use it to my advantage."

Mia writes candidly about her struggle with reading, but her words come across as empowering, as she mentions how listening to audiobooks helped her to 'think about literature in different ways compared to other students.' She also describes her circumstances as an 'advantage,' which is really inspiring. The manner in which Mia presents her circumstances is exactly how you can turn a disadvantage into an advantage, and continue to make a stellar impression.

Have a read of one more example from Sergiou, who went on to study philosophy, politics and economics at the University of Oxford. This paragraph is different to Mariah's and Mia's insofar as it appearing towards the beginning of Sergiou's personal statement, rather than at the end. In this example, Sergiou uses his mitigating circumstances to construct a compelling narrative from the outset.

Sergiou writes in paragraph five:

> "My application comes from a unique position, as I am somewhat running my life and aspirations against the clock of my own biology: since childhood, I have had to deal with a very serious illness prompting me to grasp and fully exploit every opportunity. My limited progress in primary school instilled a desire and work ethic to push beyond the bounds set by others. This determination still burns brightly in me: I want to channel my enthusiasm through academia providing enhanced depth and credibility to my ideas. I co-founded the Barts' YES Forum by contacting and persuading the CEO of the Royal London Hospital to create a facilitator for youth voices across the Trust. I have also designed and established a mentoring scheme for young people suffering from long-term illnesses. Through this scheme, I met a vast variety of people; I have therefore seen how effective activism can yield practical results and developed the skills to lobby fund managers and politicians successfully. As a member of the NHS Youth Forum, I have been chosen as a representative in the government's NHS Long Term Health Plan."

This paragraph by Sergiou is an excellent example of how you can mention something not overtly advantageous and use it to build a story in a way that is inspiring. Sergiou went the extra mile by establishing a mentoring scheme for young people suffering from long-term illnesses, and any admissions tutor reading his personal statement would be impressed by the proactive approach he has adopted. Like Mariah and Mia, Sergiou portrays his circumstances in a manner that paints him in a good light. He comes across as strong, determined and brave, and a person who leads with integrity.

The Conclusion

Now to conclude with, of course… the conclusion. The final paragraph of your personal statement is usually best kept short and sweet. It is your chance to tie all of your points together and reiterate why studying your chosen course would be of great benefit to you. Many students feel the need to be excessively flattering and sycophantic, but you should probably avoid taking that approach, and there is a persuasive argument to support this line of reasoning. If you have actually made a strong enough impression, the admissions tutors will see your value enough to know that themselves. Use this space to reaffirm your overall message and a few of the positive points that the admissions tutor now knows about you, rather than fawning over them as a final act of desperation. The admissions tutors reading your personal statement are already familiar with the merits of their institution, so try not to harp on about the university's 'incredible faculty,' their 'high ranking in the league tables,' or their 'world-leading resources' — all of which are tedious clichés. There is no need to go telling them what they are already aware of. Try not to come across as desperate, and do not overcomplicate things. Keep it simple, authentic and personal, and get straight to the point. And when you do this, do so elegantly.

Have a read of Andrew's conclusion to his personal statement for chemical engineering.

Andrew writes in his conclusion:

> "Ultimately, I believe that my insatiable curiosity and commitment to solving challenges from a systems-based approach will equip me with the necessary skills to study chemical engineering at a higher level. This is a dynamic and ever-changing field within which to commit, and I am excited by the challenges and prospects that await in this career, each of which I am eager to relish."

Andrew's conclusion is short and sweet, but highly effective. He reiterates the points made in the bulk of his personal statement and keeps it all succinct and conclusive. He does not shove new ideas our way, or bombard us with a deluge of his greatest hits and grandest achievements as his last hurrah. No. He keeps it simple, because by now he has made a strong enough impression that we already know the value that he brings to the table. My advice for the conclusion is to not overthink it, and to not introduce new narratives or new ideas. Just glide straight to the finish line in your final paragraph, and leave the reader with a warm feeling of contentment after having read a beautiful piece of writing from a person worth getting to know. That's all you have to do.

Essay Prompts

In Chapter Two: Requirements, I explained that not all personal statements take on the same format and structure, and while the six-part structure is the gold standard for a traditional personal statement, if you are given an essay prompt for a Common App essay or supplemental essay, your answers will take a different form. This requires a greater amount of discretion, as it is up to you to decide how you wish to unload your points to the admissions tutor. In addition, owing to the fact that these essays are usually rather short, you need to focus on being succinct and getting straight to the point by answering the question directly. For an essay prompt with fewer than 500 words, you should expect to write two or three paragraphs, rather than five or six as you might do in a longer personal statement. It is also more common to infuse a bit more personality and flair in these essays, particularly if you are given a set of essays to submit to the same university. In this case, you can focus on demonstrating different characteristics with each short essay that you submit, and your answers will be guided by the questions and prompts that you are given.

The best way to understand this is to see it in action. So have a read of Ricky's four essays. These essays were required as part of the application process for the management programme at the University of California, Berkeley and the University of California, Los Angeles — both of which Ricky received offers from, before going on to study economics at the University of Chicago.

The first essay prompt said the following:

"Every person has a creative side, and it can be expressed in many ways: problem-solving, original and innovative thinking, and artistically, to name a few. Describe how you express your creative side. 350 words maximum."

Ricky writes in his first essay:

"As I prepare to hit 'record,' I stare at the clay

piece on top of the slime, contemplating how I want the video to begin. Do I crush the clay immediately or let it slowly crumble into the gelatinous material? I get particular when it comes to executing my vision. Slime is a semifluid substance made primarily of glue and similar in texture to putty. Slime videos are the sole form of marketing for my business. I create slime videos daily, posting on my Instagram and TikTok accounts. These videos range from mixing slime with miscellaneous items, such as Styrofoam beads to videos of slime from my store. Manifesting my artistic ability through the slimy substance has allowed me to use my creativity productively.

My favorite videos involve making slime that resembles food or drinks. I take inspiration from the San Francisco Bay Area culture when I create new products. These inspirations have led me to formulate slime that resembles bubble tea, honey toast, and mochi, to name a few. Creating slime with ties to my home triggers nostalgia with every stretch, squeeze, and poke I make with it. Creating my 'Frog Cake' slime was a process that sticks out among the thousands of slimes I have created and filmed. The concept came from a TikTok video showcasing a minimalistic cake, complete on top with a frog made of frosting. I was enamored by this cute dessert and wanted to replicate it with slime materials. I molded the clay into the frog's shape, placed it onto some slime, and pressed record. The slime was an instant hit. The slime's complexity was far ahead of slimes I made in the past. This slime advanced my creative process, giving me the confidence to make more intricate products.

Filming slime remains challenging; it won't always hold its desired shape or will frustratingly form an invasive bubble that ruins the video's aesthetic. However, it wouldn't feel rewarding if there weren't any forks in the road. Each slime video I make, and each challenge I overcome, stimulates my creativity and keeps me reaching for more bottles of glue."

Ricky's essay immediately stands out because it is so specific, personal, original, quirky and authentic. For the average person, writing 350 words about slime might not initially jump out to us as particularly absorbing or fascinating, and yet Ricky manages to exude genuine passion for his creative works, which puts us under a spell and pulls us into his imaginative world. He does a fantastic job of answering the question, as he clearly demonstrates his 'creative side' as he has been asked to do. His narrative is one that evokes a childlike creativity and boundless imagination, which makes him very charming. Ricky keeps his answer unique to him and his writing does not come across as contrived as a result.

Having read Ricky's answer, you can see how a six-part paragraph structure would be inappropriate for an essay prompt of this kind. For example, if you received this question and started by writing about your academic background or mentioning your work experience, it would be incongruous with what is actually being asked. The prompt is simple: 'describe how you express your creative side.' So with a limit of 350 words, you ought to get straight to the point and answer the question. In addition, you may notice that Ricky used the literary device 'in medias res,' which I outlined in the previous chapter, as he dives straight into a decisive moment in his story with this line:

> "*As I prepare to hit 'record,' I stare at the clay piece on top of the slime, contemplating how I want the video to begin.*"

This draws the reader in, as we are invested in and curious to find out how the story unfolds. Overall, Ricky's essay is highly descriptive, engaging, imaginative and creative, and he does a great job of answering the question. He has the upper hand because writing about a topic that is so obscure and unique to him dissolves the competition that he might have encountered had he chosen to write about a more common outlet of creativity, such as playing a sport or musical instrument. In essence, Ricky's essay is successful because he hits the nail right on the head by writing about his own creative endeavours, and because he keeps it truly personal to him, doing so with an infectious enthusiasm and passion that makes him likeable and compelling.

Let's have a look at Ricky's second essay prompt:

"What would you say is your greatest talent or skill? How have you developed and demonstrated that talent over time? 350 words maximum."

Ricky writes in his second essay:

> "Entrepreneurship is a skill I've kept in my back pocket from ages five to seventeen, applying it in situations that require problem-solving and innovative solutions. My first lemonade stand marked the beginning of this skill's development. The rural road I live on holds only three families, but this didn't stop me from placing a 'lemonade for sale' sign in my front yard. I longed for the experience other kids got when selling lemonade curbside, so to achieve this, I made flyers and dropped them into every mailbox within a three-mile radius of mine. My marketing as a five-year-old paid off as I soon had a line of eager customers awaiting my lemonade. This event was monumental in crafting my entrepreneur-

ial skills, as it proved I could take a seemingly unworkable idea and successfully execute it. My early success in product marketing and skills in entrepreneurship helped me when I started my own business.

'RL Slimes' debuted as a small Instagram page in 2017, but has grown to become a pretty sticky empire of its own. I entered the slime market with no experience of how slime worked or how to manipulate it into a sellable product. This lack of experience did not hold me back. Entrepreneurship prompted me to assert myself in the already booming market. I quickly learned tactics from successful 'slimers' and repurposed them for myself. My assertiveness paid off, as 'RL Slimes' has become one of the leading slime businesses globally. I now travel the country and ship my products worldwide; I've sold thousands in total.

Coordinating, running, and executing the first California slime convention was another accomplishment deemed unfeasible; however, my former triumphs made me believe I could do it. As an eager 13-year-old business owner, I wanted to bring the world of slime to Sonoma County. I met with multiple event spaces until I signed a deal with DoubleTree Hotel, paying with 100% of my own money. Sonoma SlimeFest remained the largest slime convention on the West Coast for its time, and it was my entrepreneurial spirit that made it happen."

The narrative of Ricky's first essay was creativity, and in his second essay, he makes it abundantly clear that he is an ambitious entrepreneur with a bold vision that has allowed him to overcome challenges that other people may have been fazed by. Ricky starts off the essay by answering the question directly when he writes:

"Entrepreneurship is a skill I've kept in my back pocket from ages five to seventeen,"

The question is clearly asking him what his 'greatest talent or skill' is, and Ricky does not leave us in needless suspense about what it is. He gets straight to the point by mentioning entrepreneurship in the first sentence, and he continues to be economical with his writing. As a budding entrepreneur, he demonstrates many of the skills that would be required in his line of work, such as thinking outside the box and creative problem-solving. For example, when Ricky describes his yearning for a lemonade stand despite there only being three families on his street, it creates a vivid image of a young, ambitious person with a dream that simply could not be contained. This is a highly effective way of letting us know some of the most virtuous personality traits he has, without him explicitly saying, 'I am ambitious, imaginative and creative.' He focuses on showing, rather than telling. In addition, Ricky is rather poetic and intentional with his words. For example, by writing 'marketing as a five-year-old,' Ricky draws attention to the juxtaposition of someone so young undertaking a project that is far beyond the scope of skills that a person would normally have at that age. We observe a similar use of juxtaposition in the contrast between where he has come from and how far his business has taken him with phrases such as this:

"'RL Slimes' debuted as a small Instagram page in 2017, but has grown to become a pretty sticky empire of its own."

There is a clear gulf that Ricky has had to cross from first starting as a 'small Instagram page' to creating a 'sticky empire,' which is a rather creative description that makes his achievement look all the more impressive. Ricky does a great job by presenting himself as someone with gutsiness and ambition, and after this second essay, he has made a strong impression.

Now, let's have a read of Ricky's third essay prompt:

"Describe the most significant challenge you have faced and the steps you have taken to overcome this challenge. How has this challenge affected your academic achievement?"

Ricky writes in his third essay:

> "The night of October 8th was fairly calm; I worked on a project for my eighth-grade history class and FaceTimed with friends. As I turned over to fall asleep, I received an unusual text from my best friend that read, 'Do you smell the smoke?' I jolted out of bed and stuck my head out of the slider connected to my bedroom; I

didn't smell anything. Still worried, I made my way to the living room where floor-to-ceiling windows revealed a distant mountain range; here, I saw miles worth of flames. I ran to my parents' bedroom to wake them. We collected a few items and drove off. After that night, I didn't sleep in my house for six months.

Luckily, my home was able to stay standing by the grace of a team of firefighters, but the damage left it unlivable. Not only was I displaced from my home, but my middle school and the high school I was set for the following year perished as well. I moved residences and school locations in a matter of one night. I moved into a two-bedroom apartment with three animals, and my education migrated into an abandoned schoolhouse. My academics were at risk from teachers adapting to a new environment and teaching methods quickly, but I kept moving in the way I did before the fire. Knowing I was set for high school the following year meant I couldn't jeopardize my educational foundation.

The Tubb's fire prepared me for any curveball that could be thrown at my academics. Sudden changes in location and format now seem second nature. Switching to distance learning due to COVID-19 was simple compared to the effect that the fire has had on my education. The Tubb's Fire provided me with grit that I can apply in any situation that catches me by surprise. I used this grit when navigating school via Zoom and social

> life through a screen. The Tubb's Fire stole many things from me, but it strengthened my will to persevere through any obstacle or unforeseen event."

This third essay prompt introduces us to a different aspect of Ricky's journey, as this story is clearly harrowing, but beautifully written. Ricky sets the scene incredibly well by describing the moments prior to discovering the fire, as well as when he goes on to wake up his parents. The essay prompt instructs students to write about their 'most significant challenge,' and considering the imminent danger and catastrophe that Ricky faced that night, this response clearly answers the prompt. Ricky's writing manages to be gripping without being verbose, and without using flamboyant language. For example, in his first paragraph, he simply describes what happened and then ends with the following line:

"After that night, I didn't sleep in my house for six months."

This is effective because, once again, he adopts a 'show, don't tell' style of writing. The mere fact that he could not return to his own home for six months is enough to impress upon the reader the gravity and magnitude of what he went through. Ricky also goes on to answer the second part of the prompt by describing how the moment affected his academic pursuits. He demonstrates resilience and mental strength with phrases such as:

"I kept moving in the way I did before the fire."

"The Tubb's fire prepared me for any curveball that could be thrown at my academics."

"The Tubb's Fire provided me with grit that I can apply in any situation that catches me by surprise."

"The Tubb's Fire stole many things from me, but it strengthened my will to persevere through any obstacle or unforeseen event."

Ricky's forward-looking approach to adversity is highly commendable, considering all that he lost as a result of the fire. He presents himself as highly driven and pragmatic, and he is clearly a person who perseveres in spite of the challenges that he faces. Once again, Ricky has not used these words himself, which numerous students do. Instead, we have observed these meritorious traits within him, having read his deeply moving story. His skills closely align with what an admissions tutor would hope to see in a person looking to explore their entrepreneurial potential, and Ricky is passionate about his achievements, but equally gracious, strong and reflective about the challenges that he has faced. This is the optimal balance that you should strive for. Evoke passion about your high points, but just as much reflection about your low points.

Overall, Ricky has answered these first three essays brilliantly. At this point, he will have already made a stellar impression on the admissions tutor such that it would take a complete bungling of the fourth essay for him to jeopardise his entire application. Let's see how Ricky manages the final essay of this set of four.

Ricky's final prompt says the following:

"What have you done to make your school or community a better place? 350 words maximum."

Ricky writes in his fourth essay:

"My relationship with slime is light-hearted. I used to see slime simply as a playful toy, but now I understand its value as a tool. Four out of five of the human senses get used when playing with slime, which makes it serviceable for people with sensory processing disorders like autism. I wanted to turn my business into something that could help people more directly, which urged me to reach out to a local elementary school for students with autism. The Anova Center for Education's staff was eager to partner with me, as slime was already being used as one of their sensory tools. Before reaching out, I had no direct relationship with anyone on the autism spectrum and was truly naive about the disorder. Working alongside the staff has allowed me to educate myself on autism and grow connections with amazing students.

The genuine joy I see as the students work with their slime leaves me incredibly grateful for finding a community that can utilize slime beyond its conventional use. I want slime to

> be something the students can use to express themselves, not just a tool for in-class productivity. I'm planning an art project where the students will design a slime and then make it with food dye, glitter, and scents. I've been getting to know each of the ten students personally through our sessions; the last session included our favorite smells. Our next sessions will involve individual slimes according to each student's favorite smell, hopefully making them feel special while introducing a new sensory factor.
>
> Getting to know the students has made me want to further research autism and slime's applicability, locating which factors make slime so valuable for the autism community. With this research, I want to find a way to make slime an even more accessible tool to more students. Witnessing the students' reactions to slime has enlightened me about the incredible capability slime has to offer. Seeing how slime has been conducive for the group of kids I've worked with has made me want to deliver slime to more students with autism."

In a similar manner to how a six-part structure for a personal statement communicates different points — such as your academic insights, work experience and other projects — you should strive to do the same with your essay prompts. Notice how Ricky has covered four key areas in his four essays:

Essay 1: **Creativity**
Essay 2: **Entrepreneurship**

Essay 3: **Overcoming Adversity**
Essay 4: **Making a Difference**

I strongly advise that you follow this approach of covering different areas in order to convey different aspects of your character, so as not to be repetitive. Each essay has its own theme, and Ricky maintains that individual narrative for each essay and then seeks to cover a new facet of his overall character. Crucially, he does not labour on the same points too much, despite exploring a topic that he has mentioned before: his slime business. The question asks the student to consider what they have done to 'make their school or community a better place.' Ricky's work to help people with autism shows that he is not only creative, entrepreneurial and resilient in the face of adversity, but that he also seeks to make a meaningful impact on others. In addition, Ricky starts the essay with the line:

"My relationship with slime is light-hearted."

Considering that we know so much about Ricky's passion for slime already, this sentence grabs our attention, as it does not reveal in what way his relationship with slime is 'light-hearted,' thereby encouraging us to read on and find out. Overall, Ricky has answered these prompts with great skill, aplomb and flair — both in terms of his knack for writing and the substance of the topics he covered. With each essay, we have gotten to know a part of Ricky's character, and each essay stands strong on its own. When writing answers to essay prompts, your number one focus should be to get yourself as close as possible to what the prompt is asking of you, and to keep it personal and authentic to you, just as Ricky has done. Remember that your writing will be much more compelling when you make it personal to you, because it is always better to be a first-rate version of yourself than a second-rate version or bad imitation of someone else. When you try to imitate a person that you are not, you are less likely to be impressive or convincing, because most readers will sense that something about you is a bit askew. While you should always follow the fundamental tenets of 'good writing,' a personal statement or any college admissions essay is subjective in the way that people have different styles and tastes. So your best bet is to be your authentic and fully expressed self, and write with passion and candour.

Scholarship Essays

Being transparent, authentic and reflective is a central component of coming across as endearing to a reader, and this certainly applies to scholarship essays. If you are asked to write one, this is an excellent opportunity to offer a fresh insight into a deeply personal aspect of who you are that goes beyond anything academic or professional. Once again, I strongly advise that you do not fawn over the university in a scholarship essay — instead, keep it personal to you. I also advise that you focus on one highly specific aspect of your journey or something that you care about, and prioritise depth rather than breadth. A student named Brielle managed to receive numerous scholarships — some of which were worth up to $80,000 — from more than ten universities, including the University of Cincinnati, the University of North Carolina, Greensboro, and Ohio University.

In the next section, have a read of Brielle's scholarship essay in response to her prompt, which was:

"Discuss an accomplishment, event or realisation that sparked a period of personal growth or new understanding of yourself or others."

Brielle writes in her scholarship essay:

> "Growing up, questions like 'who are you and what sets you aside from others?' were always the hardest ones to answer. In my mind, I felt as if it was almost impossible to be unique in such a big world — which is why I never really knew how to answer this question. It wasn't until I entered the college application process that I began to ponder this question again. As I thought deeply about it, I confronted a repressed memory — a memory of a story my grandmother had told me about the origin of my last name. The one unique thing about myself that I hated the most. One of my great grandfathers, Levi, was an enslaved man who managed to escape from slavery after fighting in the American Civil War. After becoming a free man, he knew that he wanted to reclaim the power that was once stripped from our ancestors. He no longer wanted the constant reminder of oppression, genocide and generational pain attached to his identity. He decided to change his last name

from the name that was assigned by his slave master. When he opened his eyes on his first day of freedom, the first thing he saw was a rug. A muddy, worn-out rug. But it was his. Levi Ruggs is what he decided to call himself. This last name has trickled down into my family tree for over 150 years. It was given to my grandfather, my father, and now me.

Is it possible that my great-grandfather purposely chose a name that he knew would give his descendants a unique and powerful addition to their character? Have I betrayed my grandfather by hiding this part of who I am? Would he want me to feel ashamed when people made fun of it? Or would he want me to stand confidently and pass down this legacy he created to my own children? The more I thought about his intention, the more inspired and uplifted I began to feel. I no longer felt the shame and humiliation that I'd once felt before. I began to feel proud that I didn't have a symbol of hatred, trauma and unthinkable doings weighing down on my identity. I was free of the shackles that were once forcibly attached onto the spirits of my ancestors and for that, I am forever grateful.

I have learned to embrace a part of myself that, for a long time, I had felt was unworthy of being embraced. I no longer feel that I have to hide a part of myself to fit in with the rest of society, because now I understand that uniqueness is meant to set you aside from everyone else. So

> now when people ask me who I am, I say that I am proud, confident and artistic. I am a modern-day symbol of the perseverance and hope of my ancestors. I am a powerful black woman with caramel skin and perfect kinky curls. But most importantly, I say, I am Brielle Ruggs."

Brielle's scholarship essay is an excellent example of how to make your writing 'personal' to you, despite the subject matter of this essay concerning her great-grandfather's surname. Brielle does not beg the universities for sympathy, and her essay does not come across like a sob story, but rather like one of triumph, while acknowledging a dark past.

This line was particularly profound:

"I was free of the shackles that were once forcibly attached onto the spirits of my ancestors and for that, I am forever grateful."

Brielle's story is captivating, and the symbolism of slavery and the figurative language used with 'free of the shackles' is beautifully written, introspective and reflective. She is open about her discomfort with her name and its history, but goes on to demonstrate a development of her character and perspective. Importantly, Brielle answers the question directly, as it required that the student write about something that demonstrates 'personal growth or a new understanding of oneself or others.' This essay does exactly that. Overall, Brielle's essay stands out because she keeps it authentic to who she is. Focussing on keeping it personal means that she stands in a league of her own and remains compelling. Once again, I advise that you focus on keeping your essays or personal statements 'personal' to you; remember to 'write what you know' and 'show, don't tell.'

A Quick Summary

With that, you have explored how to approach essay prompts of various kinds. You also now know the classic six-part paragraph structure that will help you to communicate your experiences neatly, logically and coherently for your personal statement. As I pointed out before, you are free to rearrange your paragraphs as you see fit, but starting with this classic structure ensures that you cover the important bases first. Afterwards, you can refine, revamp and rejig your structure in a creative or inventive fashion.

Let's have a quick recap of the six-part structure before you move on to the next chapter:

- **Paragraph one** was your introduction, where you set the scene and introduced your narrative.

- In **Paragraph two**, you covered your academic foundations and intellectual perspectives.

- In **Paragraph three**, you went into detail about how your skills were applicable in the real world, through your work experience or other related projects.

- In **Paragraph four**, you took the chance to either build upon your work experience or write about other projects or insights.

- **Paragraph five** was your chance to tell the admissions tutor about your extracurricular activities or other mitigating circumstances.

- **Paragraph six** was your conclusion, where you reiterated your message and tied your points together.

Whether you are using this classic six-part structure or are given an essay prompt to answer, at this stage of the writing process, you should have a good draft to work with, which you can further build upon. This draft is akin to the first sketches of what will become a beautiful painting. As you continue to fine-tune your writing, you will need to ensure that you are writing reflectively and coherently, which I will cover in the next two chapters before going on to the final stage of this process of crafting an excellent personal statement — which is refinement. You have come a long way, and you should feel proud that you have taken these steps towards producing a stellar personal statement. Keep going. It will pay off in the end.

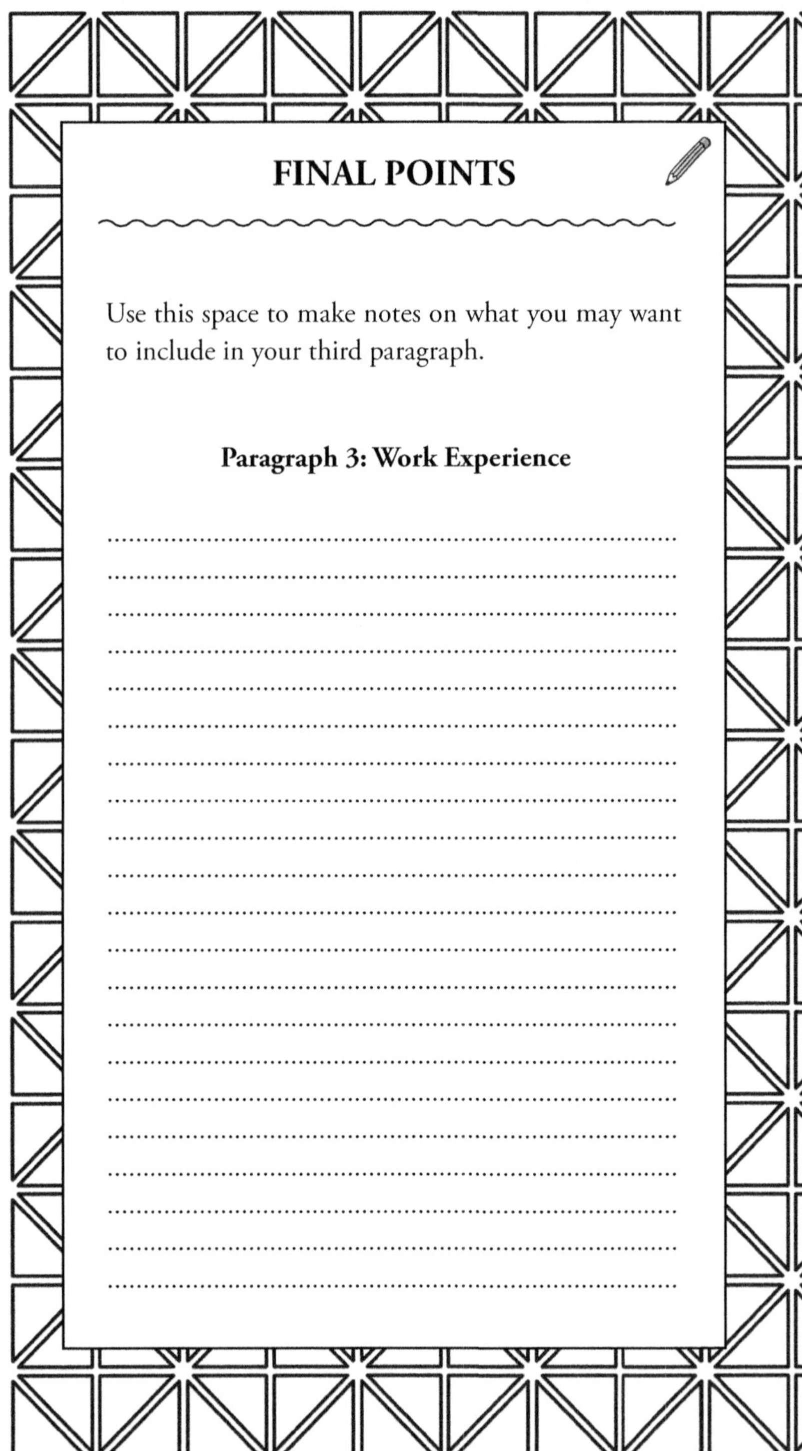

FINAL POINTS

Use this space to make notes on what you may want to include in your third paragraph.

Paragraph 3: Work Experience

....

....

....

....

....

....

....

....

....

....

....

....

....

....

....

....

....

....

....

....

....

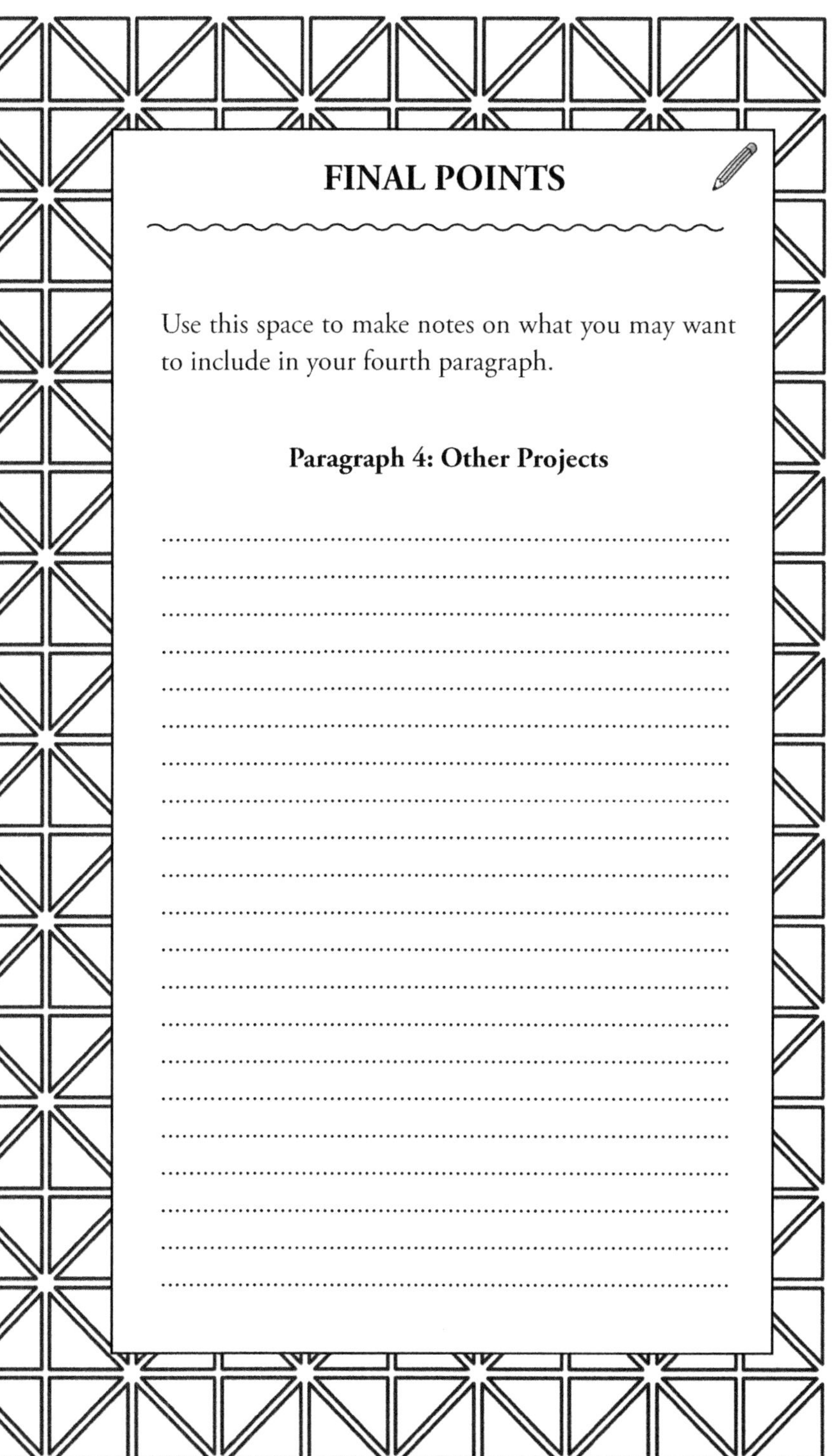

FINAL POINTS

Use this space to make notes on what you may want to include in your fourth paragraph.

Paragraph 4: Other Projects

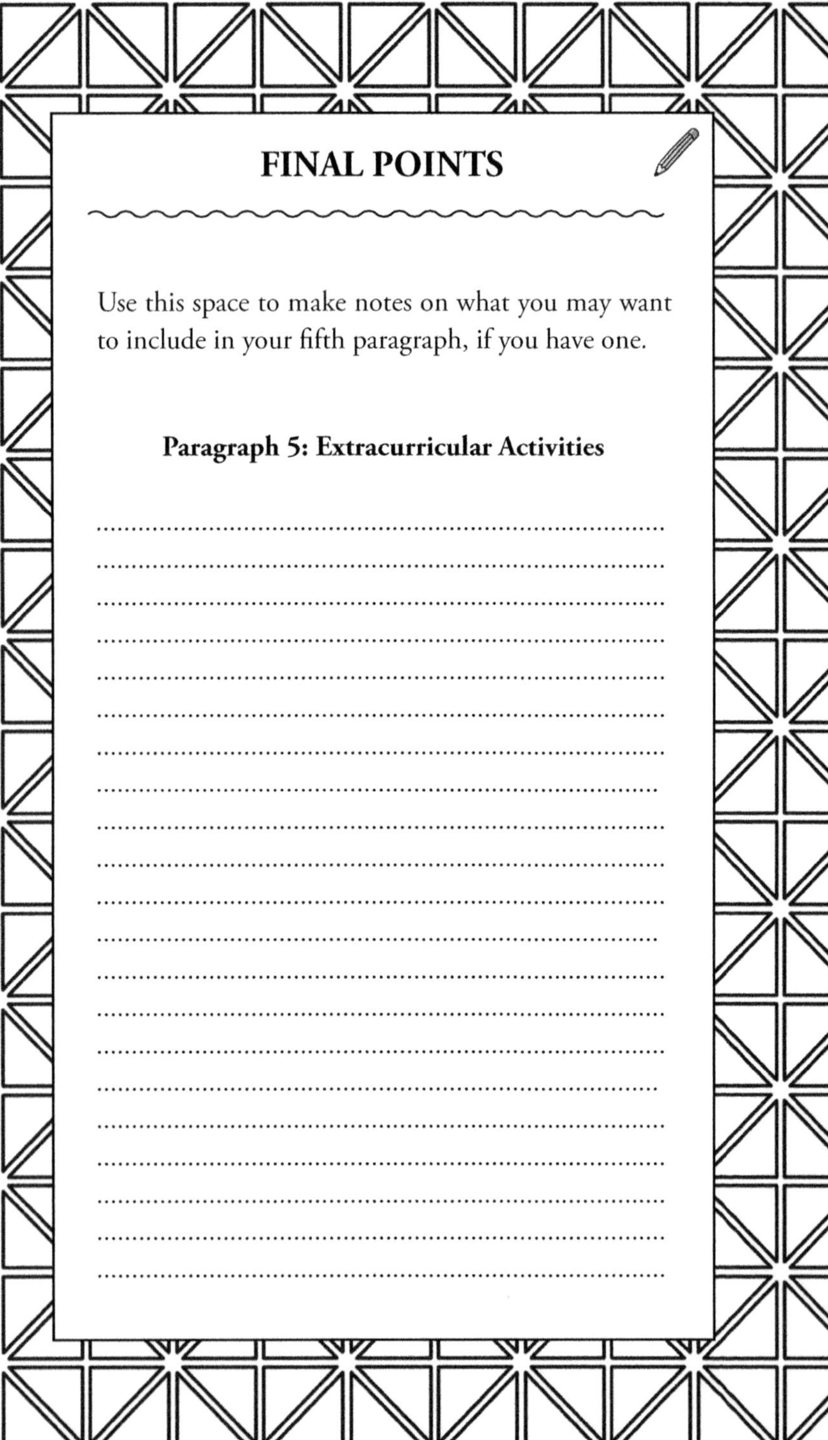

FINAL POINTS

Use this space to make notes on what you may want to include in your fifth paragraph, if you have one.

Paragraph 5: Extracurricular Activities

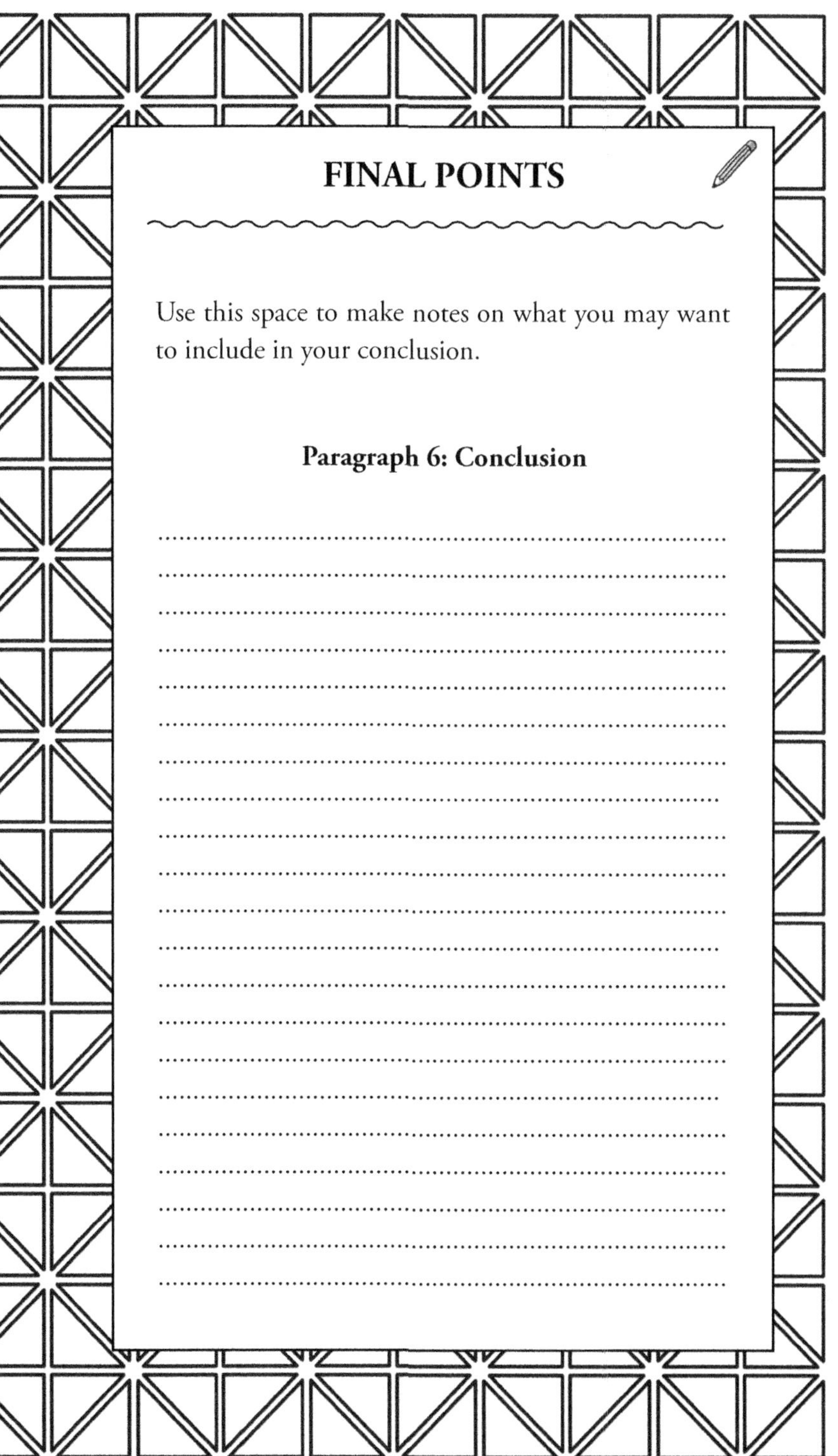

FINAL POINTS

Use this space to make notes on what you may want to include in your conclusion.

Paragraph 6: Conclusion

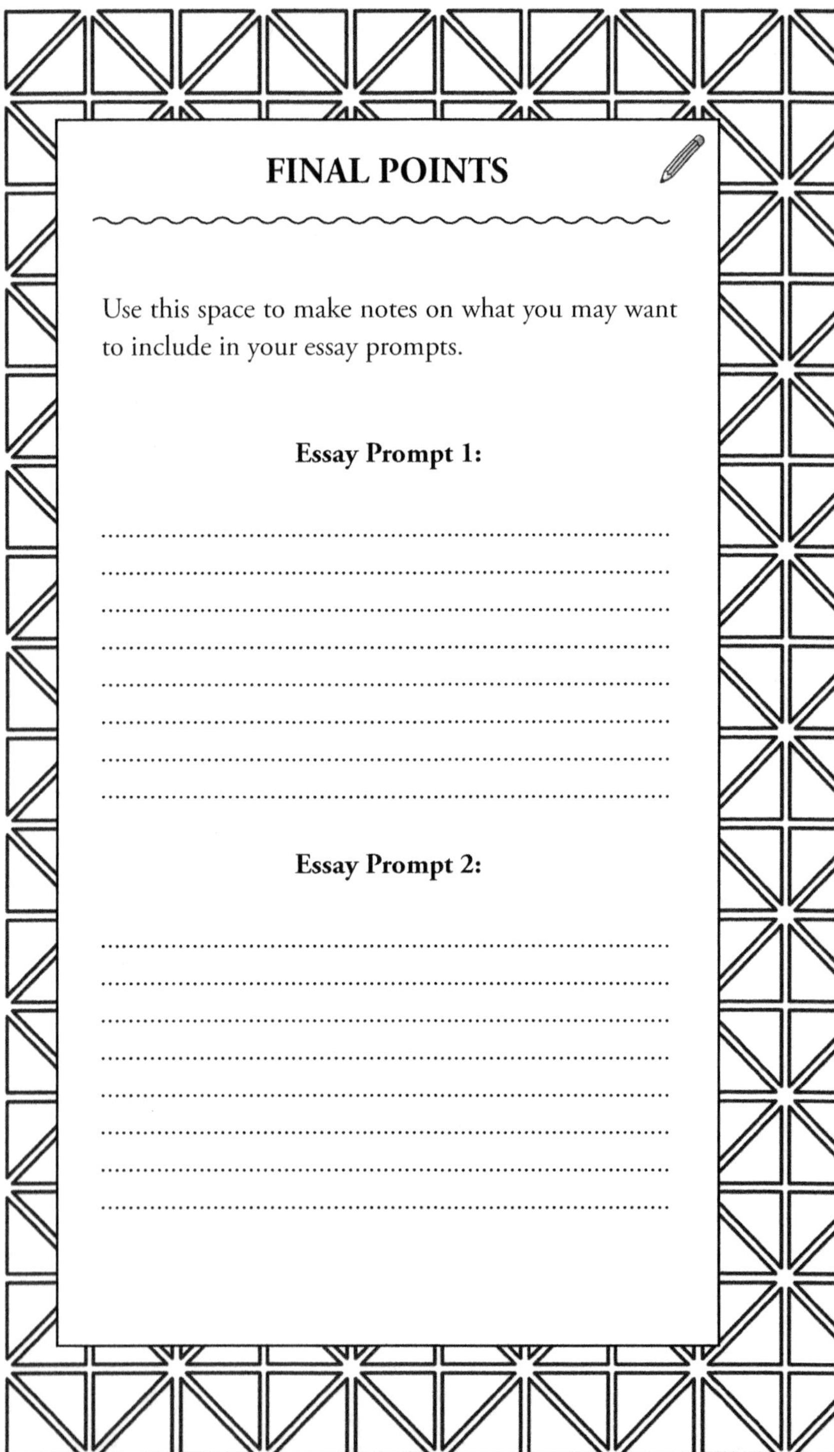

FINAL POINTS

Use this space to make notes on what you may want to include in your essay prompts.

Essay Prompt 1:

Essay Prompt 2:

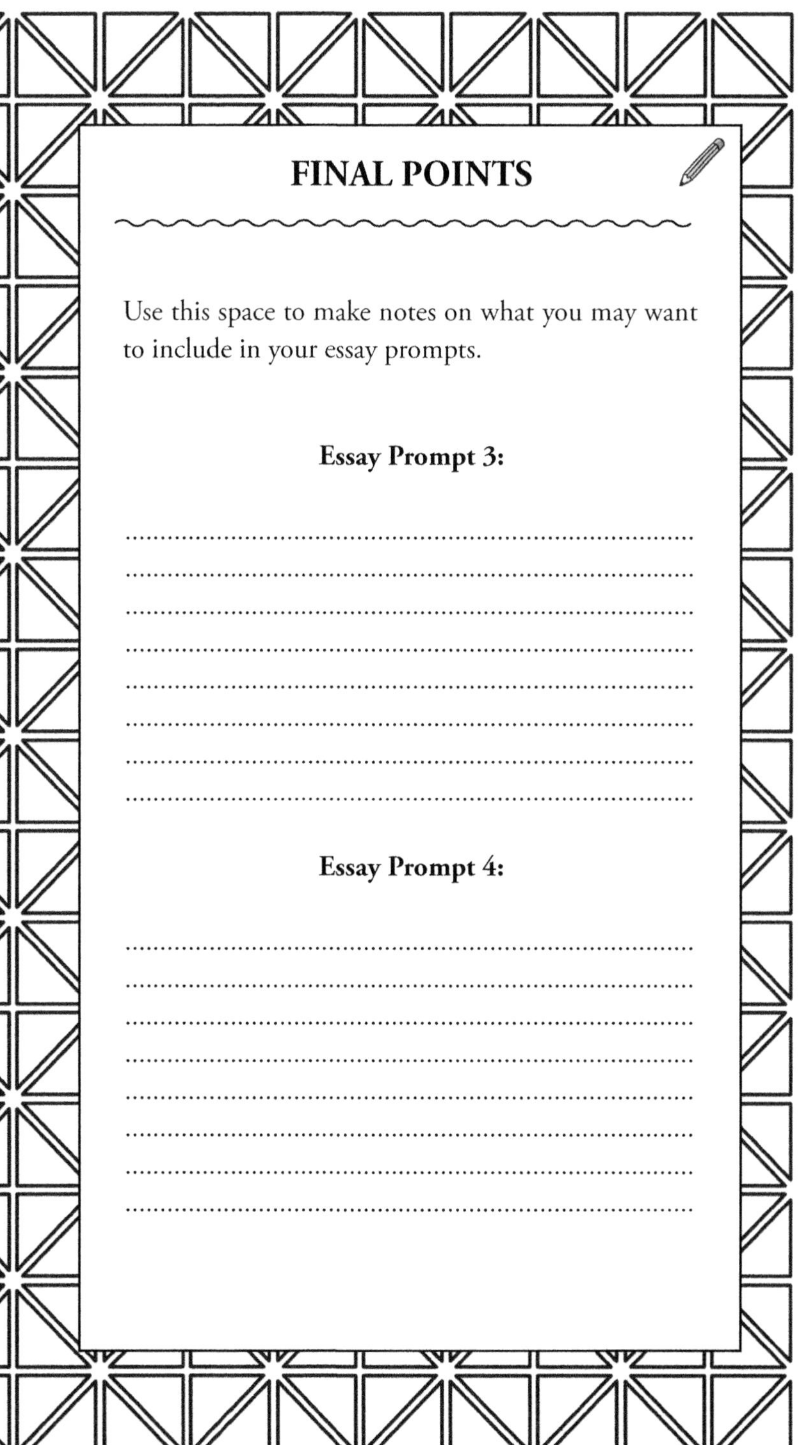

FINAL POINTS

Use this space to make notes on what you may want to include in your essay prompts.

Essay Prompt 3:

Essay Prompt 4:

Chapter Six: Reflection

Congratulations on making it this far. You should now have a good personal statement draft that you can build upon. The previous two chapters on structure taught you how to form the basic skeleton of an excellent personal statement with a six-paragraph framework and gave you examples of how to address essay prompts. In this chapter, you will learn how to write in a manner that is compelling, comprehensive, and most importantly... reflective.

Writing Reflectively

What does it actually mean to write reflectively? It means to critically analyse your experiences, ideas and beliefs. It requires that you evaluate how your experiences have impacted your life or how you think, and perhaps how your experiences, beliefs and ideas have influenced what you will do in the future. One of the features of reflective writing is that it is not just descriptive, but analytical too. This means that rather than simply giving the reader an account of how an event unfolded or an explanation of a subject that you are interested in, you ought to inject your own opinions, insights and perspectives along the way. Reflective writing strikes the right balance between being objective, by stating how things are, and being subjective, by shedding light on your own interpretation of facts, theories, events, situations, rules and topics, and sometimes challenging or scrutinising firmly held assumptions.

Writing reflectively is a hallmark that distinguishes a basic personal statement from one that is remarkable, memorable and excellent — so it pays to know how to formulate answers in this manner. One of the most common mistakes that students make in writing a personal statement is thinking that an admissions tutor will be impressed by a laundry list of achievements and experiences. But this is far from the truth. Firstly, your academic record speaks for itself, so rattling on about what can clearly be seen on a CV or other reference is not a good idea. Instead, the answer lies in being reflective and insightful, and exploring your own personal contributions and remarks on what you are discussing. In addition, when you write reflectively, it is almost always a more compelling read for an admissions tutor if you strive to dig deep into a select few curated experiences or illuminating ideas that genuinely resonate with you than to spread yourself too thin by exploring multiple experiences or points superficially. Remember, 'write what you know.' But perhaps I should add 'write about what makes you come alive' or 'write what galvanises you into action.' The reader will feel your passion.

The R Funnel

One of the ways that I recommend that you write reflectively is by using what I call an R Funnel, an original concept that I devised. Practically every personal statement or essay prompt follows the R Funnel — even unknowingly.

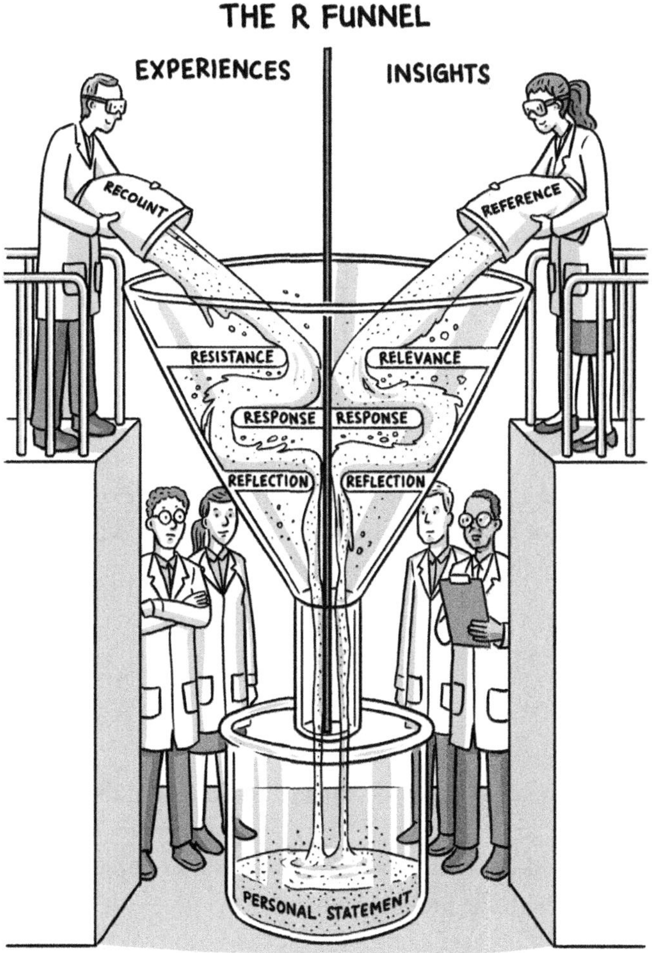

The more you read through personal statements, the more you will realise how often this actually appears in writing. The R Funnel is a framework that you can use within your own personal statement in order to tell the admissions tutor what they want to hear, how they want to hear it.

There are two versions of the R Funnel, as each is used in two separate scenarios. The first is used as a means to describe experiences that you have had, while the second is used to explore your insights about an intellectually illuminating topic. The first version of the R Funnel, which I will call 'R Funnel 1,' is '*Recount, Resistance, Response, Reflection*,' while the second version, which I will call 'R Funnel 2,' is '*Reference, Relevance, Response, Reflection.*'

Let's start with R Funnel 1:

1) Recount.

This is where you provide context to an experience that you had. Make sure that you pick out the most relevant details, and do your best to filter out the rest. This should be limited to no more than three sentences, ideally.

2) Resistance.

This is where you provide further information about what resistance you faced, what obstacles you had to overcome, what the risks were, and perhaps why it was so important that you dealt with the problem at hand.

3) Response.

Now that you have provided context for what you had to face, it is only natural for an admissions tutor to want to know what your response was and how you went about remedying the problem. This is the critical part, because this is where an admissions tutor gets a clearer picture of you as a person and how you react to problems and adversity. So, in response to the task or challenge, ask yourself:

- What did you do about it?
- What was your thought process?
- What was your strategy, if you had one?
- What were the stakes?

A quick tip — if you were working in a group, make sure that you are clear about what your individual role was, as opposed to writing that 'we' did A, B, C or D. If you write 'we did,' rather than 'I did,' it is not clear exactly what your specific role was within the wider task, and thus, it is harder to see what skills you actually showed. Instead, keep your reflective writing in the first person, not the third person.

4) Reflection.

This is the juicy bit, as it is the part that helps you to portray intriguing and personal insights about your experiences. Try to think about the following questions:

- What did you learn?
- What surprised you?
- What qualities did you gain from your experience?
- How have your beliefs, ideas or opinions changed over time, if at all?
- What really 'hit home' for you?
- How is this experience going to help you in your university application?
- Does this experience affect you in your daily life today, and in what ways?

Let's see R Funnel 1 in action, with this example from Reece — a medical student at Yale University.

Reece writes in his personal statement:

Recount:

"I observed a week of various medical professions, rotating between specialties each day."

Resistance:

"On the third day, I was asked by a doctor to keep one of the stroke patients company who did not have any family close by. This was a bit nerve-wracking as she struggled to remember some words and was clearly upset."

Response:

R "I remembered observing a doctor from another ward putting a patient at ease the day before, and how her attitude made the patient calmer. In response, I tried to emulate this coolness and equanimity under pressure. I made eye contact and smiled, and told her that I understood and empathised with her situation. I then asked if she would like to play a game of dominoes."

Reflection:

R "This moment with the stroke patient attuned my mind to the value of empathy, and how much of a difference the simple act of human interaction could have on a person. From that point onwards, I have strived to be the kind of doctor who always sees patients as people first, and comforts them in their moments of vulnerability and hardship."

Reece does an excellent job of taking us through his experience with the stroke patient by recounting his experience to establish the context and then explaining the resistance that he faced. Thereafter, he provides evidence of how he responded to the resistance that he faced by trying to emulate the 'coolness and equanimity' that he had observed from a doctor on another ward. Finally, Reece reflects on his experiences by providing insights into how he hopes to be an empathic doctor, and the importance of seeing patients as 'people first.' As Reece's example shows, using the R Funnel, in this case, has allowed him to hit all of the right notes by providing just about enough context, and then lasering in on his responses and his reflective statements in order to demonstrate key skills that any budding medical student and future doctor would need to display.

So, now that you have seen R Funnel 1 with Reece's example, let's have a look at R Funnel 2, which is used as a framework to help you to explore your thoughts, perspectives and insights about a theoretical topic, rather than an experience.

1) Reference.

This is where you introduce a topic or observation that has interested you, which is usually something of intellectual value.

2) Relevance.

This is where you expound on why this particular topic matters so much to you, its significance within a wider debate or larger issue, and perhaps how this topic has challenged your previously held beliefs or surprised you. Strive to answer these questions:

- Why does this topic matter to you?
- What impact does this topic have on other people?
- How has this topic surprised you?
- How has this topic challenged your ideas?

3) Response.

In this part of the R Funnel, you ought to write about what you have done to explore your topic of interest at a deeper level, and perhaps mention the sources that you have used to broaden your horizons, such as books, research, articles, lectures or conversations with notable thought leaders in your chosen field.

4) Reflection.

The final part is your chance to reflect upon all of your ideas and discoveries, and perhaps what you hope to do with this newfound knowledge. You should also think about how your chosen degree may help you to further explore your topic at a higher level, or how you want to infuse the insights that you have gained within your long-term career.

Let's see R Funnel 2 in action with this example from Hamish — a student in computer science and engineering at the Massachusetts Institute of Technology.

Hamish writes in his personal statement:

Reference:

"Having grown up during a period of technological metamorphosis, I hope to study computer science and engineering to allow me to intertwine my passion for technology in a manner that makes a difference in people's lives. Recently, I have become increasingly fascinated by the advent of artificial intelligence (AI), which I am keen to explore at a higher level.

Relevance:

"Equally, I remained wary of the potential dangers that artificial intelligence might bring upon various industries and our personal lives, such that I took the steps to investigate the benefits and risks of this technology."

Response:

"After attending a conference and reading articles about the use of artificial intelligence in buildings, roads, cities and other infrastructure, I gained a greater insight into the multiple benefits of AI. I learned about 'smart cities,' and discovered that AI can help us to take a bolder step towards improving productivity, efficiency and safety, while also promoting a more sustainable and greener environment."

Reflection:

R "I now believe that artificial intelligence, like many other forms of innovation, holds an enormous amount of potential if harnessed responsibly. We still have a long way to go in understanding the full potential of AI, but I get the impression that we stand to lose a lot more by not embracing this technology than if we step boldly into the unknown. The opportunities to truly make an impact through the use of AI deeply excite me, and I very much look forward to exploring such topics amongst your esteemed faculty."

With Hamish's example, you can hopefully see how R Funnel 2 helped him to outline his ideas logically. He first referenced the context of the topic that he wanted to write about — artificial intelligence. He then went on to explain why the topic of artificial intelligence is important to him and wider society. Critically, by attending a conference and reading books about the use of artificial intelligence in buildings, roads, cities and other infrastructure, Hamish demonstrated a genuine passion to broaden his horizons. Thereafter, he reached a conclusion in a reflective manner, drawing from his intellectual explorations in order to provide a well-reasoned statement about the need to balance the benefits of artificial intelligence with the potential risks posed. He articulates his thoughts clearly and reflectively, and injects his own personal perspectives on the topic of artificial intelligence rather than simply stating that he is 'fascinated by artificial intelligence' and leaving it at that.

As you build upon the aforementioned six paragraphs or essay prompts from the two previous chapters, the R

Funnel will provide a framework that will allow you to write about whatever situation or ideas exemplify the quality, skill, narrative or trait that you are trying to get across with greater ease. The R Funnel, when used in moderation, is handy in that it stops you from overexplaining or labouring a point, or shooting off at a tangent. In addition, for people who are averse to self-promotion, the R Funnel helps with the often uncomfortable nature of writing effusively about yourself or your experiences. It may also be helpful in coming up with answers to points you might struggle to articulate in a comprehensive way.

Now that you know what it means to write reflectively, and you know about the R Funnel, go back to your personal statement draft. To start off with, find a topic or experience that you wrote about — for example, a work placement, internship or your commentary on a subject of interest to you. Try to work through your writing to identify if your sentences reflect the R Funnel.

Remember — if you are describing your tangible experiences, it is R Funnel 1. If you are describing your thoughts, ideas and insights about a subject, it is R Funnel 2. It is not a hard-and-fast rule, but it helps to be aware of the logic and flow behind what makes your writing reflective.

You are now in a position where you can confidently describe an experience that had a meaningful impact on you and articulate your points on an important issue in a reflective and thoughtful manner. As I mentioned before, being reflective, insightful and compelling is the hallmark of a personal statement that is a cut above the rest. This is because it is your reflections and how you respond to situations that reveal the most about you — not just the experiences or topics themselves. This is good news for you, because it means that a medical student who has been fortunate enough to witness the ingenuity of brain surgery during their work experience would not necessarily have the upper hand or a superior personal statement over another medical student who has served lunch to residents in a nursing home. Focussing on a student's reflections and insights, in effect, 'levels the playing field.' It is your chance to be candid about how you really respond to problems, and how you really think. Ultimately, it means that your ideas and personal insights are what add value to your character.

As you go through your statement, scrutinise every experience that you have mentioned, and focus on the million-dollar word: reflection. The more you do this, the closer you are to producing an excellent personal statement.

Curiosity

While the R Funnel is an effective way to convey reflective thoughts about your experiences and insights, you do not need to always follow it to a tee. For brevity, you might deem it necessary to compress the R Funnel by focussing solely on the first and last 'R's' — e.g. 'recount' and 'reflection' for R Funnel 1 and 'reference' and 'reflection' for R Funnel 2. In addition, in cases where your essay prompt requires that you reflect on a subject in an open-ended and creative way, the best way to convey reflectiveness in your writing is by focussing on one word: curiosity — which is another way to be reflective that does not follow a predetermined structure.

To be curious means that you are:

"Interested in learning about people or things around you."

When it comes to personal statements and college admissions essays, curiosity is contagious, particularly when you take an interest in something very specific and niche. The most impressive personal statements and admissions essays focus on depth rather than breadth, and the writing tends to demonstrate a genuine passion to explore the topic in question, rather than merely covering bases for the sake of 'ticking a box.' The most compelling personal statements to read are from students who not only state facts, but take an incisive and analytical stance on issues, beliefs or observations that challenged their understanding of a topic. In addition, as your write, you need to constantly remind yourself of the big question:

What does this say about me?

As I mentioned before, by implanting your own perspectives, ideas, questions and opinions into the topics that you discuss, you avoid the risk of being overly descriptive. You remind the admissions tutor that your insights are valuable to the discussion at hand. This is what makes you curious and enhances your reflective statements.

Let's have a look at an essay prompt that embodies what it means to be curious, analytical and reflective. Ricky — whose essay prompts I covered in the previous chapter — was asked to submit an 'Uncommon Essay' by the University of Chicago for his application to study economics, and this was his prompt:

"In the spirit of adventurous enquiry, pose your own question or choose one of our past prompts.

Be original, creative and thought-provoking. Draw on your best qualities as a writer, thinker, visionary, social critic, sage, citizen of the world or future citizen of the University of Chicago. Take a little risk and have fun."

Ricky writes in his 'Uncommon Essay:'

"Did curiosity really kill the cat? As a student, I'm always told to never limit my brain's capacity and to be on the constant search for ways to explore my own curiosities, so why haven't I been killed? I mean there are circumstances when overstepping boundaries will get you a bullet in the head, like taking a deep dive into a drug deal to see the type of crack being sold, but that's more of an exception. Einstein wasn't assassinated for challenging the laws of physics, nor was Marie Curie when researching radioactivity. Why would such a common phrase suggest that having a mind driven by curiosity is dangerous?

Let's look at the exceptions: listening in on a private conversation will kill the cat, running to check the basement after hearing sounds of a killer intruder will kill the cat (note late 90's slasher films), and snooping through your partner's text messages will most definitely kill the cat. Now, these exceptions absolutely do not define the rule. I lead a life driven by curiosity, and it's not like every teacher from every class I've taken since preschool hasn't encouraged this. I place no limits on my curiosity and have yet to find myself in trouble because of it. The implication of the phrase is not completely applicable to the overall statement, so why exclaim a phrase that has a lack of relevant value? The curiosities that 'curiosity killed the cat' attacks are rather minute. The phrase carries a much heavier weight that seems to extend to all types of curiosity; rather misleading isn't it?

I feel even the phrase 'curiosity got the cat a bowl of milk' makes far more sense than its fallacious opposite. Painting the picture of an entirely negative outlook on curiosity makes an outside-the-box thought unappealing. If the phrase were to get reworked to uplift inquisitiveness rather than demean it, I'm sure the results of increased curiosity would follow. Contrary to the idea proposed in the phrase, I have been led (almost) nowhere but to positive places by curiosity. Curiosity allowed me to uncover a unique process of making slime for my business.

Now, I must be honest, there were circumstances when playing curiously with slime killed the cat. My initial curiosity with slime resulted in it spilling and settling on top of the beads of my carpet, which got me into a bit of trouble with my mom. Whoops. Getting a little messy with slime paid off, though. My curiosity helped me achieve what many considered a breakthrough in the slime world: conquering 'icee' slime. When I first saw this peculiar texture online, I knew I had to get my hands on the recipe; the only thing stopping me was that a mere two people knew how to make it. This is when my bowl-of-milk-receiving curiosity kicked in, and I marathon-ran through countless recipes until I finally conquered it. Curiosity rewarded me with a new best-selling texture that I have been selling for three years now. Thanks, curiosity!

The phrase itself is far more dangerous than the alleged scenario it proposes. If people led by 'curiosity killed the cat,' then the researchers of the world would lack the incentive to find a cure for cancer, theoretical physics would be non-existent, and I wouldn't have cared to learn how to make icee slime. A simple, 'cute' phrase unpacks a whirlwind of misguidance. What is the author of this phrase proposing? Do they expect the children of the world to be led by dull thoughts and to accept all realities rather than exploring, uncovering, and predicting new ones? Are your doctors not supposed to research breakthrough medical miracles to uncover a pattern that can be relayed to future cases? Seems pretty careless. I bet the initial pioneers of the world roll in their graves each time someone exclaims how 'curiosity killed the cat,' at least I know I will."

This answer to the University of Chicago's 'Uncommon Essay' prompt is superb because it nails the idea of 'adventurous enquiry' and 'micro musings,' as I mentioned in chapter one. Ricky's initial essays on slime were already rather niche, and they set him apart from other candidates. This essay follows a similar style insofar as focussing on challenging the aphorism 'curiosity killed the cat.' What makes this essay interesting is the way that Ricky challenges, dissects and evaluates this commonly used phrase, and then goes on to offer his own adjustment of the phrase, from 'curiosity killed the cat' to 'curiosity got the cat a bowl of milk.' Throughout this essay, Ricky uses his own experiences to present a compelling case on the benefits of curiosity, and his arguments are very persuasive and cogently written. In addition, the style of writing strikes the right balance between being informative and occasionally injecting a bit of humour and a colloquial tone. For example:

"Running to check the basement after hearing sounds of a killer intruder will kill the cat (note late 90's slasher films)."

"Snooping through your partner's text messages will most definitely kill the cat."

"This is when my bowl-of-milk-receiving curiosity kicked in."

Ricky also incorporates a lot of rhetorical questioning throughout the essay from the first line, which proves highly effective for this style of essay, as it allows the reader to engage in the thoughts that Ricky has about the phrase 'curiosity killed the cat,' and perhaps question their own beliefs too. Ricky's essay has a quality to it that is difficult to engineer without genuine curiosity, and perhaps that is why his writing reads so authentically. It is a skill to be able to take a singular topic or phrase, such as 'curiosity killed the cat,' and extrapolate that into an entire essay that still remains interesting. Yet Ricky manages to do this excellently.

If you are given a question that requires that you demonstrate reflection and curiosity, it is always best to focus on something specific, just as Ricky has done. Your writing will always read better when you fully explore a select few curated topics, rather than trying to cover as many bases as possible with a superficial and contrived answer that has not been explored to its full potential. Keep it personal, write deeply and reflectively, and be yourself.

That's all for this chapter. In the next chapter, I will show you how to 'thread the needle' by seeing your personal statement from a 'bird's eye view.' I am sure you want to know what all of that means, so come along.

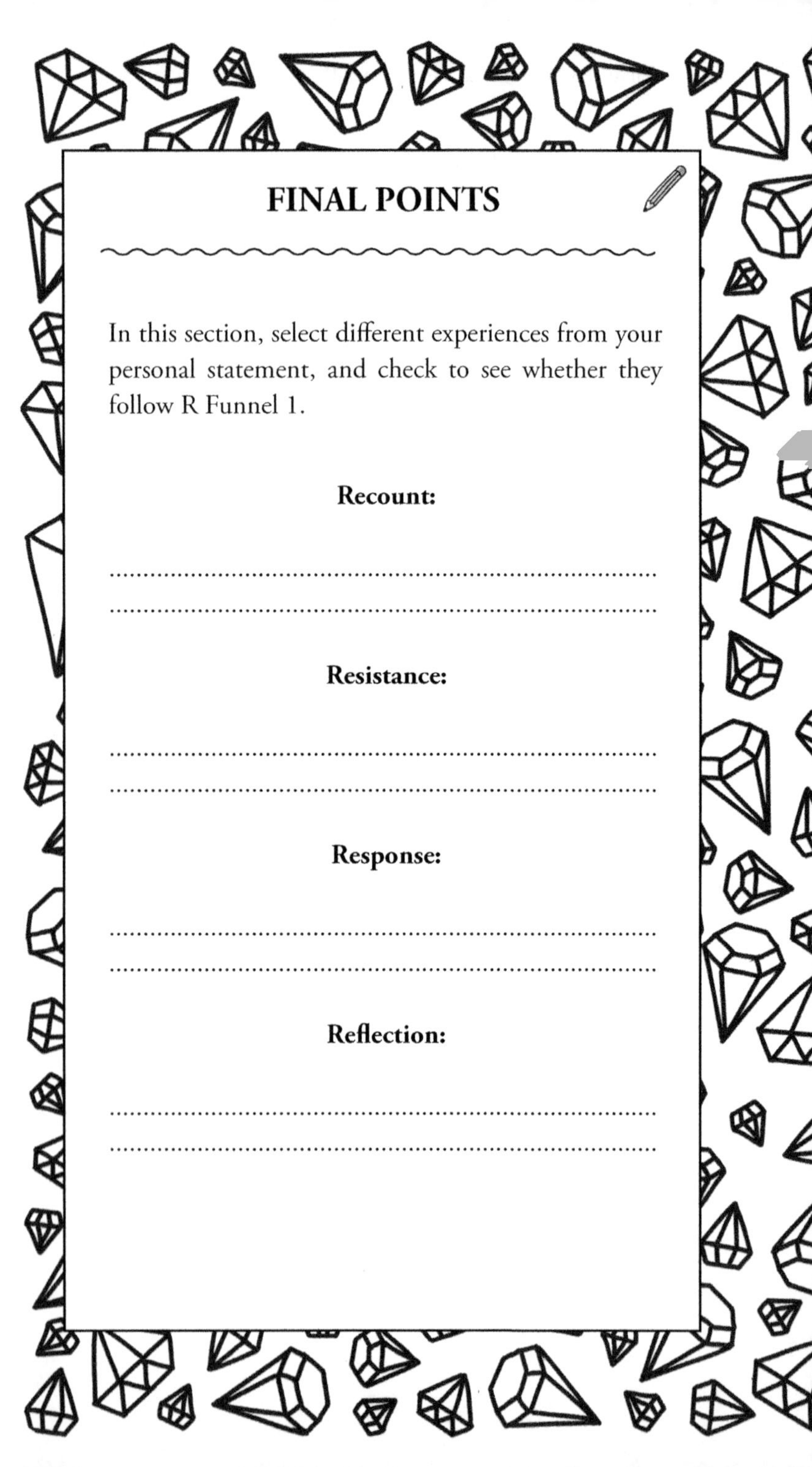

FINAL POINTS

In this section, select different experiences from your personal statement, and check to see whether they follow R Funnel 1.

Recount:

....

....

Resistance:

....

....

Response:

....

....

Reflection:

....

....

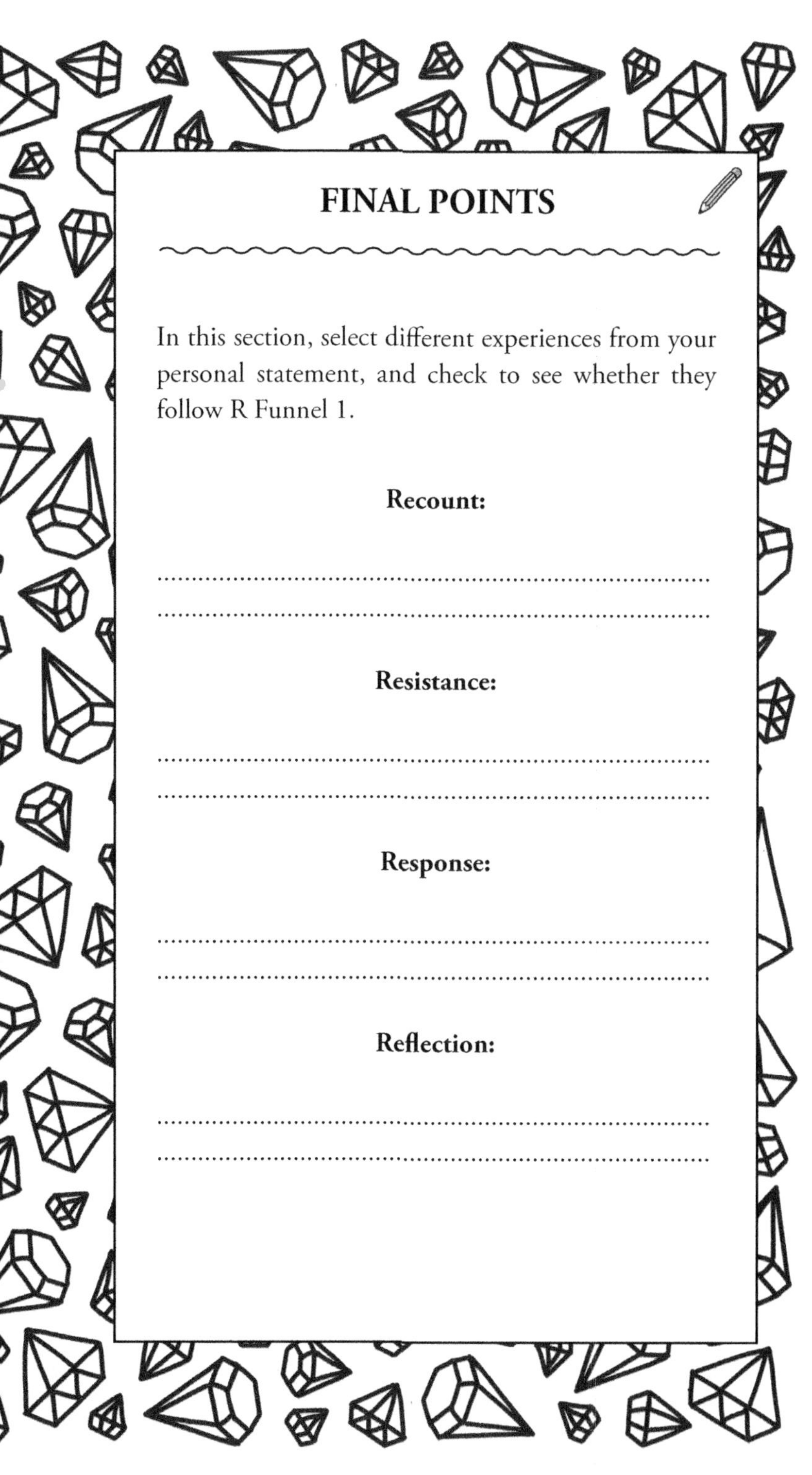

FINAL POINTS

In this section, select different experiences from your personal statement, and check to see whether they follow R Funnel 1.

Recount:

....

....

Resistance:

....

....

Response:

....

....

Reflection:

....

....

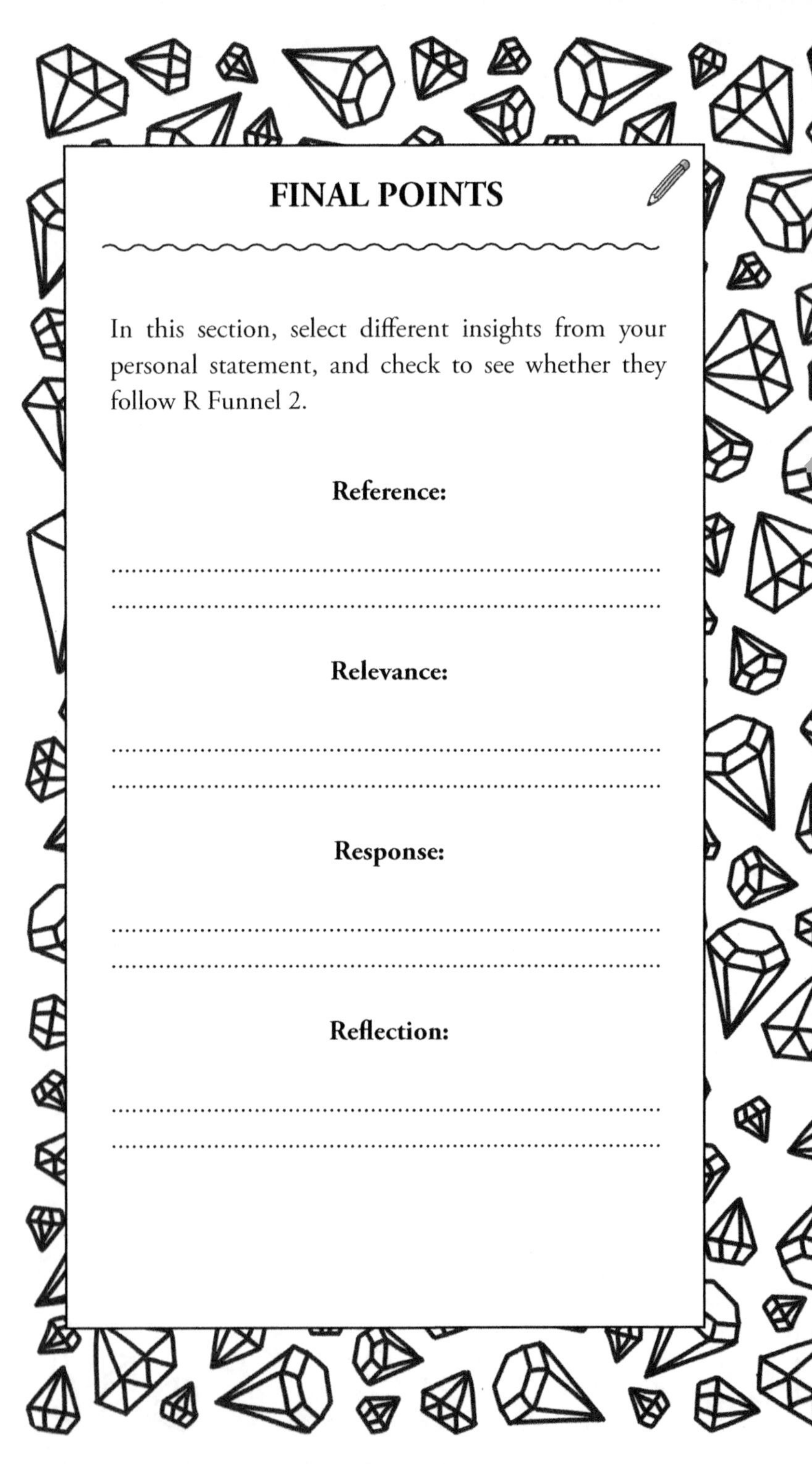

FINAL POINTS

In this section, select different insights from your personal statement, and check to see whether they follow R Funnel 2.

Reference:

....

....

Relevance:

....

....

Response:

....

....

Reflection:

....

....

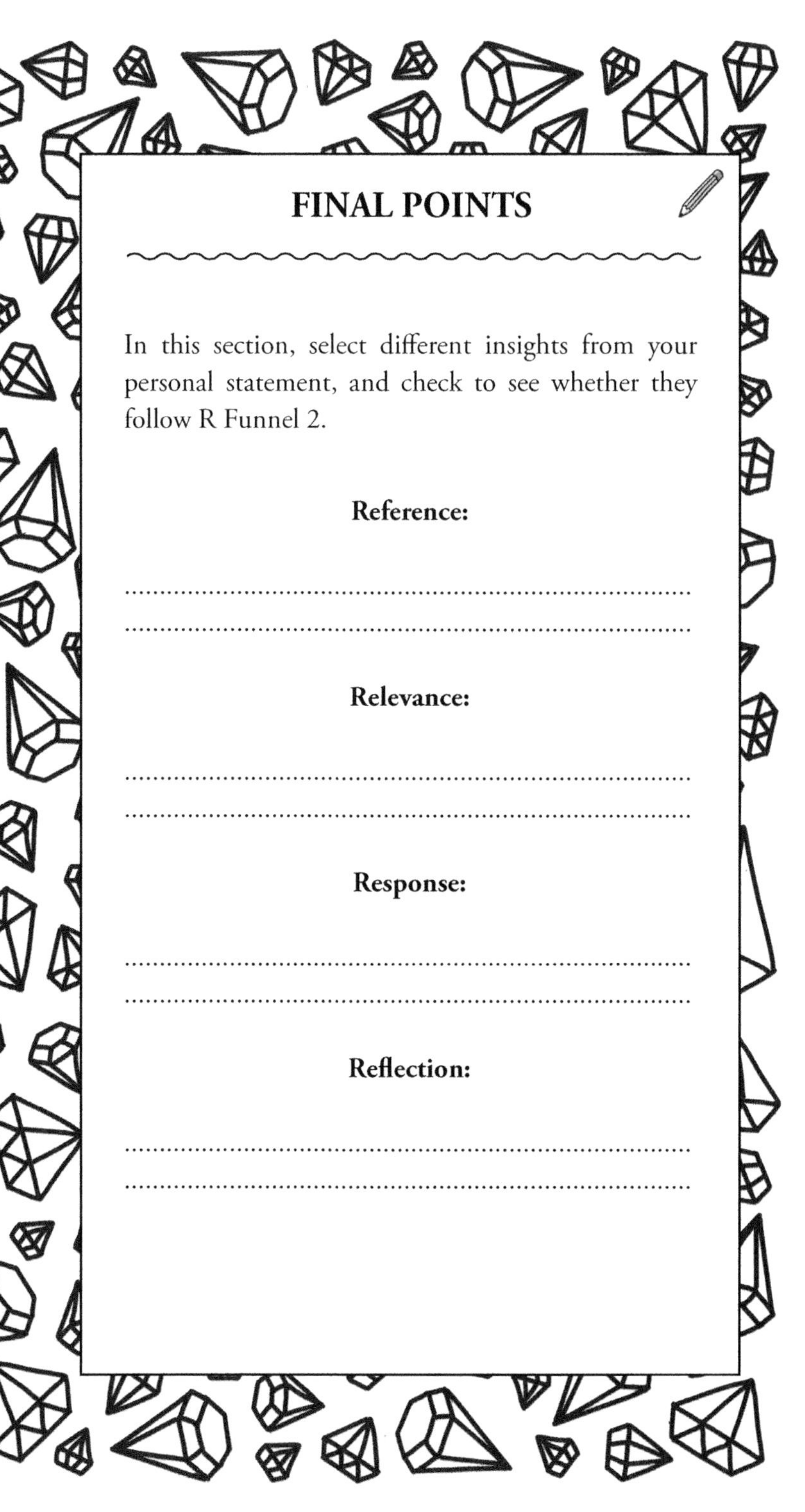

FINAL POINTS

In this section, select different insights from your personal statement, and check to see whether they follow R Funnel 2.

Reference:

....

....

Relevance:

....

....

Response:

....

....

Reflection:

....

....

Chapter Seven: Coherence

Let's take a brief trip back to the first chapters of this book. If you recall from earlier on, I referred to a personal statement as a 'six-course meal.' This is important because while it is crucial that you maintain sound logic and flow from one word to the next, and one sentence to the next, it is equally important that you are aware of the sequence and progression of your paragraphs when the personal statement is taken as a whole.

Threading the Needle

If you imagine that each of your six paragraphs is a small ring, you want to metaphorically guide a thread through each of those six rings, so that they come together as one. This is what I mean when I refer to 'threading the needle.'

The dictionary defines it as follows:

"To find harmony or strike a balance between conflicting forces or interests."

You need to make sure that your flow, logic and structure are all coherent, intelligible, and frankly, that they all make sense and match your original theme or narrative from the 'top level' of your writing, and not just within each individual paragraph.

One of the ways to thread the needle is to condense each of

your paragraphs into one short sentence, and analyse the essay in a summary format. Let's say that you have six paragraphs in your personal statement. You will need to check to see if these six sentences make logical sense when tied together as one storyline. I will show you a few examples, but before that, let's remind ourselves of the classic six-paragraph structure that is typically seen in a personal statement.

- **Paragraph one** was your introduction.
- **Paragraph two** was about your academic background and intellectual perspectives.
- **Paragraph three** was about your work experience.
- **Paragraph four** was the space for continuing to write about your work experience, as well as your other related projects, insights, achievements and interests.
- **Paragraph five** was for your extracurricular activities or mitigating circumstances.
- **Paragraph six** was your conclusion, where you tied everything together in the end and reiterated your main points.

Remember that even if you do not use the six-paragraph structure, you can still attempt to thread the needle with your own arrangement of paragraphs and structure. The same principle of ensuring your logical progression of ideas still applies. Once again, all you have to do is summarise what is being said in each paragraph into a sentence and read through each of them.

So let's have a look at a few examples of paragraph summaries for candidates who applied to different subjects.

Threading the Needle Well: Economics

Student A is applying to study economics, and upon summarising what they have written in each paragraph, this is what emerges.

In *paragraph one*, the student remarks on recent global events in economics, and shares their personal insights.

In *paragraph two*, the student mentions how their academic projects helped to shed further light on key issues in economics.

In *paragraph three*, the student writes about how working at a bank allowed them to see economics and finance in action.

Paragraph four gives us insights into how the student's previous work inspired them to establish a start-up.

Paragraph five goes into detail about how this start-up experienced enormous success, and they go on to mention that they won awards.

And, in *paragraph six*, the student makes a final statement to reinforce their qualities and genuine enthusiasm for their course.

Hopefully, you can see how the student manages to thread the needle rather well here, as each paragraph builds upon the next one logically.

Threading the Needle Well:

Dentistry

Now, let's see how **Student B**, applying to study dentistry, threaded their needle.

In *paragraph one*, they explore an insightful study about innovative procedures in dentistry.

In *paragraph two*, they mention how their studies piqued their interest, and that they pursued the sciences as a result.

In *paragraph three*, they write about how they worked in a dental clinic and saw procedures firsthand.

In *paragraph four*, they provide insights into their experience of volunteering at a food shelter, which helped to build their communication skills and empathy.

In *paragraph five*, they write about how they enjoy sculpting as a hobby, which helped to build their manual dexterity.

And finally, in *paragraph six*, the student expands on why their skills make them suitable for dentistry.

Once again, this student has managed to thread the needle, and their paragraph progression is coherent and logical.

Threading the Needle Well: Medicine

Here's another: **Student C**, who is applying to study medicine.

In *paragraph one*, the student mentions that they overcame a debilitating illness as a child, which sparked a curiosity about biology.

In *paragraph two*, the student writes passionately about how they excelled in the sciences, and sought to apply their skills to help others.

In *paragraph three*, they write about undertaking work in a hospital, which provided practical experience.

In *paragraph four*, they mention that they founded a charity to raise awareness of children's diseases.

Paragraph five sees the student sharing their hobbies beyond the classroom — namely that they captained the school basketball team, which solidified their leadership skills.

And finally, *paragraph six* is the student reaffirming their commitment to medicine.

You won't be surprised to learn that this student managed to thread the needle too. Now, let's have just one more example of a student doing this rather well.

Threading the Needle Well:

Law

Student D is applying to study law, and in *paragraph one*, they outlined their observations on a legal principle and landmark case.

In *paragraph two*, they write about how their studies have provided context for their aforementioned legal topics.

In *paragraph three*, they write about how working at a law firm helped to cultivate a legal lexicon and mindset.

In *paragraph four*, the student writes about how further work at a barrister's chambers strengthened their analytical skills.

In *paragraph five*, the student writes about taking part in a school mooting competition, and how they created a law podcast.

And finally, in *Paragraph Six*, the student manages to weave all of the points together, and expresses their future career plans.

So, hopefully, you can see that from paragraph one to paragraph six, the subject matter of each paragraph follows on from the next, gradually building to a summary in the conclusion. Each of these paragraphs 'threads the needle', and they complement one another.

Not Threading the Needle: Nursing

Now that you know what to do, it is important to know what not to do. Here's an example of a student who did not manage to thread the needle effectively. Hopefully, you will notice the difference.

Student E is applying to study nursing.

In *paragraph one*, they wrote about having a childhood passion for video games and being creative.

Paragraph two focuses on the student studying art at school, and playing an active role in various sports clubs.

Paragraph three sees the student lamenting the time spent working at an accountancy firm over the summer, which they eventually concluded was a waste of time.

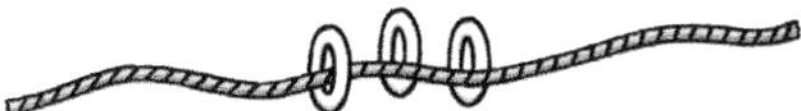

In *paragraph four*, the student writes about how they randomly watched a Netflix documentary about the flu and thought they would try nursing because of it.

Paragraph five lists several inspiring quotes from personal development books that the student has read.

And finally, in *paragraph six*, the student concludes by attempting to make a questionable connection between video games and nursing.

A structure such as this might, in fact, be the student's real story, but it is hard to follow because it jumps from video games to studying art, then sports, and then all of a sudden accountancy enters the storyline before the nursing bomb is dropped from out of the blue. If your structure looks like this, you leave the reader in suspense, and the reward is usually not as satisfying as you might think. You might be surprised to discover how common a paragraph structure such as this actually is, but do not feel deterred if you have done this. The reason why threading the needle can be hard to achieve is because you need to write from the perspective of the individual words themselves, the overall paragraph's logic, and the essay's logic at the same time.

Imagine trying to draw a circle on a sheet of paper with a pencil in your hand, versus trying to draw a gigantic one on a massive, sweeping field. For the latter, it would be easier if you could see where you were going from a bird's-eye view — and writing is no different.

So it is important not to follow the logic demonstrated by this nursing student who conjured a vague narrative only towards the end of the personal statement. Rather, you should strive to make your narrative, direction and intentions clear no later than paragraph two. And thereafter, your subsequent paragraphs should build upon what you have already written.

In effect, hook the reader in from the start, and then carry it through right till the end. Even if you mention something that casts doubt on your commitment to study your chosen subject, you can use that in your favour to show how your character has developed over time. But just bear in mind that every point should relate back to your overall message and narrative, which is your desire to study the subject that you are applying for. Also, remember that admissions tutors are quite literally searching through hundreds of personal statements from other students just like you. While you do not need to go down the route of being gimmicky, eccentric or over-the-top for the sake of getting attention, it is important to demonstrate your genuine passion for your chosen subject, and not leave the admissions tutor with any doubt as to your suitability for your chosen course.

If you have managed to produce your paragraphs, write reflectively and thread the needle from paragraph to paragraph, you should give yourself a well-deserved pat on the back, and perhaps treat yourself for your hard work. But, do not relax too much, because there is still a little bit more to do as you move from the Writing stage to the Refining stage, and I will discuss all of that in the next chapter.

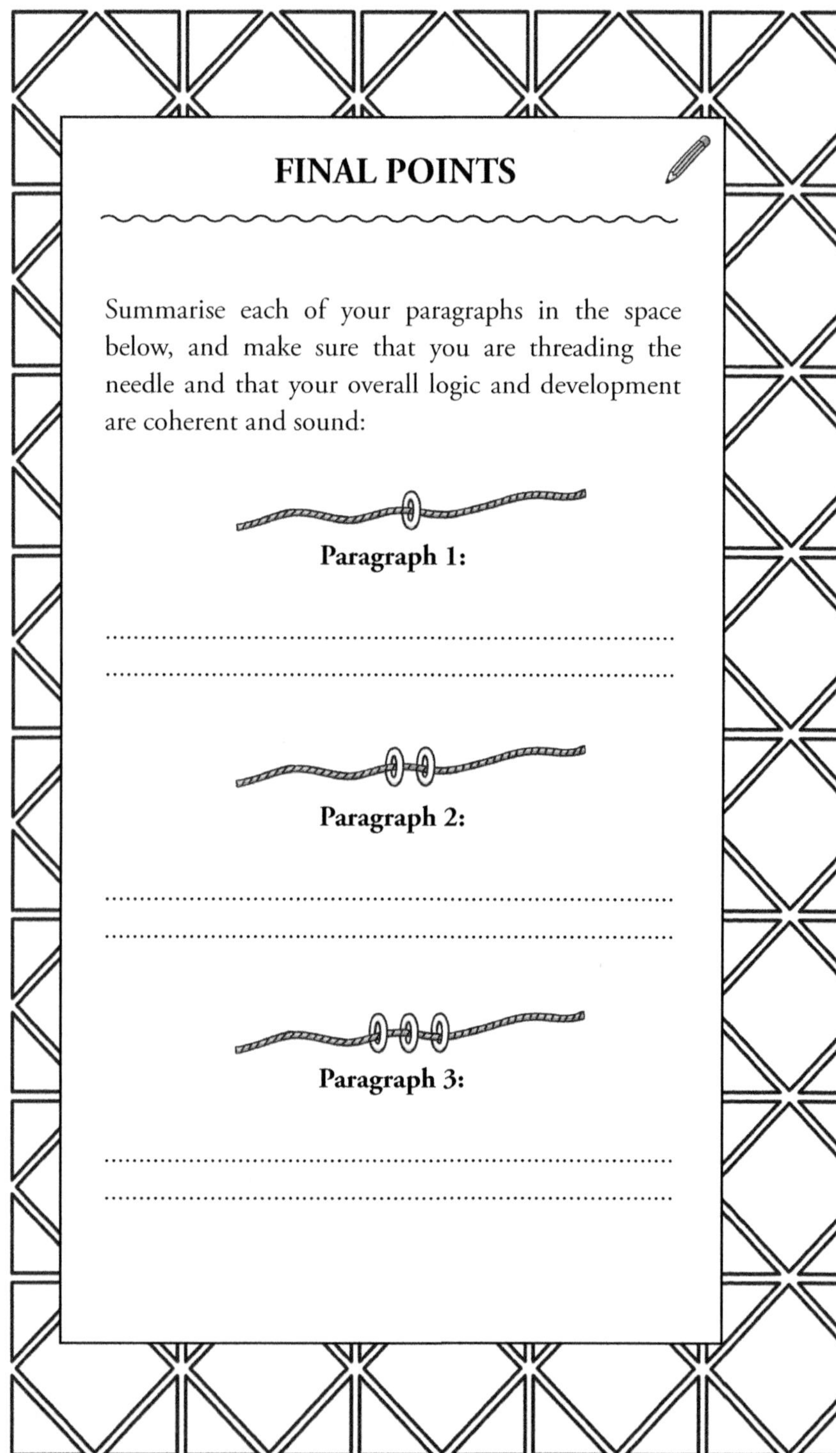

FINAL POINTS

Summarise each of your paragraphs in the space below, and make sure that you are threading the needle and that your overall logic and development are coherent and sound:

Paragraph 1:

....

....

Paragraph 2:

....

....

Paragraph 3:

....

....

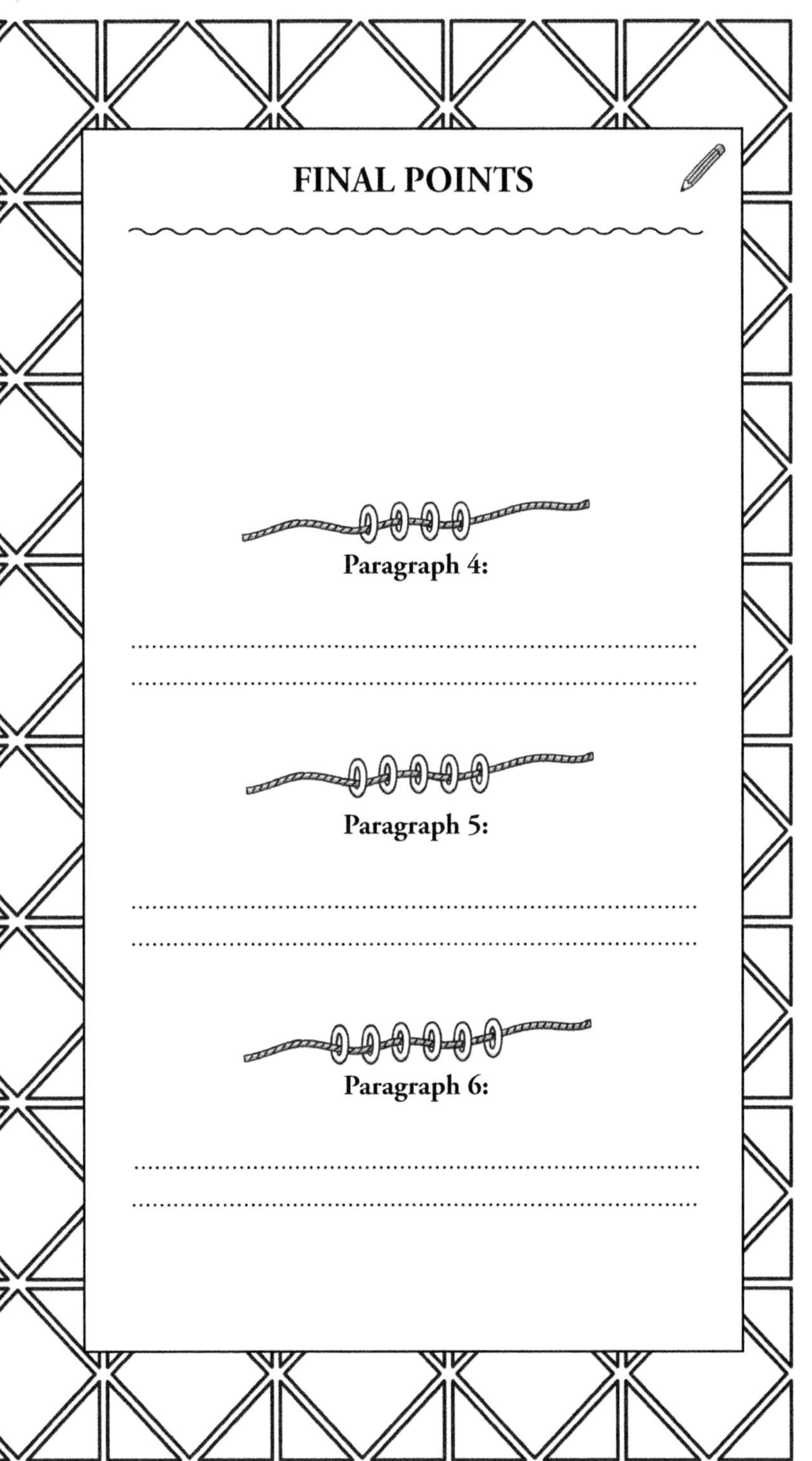

FINAL POINTS

Paragraph 4:

....

....

Paragraph 5:

....

....

Paragraph 6:

....

....

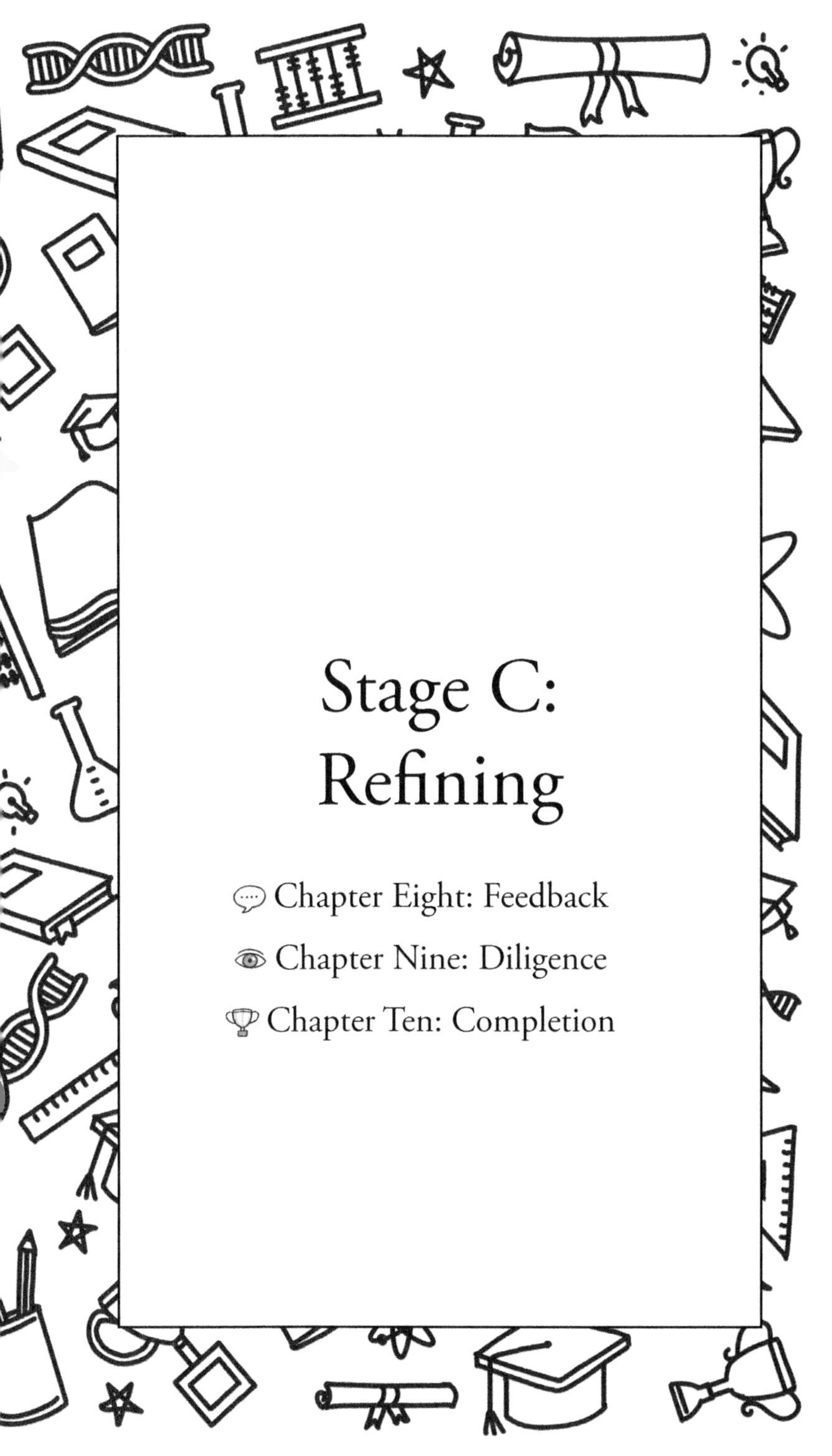

Stage C: Refining

Chapter Eight: Feedback

You have now covered two very important stages of crafting a personal statement: the Planning stage and the Writing stage. If you have followed my instructions to the letter, you should now have an excellent draft that you can improve, enhance and continue to make your own. This next stage of the process is about refining. By producing a draft, you have gotten over the major hurdle of actually getting some text down that you can work from, and now you can breathe a sigh of relief. You have just overcome the thickest and hardest part of writing a personal statement. The refining process is about sharpening, tweaking and potentially rewriting parts of your personal statement to elevate your writing as close to perfection as possible.

With that said, it is important to be reminded of the famous quote:

"A work of art is never finished, merely abandoned."

So while it pays to be meticulous, do not get too caught up in this Refining stage, because you run the risk of ruining something that was already excellent to begin with. It is all about balance. At its core, the goal of refining is to edit your writing in a way that helps to bring your narrative to light even more, and perhaps make your writing more persuasive, compelling or powerful. It is a chance for you to check for coherence and that you are threading the needle, as I explained in the previous chapter. It is also an opportunity for you to make sure that your writing is reflective, and that it presents your skills and accomplishments in the best light.

Finally, this stage of the writing process allows you to take your draft and adapt it to other universities, or even other courses at the same university, if you are applying to more than one course there. This is important because specificity can make a big difference in the success of your application, so if you manage to edit your personal statement in a way that adapts to and is tailored to your course, it will make a stronger impression than a personal statement that is too generic. You can improve this 'specificity' by mentioning individual modules from that course, and quite often, candidates will rewrite the first and last paragraphs of their personal statements in order to apply to more than one programme.

A Fresh Pair of Eyes

Anyway — back to the main point about refining. While you might be incredibly self-aware, it is usually a wise choice to get another person to have a look at your personal statement. This is because during the process of writing your personal statement, you are most likely to see your writing from your own perspective, and you might miss key details or mistakes that may be obvious to someone else. The best way to figure out any areas that may require improvement is to hear opinions, critique and feedback that will strength-test your writing.

A good place to start is by sharing this draft with a handful of people — those who know you well, but equally, those who do not know you well. Sharing your draft with someone who does not know you on a personal level is a great way to receive an unvarnished and unbiased opinion about you from a fresh pair of eyes.

Who to Seek Feedback From

When it comes to feedback, there are two kinds of people that you will encounter. In one group, you will find the passive, perfunctory and pandering types. These are the people who, with the best of intentions, will not really get into the details of your writing or tell you when something is wrong. Their greatest priority is not to upset you, so they will avoid criticising your writing. They are easy to deal with, but ultimately, not as valuable in improving your application in the long run. In the other group, you will find the punctilious, pettifogging and perfectionist types. They might be your parents, teachers or academic advisors who are more likely to point out the areas that require improving. This can be irritating, particularly when you disagree with their opinions, but I strongly recommend that you associate yourself more with people of the second type rather than the first. Because even if you think that their comments about your personal statement are wrong, you would have at least taken the time to hear them out, and can privately consider whether you want to take their advice on board. It is much better to receive criticism and go on to craft an excellent personal statement than to feel too proud of your writing to accept feedback and go on to submit something sub-par, which may result in a rejection.

Surely, you'd rather achieve your goals with humility than fail with pride, right?

Regardless of who you consult for feedback on your personal statement, be sure to ask them these three key questions:

1

Number One:

What did you learn about me after reading my personal statement?

2

Number Two:

What did you like about my personal statement?

3

Number Three:

What did you not like about my personal statement?

Make sure that you ask these questions in that exact order. The importance of the first question, 'What did you learn about me from my personal statement?' is that it immediately highlights the parts that were most revealing or surprising about you — for better or for worse. This is good because it suggests that the information included was interesting to the reader, or that it educated them in some way.

The second question, 'What did you like about my personal statement?' is very simple, and encourages the reader to point out your strongest attributes. If enough people mention similar strong features of your personal statement, you will feel more confident about including them.

The third question, 'What did you not like about my personal statement?' forces the reader to do something that most of us are somewhat uncomfortable with — give criticism and receive criticism. The power of asking this question is that you give the reader permission to be completely honest — as brutal and sobering as it may be. If enough people mention similar points of improvement, it will register in your mind that perhaps those parts could be changed.

Receiving feedback from others can be revelatory and often uncomfortable, so do not be surprised if you feel a little bit embarrassed or offended by the critiques that come your way. At the same time, it is healthy to bear in mind that every person may have an opinion, but the ability to harbour one does not automatically make their opinion the truth. When all is said and done, this is your personal statement. So you need to strike the right balance between taking advice openly and with humility, but also being wary of other people potentially draining the life and soul from the writing that is uniquely yours. It is a fine balance, and you will know that you have gotten it right when your personal statement is authentic to who you are, and still manages to impress those who do not know you personally.

Fundamentally, the goal is to get into your chosen degree, so whatever path you took to get there will not matter as much when you look at the whole process one day in the future. As long as you get into your chosen university, that is all that will count in the end. Do not lose sight of the end goal.

That is all for this chapter. In the penultimate chapter of

this book, you will learn about the final checks that you will need to make before your submission. You have done a great job in reaching this stage of the book, so you might as well come along.

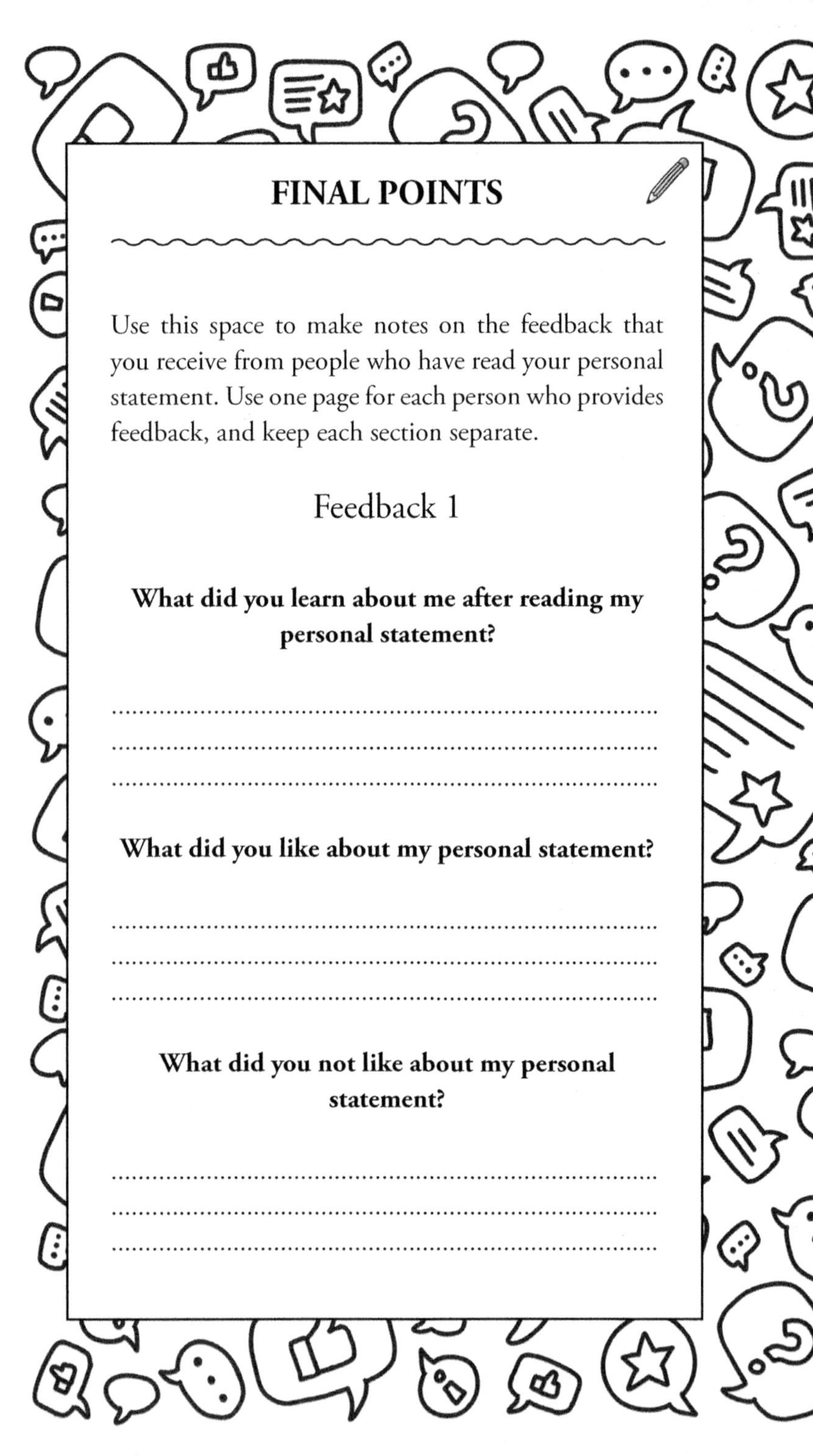

FINAL POINTS

Use this space to make notes on the feedback that you receive from people who have read your personal statement. Use one page for each person who provides feedback, and keep each section separate.

Feedback 1

What did you learn about me after reading my personal statement?

....

....

....

What did you like about my personal statement?

....

....

....

What did you not like about my personal statement?

....

....

....

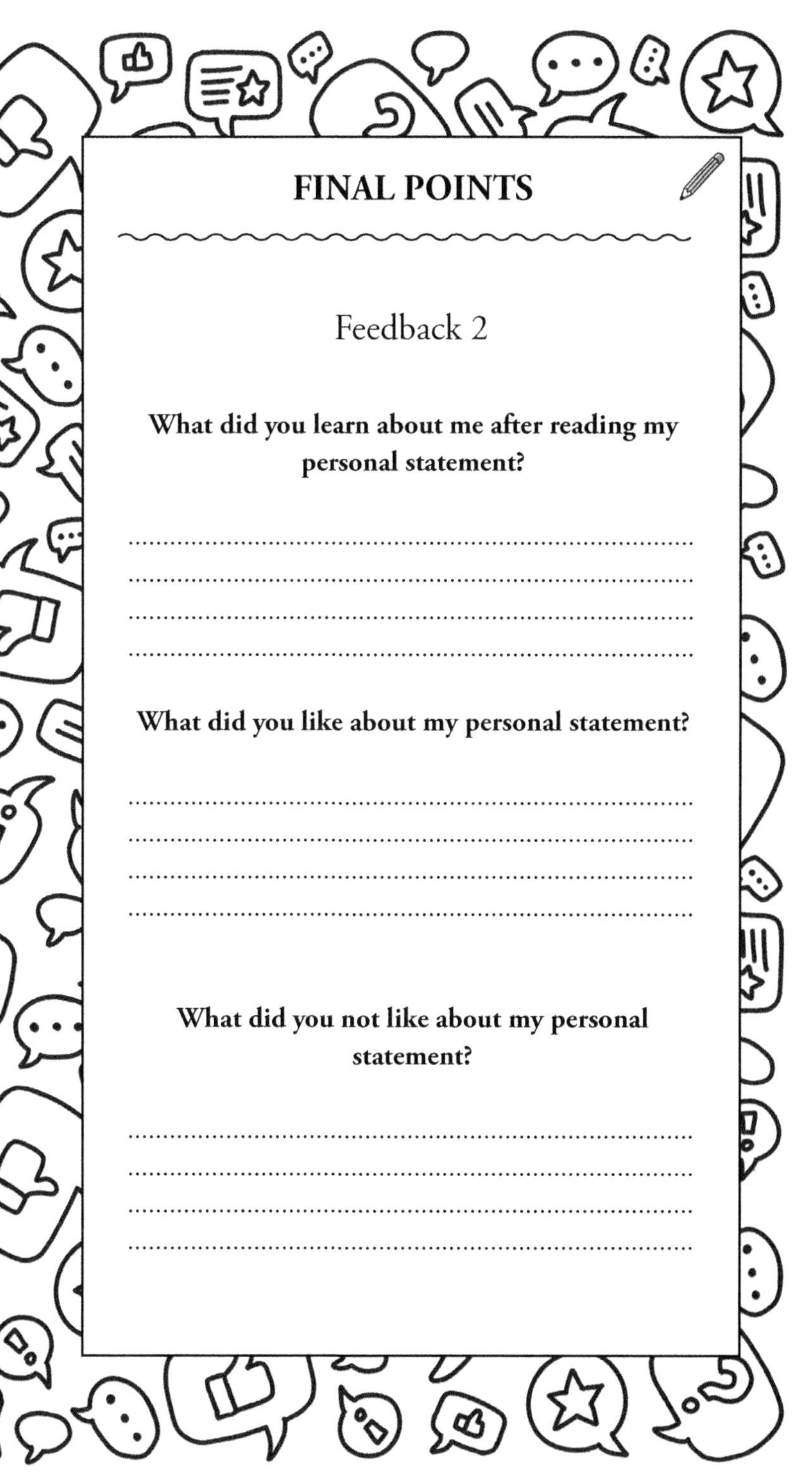

FINAL POINTS

Feedback 2

What did you learn about me after reading my personal statement?

....
....
....
....

What did you like about my personal statement?

....
....
....
....

What did you not like about my personal statement?

....
....
....
....

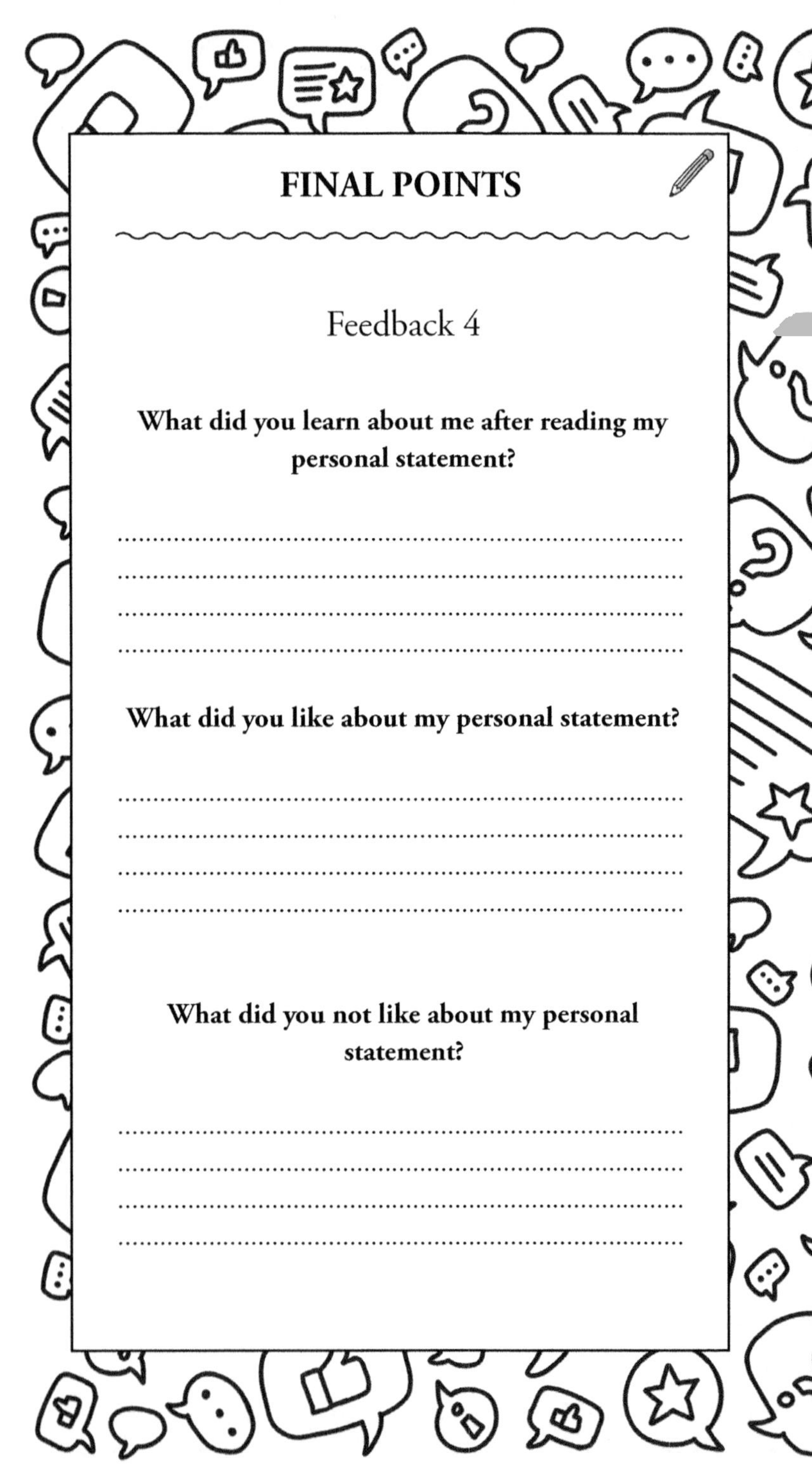

FINAL POINTS

Feedback 4

What did you learn about me after reading my personal statement?

....

....

....

....

What did you like about my personal statement?

....

....

....

....

What did you not like about my personal statement?

....

....

....

....

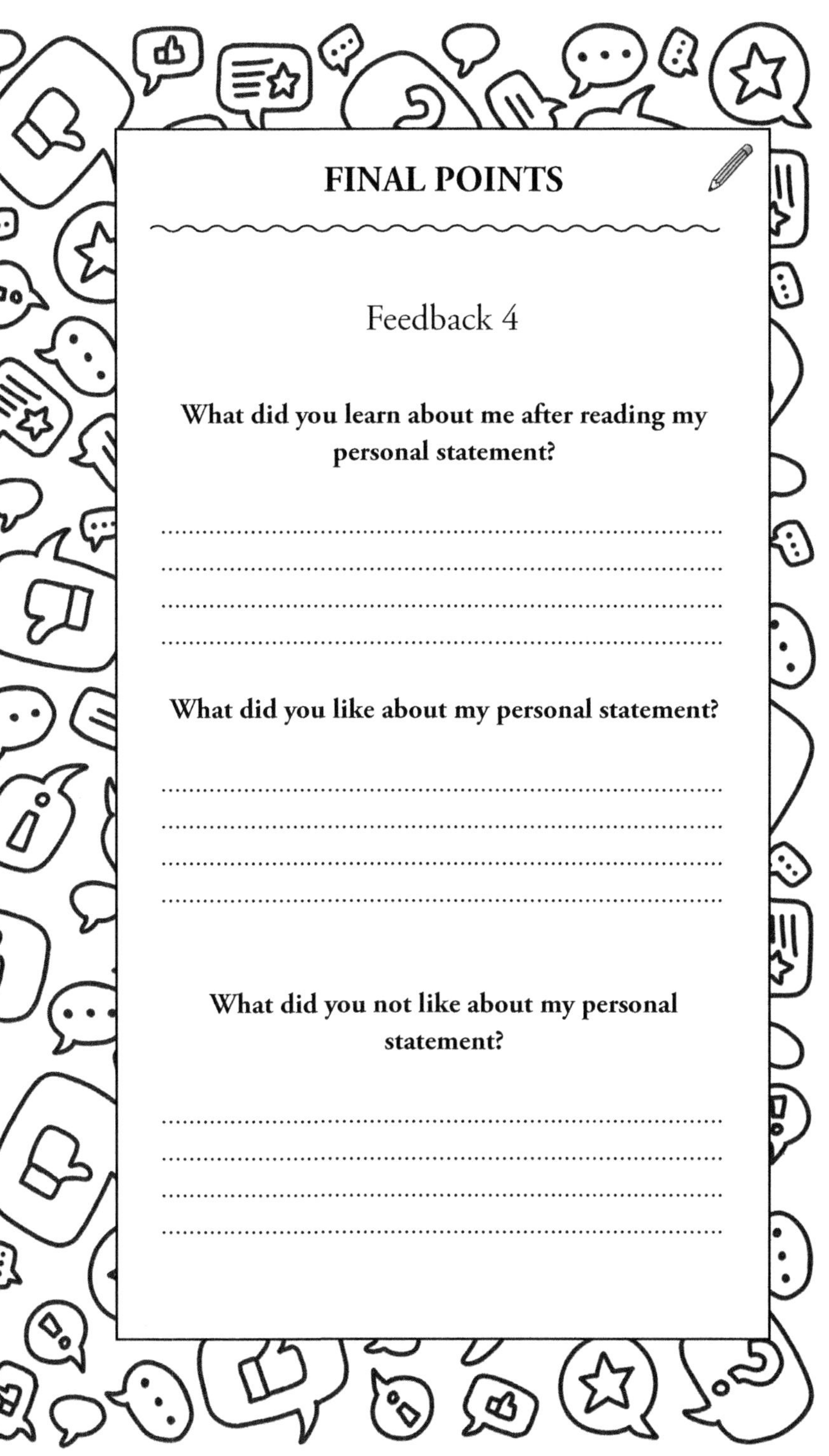

FINAL POINTS

Feedback 4

What did you learn about me after reading my personal statement?

....

....

....

....

What did you like about my personal statement?

....

....

....

....

What did you not like about my personal statement?

....

....

....

....

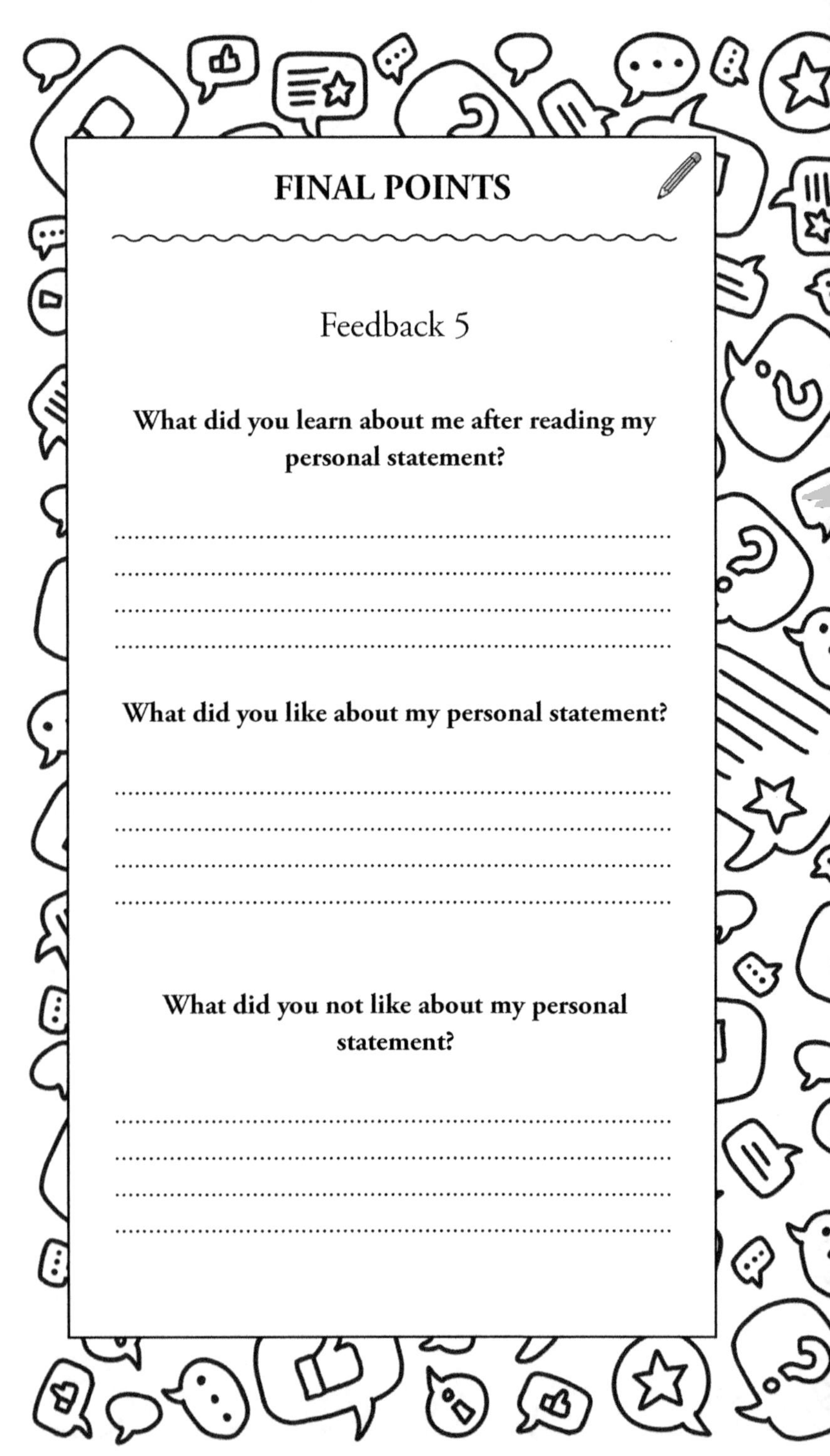

FINAL POINTS

Feedback 5

What did you learn about me after reading my personal statement?

....
....
....
....

What did you like about my personal statement?

....
....
....
....

What did you not like about my personal statement?

....
....
....
....

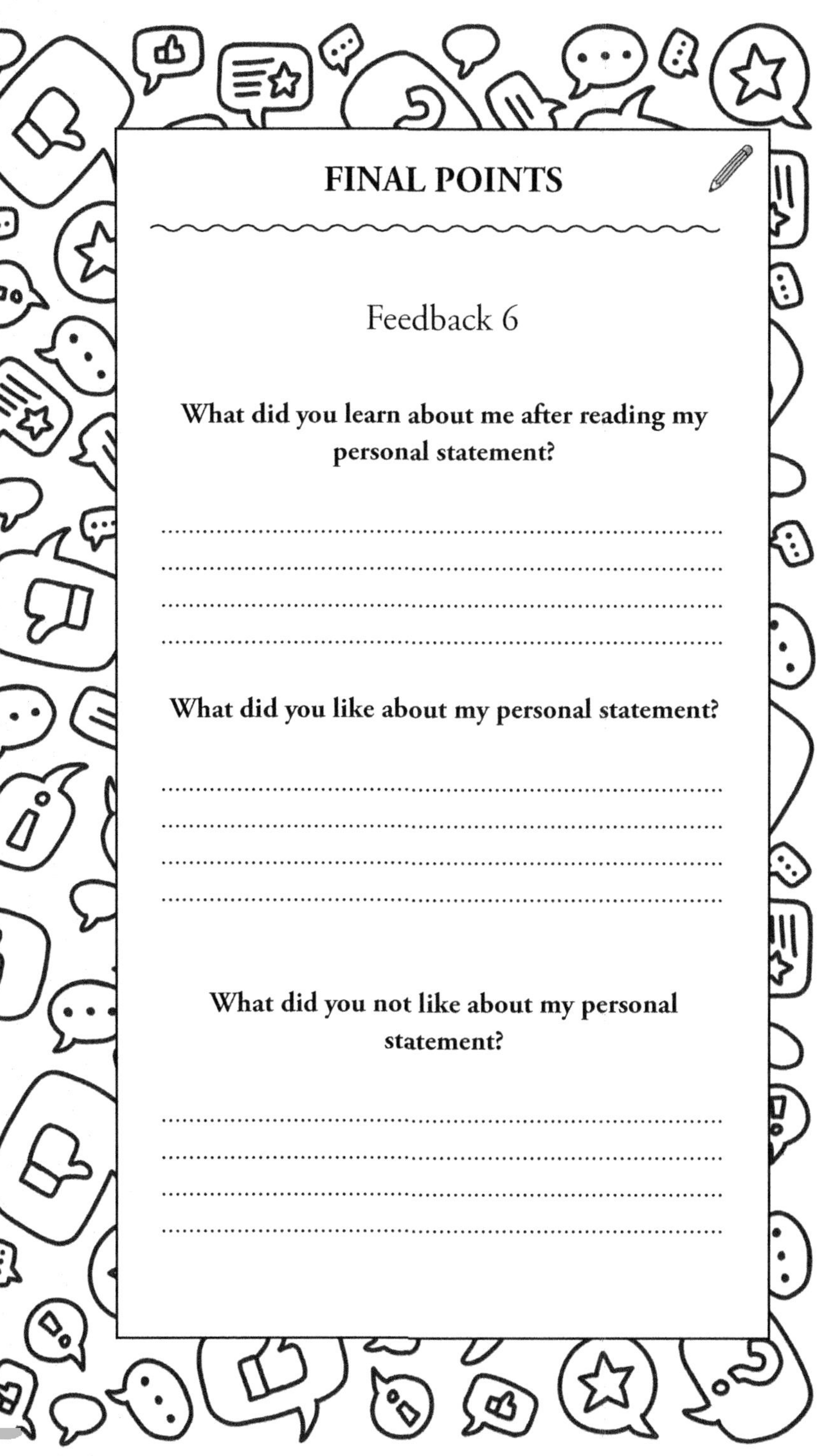

FINAL POINTS

Feedback 6

What did you learn about me after reading my personal statement?

....

....

....

....

What did you like about my personal statement?

....

....

....

....

What did you not like about my personal statement?

....

....

....

....

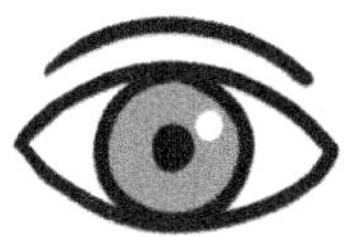

Chapter Nine: Diligence

In this penultimate chapter of *How to Write an Excellent Personal Statement*, I will cover the final points that you ought to address in order to ensure that your personal statement is ready to be sent as part of your application to your chosen programme. These last steps are you doing your due diligence and making sure that you have dotted the i's and crossed the t's. This chapter will laser in on your grammar, style and minute details that will enhance your writing. This may all seem a bit pedantic, but remember that academics and admissions tutors can indeed be pedantic, so you might as well do the relevant checks now while you have the chance. You do not want to leave any stone unturned or risk having your personal statement dismissed on technical or style issues, despite the substance of your writing being of a high standard.

Some students overlook this stage of the refining process to their detriment, thinking that admissions tutors will overlook a small mistake. Do not be that person. As you get deeper into reviewing and revamping your statement, you will want to keep an eye out for some common pitfalls that students make, and I am going to go through each of them in this chapter.

So, let me introduce you to 'The Personal Statement Checklist.'

The Personal Statement Checklist

There are 50 areas that you will need to pay attention to and address so that you can refine and perfect your personal statement and bring out its true potential. This checklist is divided into the following six sections:

1) The Basics
2) Punctuation and Characters
3) Words
4) Sentences
5) Style
6) Tight Writing

As you go through this checklist, thoroughly read each area covered, and at the end of the chapter, try to tick off each point when you can comfortably say that you have met the requirements set out in this checklist.

1. Plagiarism

Number one on the list is the dreaded 'P' word. If you plagiarise writing, you are really playing with fire, and this may be the fatal blow to your application in the long run. So please do not be tempted to copy work that is not yours. You might be caught, you will regret it immensely, and it may leave a negative stain on your record. Instead, just take the time to actually write your own work, even if you think it would be better or easier if you nabbed someone else's. On extremely rare occasions, you might be one of the unlucky few to have accidentally included sentences that are identical to another student's. For your own peace of mind, you may wish to copy and paste the text from your personal statement into a plagiarism checker, which you can find online. As they say, it is better to be safe than sorry.

2. Spelling

If you are about to study at university, you do not need to be told that spelling mistakes can be the reason why your application is thrown onto the rejection pile. Whether these errors are a result of not knowing how a word is spelt or a simple case of slippery fingers, the outcome is still the same. It shows sloppiness and carelessness, and you ought to think that if other students have taken the time to make these checks and you have not, it is only fair that you could be put at a disadvantage — no matter how good you are in other areas. Do not rely on admissions tutors simply overlooking spelling errors, because they might not. Microsoft Word, Google Docs and other word processors have their own spelling checkers for you to use, and you may wish to seek an in-depth analysis from software such as Grammarly. The options are there, so use them to your benefit.

3. Flow and Structure

For this stage of doing your due diligence, I recommend going back to Chapter Seven, Coherence, to ensure that your personal statement threads the needle. In addition, it pays to look at your paragraphing and make sure that each one has a distinct point or message that adds real value to your writing. You do not want verbose writing or needlessly complex words for their own sake. So look out for that too. Every word, every sentence and every paragraph needs to be there for a reason. If any part of your personal statement comes across as repetitive or meaningless, do not be afraid to trim the fat. It is better to have a short personal statement that packs a punch with value and impact than one that is long-winded and lacks depth or substance.

Ask yourself:

- Are my sentences written succinctly, or am I waffling?
- Do my sentences tend to follow logically from the previous ones, or do they seem to appear from out of nowhere?
- Does the style of my writing sound anywhere close to how I would naturally express myself, or does it look like I have used a thesaurus to insert big words just to impress the reader?
- Am I sticking to the main message and narrative of why I want to study my chosen course, or am I being overly descriptive with my stories in a way that will bore the reader?

In summary, double-check that your writing makes sense from top to bottom and threads the needle, and keep your writing clear and to the point.

4. Fact-Checking

When you mention the author of a book, publication or study, or quote the date of a historical event or other information that you reference in your personal statement, it is your responsibility to ensure that your facts are accurate. You do not want your personal statement to lose credibility because you did not have the time to check that what you were writing was true and up-to-date. Keep it truthful and accurate, and do the extra work to double-check the assertions and statements that you make. Also, some students erroneously think that they need to include academic-style references in their personal statement. In most cases, you should not include any references at all.

5. Tenses

The fifth point seems straightforward, but when writing reams and reams of text, you might find yourself drifting into different tenses randomly. When recounting stories in a written format, students will sometimes start writing in the present tense and then glide back into the past tense — and vice versa.

For example:

"I wake up in the morning, go to morning registration, and at that moment, I realise that today is the day I will be doing my presentation in front of the class. Instantly, I felt a sense of trepidation about the ordeal, but knew that it was a chance to showcase what I had learned."

As you can see, the student drifts from present tense to past tense.

The excerpt would be better written like this:

"I woke up in the morning, went to morning registration, and at that moment, I realised that it was the day that I would be doing my presentation in front of the class. Instantly, I felt a sense of trepidation about the ordeal, but knew that it was a chance to showcase what I had learned."

When telling stories, I recommend that you write in the past tense, and that you try to stick to it where appropriate. In addition to drifting into the wrong tense, students miss out on writing more persuasively by not utilising the power of writing in the most optimal tense when communicating specific messages or points. This is important because different tenses have different effects on the reader, so it is important to be mindful of how you use them. It is completely normal to combine different tenses when writing, and this is particularly effective when writing reflectively. But it needs to be executed correctly. For example, if you were to describe your experience of working at a laboratory, you could write:

"When I worked at the laboratory, it was fascinating to witness the ingenuity and brilliance of the scientists first-hand."

As you can see, this sentence indicates that you were fascinated at the time of working at the laboratory. It starts off with a subordinate clause — which is essentially a part of a sentence that depends on another part (the independent or insubordinate clause) in order to be complete. The subordinate clause 'when I worked at the laboratory' is then followed by the independent clause that references how you felt in the past. This kind of statement is commonly used in the earlier paragraphs of personal statements when students describe their work experience, and it reads well — so there are no problems there.

However, now have a read of this:

"Having worked at the laboratory, I now understand the ingenuity and brilliance that is required of scientists."

This second sentence communicates a similar message to

that of the one before it, but it reads in a more 'conclusive' way, which is extremely effective when reaching the end of a paragraph. It has an air of finality to it, as it brings the reflective statement of the independent clause into the present tense. It communicates what the student feels today, rather than solely communicating what they thought at the time of working at the laboratory. Both versions of the sentence are good, and both of them communicate almost the same message, but in a different way. Being aware of how you can use your tenses will give you the vital tools in your arsenal to maximise the impact of your assertions and remarks.

For your reference, it may help you to know the differences between the tenses. So let's quickly go through each of them with a few examples.

Present simple:

This is used when you want to state the facts and describe events occurring in the present moment.

For example:

"I play football."

Past simple:

This describes events that occurred in the past.

For example:

"I played football."

Future simple:

This describes an event that is to be completed in the future.

For example:

"I will play football."

Present perfect:
This describes events that began in the past and are expected to continue. It is also used to emphasise the importance of past events within the present moment.

For example:

"I have played football."

Past perfect:
This describes events that happened prior to other events in the past.

For example:

"I had played football prior to getting the injury."

Future perfect:
This describes events that will be completed between now and a specific point in the future.

For example:

"I will have played a lot of football by the end of the season."

Present continuous:
This describes currently ongoing actions which are usually temporary.

For example:

"I am playing football for the school team."

Past continuous:
This describes ongoing past events, often in relation to the occurrence of another event.

For example:

"I was playing football for the school team when I got injured."

Future continuous:
This describes future events that are expected to continue over a period of time

For example:

"I will be playing football throughout the year."

Present perfect continuous:
This describes events that started in the past and continue into the present or were recently completed, emphasising their relevance to the present moment.

For example:

"I have been playing football all season, and now need to take a break due to my injury."

Past perfect continuous:
This describes events that began, continued, and ended in the past, emphasising their relevance to a past moment.

For example:

"I had been playing football all season, and needed to take a break."

Future perfect continuous:
This describes events that will continue up until a point in the future, emphasising their expected duration.

For example:

"I will have been playing football for six years when I graduate."

So hopefully, that was not too confusing. If you need to refer back to your tenses, use this as a resource to brush up on any obscure areas.

6. Grammatical Person

When writing a personal statement, you should stick to the first person (I, we) and the third person (she, he, they or it). Try to avoid using the second person (you) when addressing the admissions tutor.

For example, do not write:

"Clearly, you can see why that moment had such a profound impact on me."

A sentence like this is too informal and unconventional for a personal statement. Instead, keep your language simple, and write from your own perspectives without summoning the reader's reactions within your writing. It should actually read something like this:

"Clearly, this moment had a profound impact on me."

7. Formatting

The final point of the Basics of the Personal Statement Checklist is your formatting, and that means paying attention to your word count, character count, page count, line count, and text formatting, as I mentioned in Chapter Two: Requirements. This all goes without saying, but there are no excuses if you cannot stick to the most basic of these requirements. So keep your personal statement within the standard format, as instructed. If you really need to, it does not hurt to double-check on your university's programme page to make sure that you are adhering to the exact guidelines that they stipulate. In addition, not all personal statements take the same form, as some will have lists of questions that will require your response. At other times, you may be asked to copy and paste your answers into an online form or questionnaire, thereby rendering your font, font size and page formatting immaterial and inconsequential to the success of your application. But, when you do need to adhere to the correct formatting, do not stray from the standard instructions. As a quick reminder, the text in your personal statement should usually follow these guidelines:

- Times New Roman
- Size 12 font
- 1 inch margins (2.54 cm)
- Single- or double-spacing.

8. Full Stops or Periods

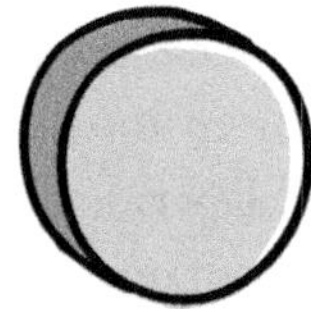

Whether you refer to this form of punctuation as a period or a full stop, no one can dispute the important role that it plays in making your writing intelligible and clear. As a general rule of thumb, if you find that you have run out of breath when reading a sentence from your personal statement out loud, you definitely need a full stop there. A full stop is followed by a space, including in the titles that you use to address someone. So it is 'Mr. Smith,' and not 'Mr.Smith,' but 'Mr Smith' is also acceptable in British English. In addition, when you use quotation marks, the full stop should be placed before all closing quotation marks for American English and British English grammar. On occasion, you can use your discretion with regard to whether you place quotation marks before or after a full stop in British English. The same rule applies to commas, question marks and exclamation points. When it comes to parentheses, periods have two options. Firstly, when part of a sentence is inside parentheses and part of it is outside, the period goes outside of the closing parenthesis.

For example, this is incorrect:

"I love being alone (at least for now.)"

But this is correct:

"I love being alone (at least for now)."

On the other hand, when a whole sentence is inside the parentheses, the period has to go inside the closing parenthesis.

For example, this is incorrect:

"Do you like my bat? (I'm referring to the animal, not the thing you use in baseball)."

This is correct:

"Do you like my bat? (I'm referring to the animal, not the thing you use in baseball.)"

This is a small detail that many students slip up on, but taking the time to understand these principles will help you to avoid making these needless mistakes.

9. Commas

The comma is to the period what salt is to pepper — they go hand in hand to make the reading experience more pleasant. Fundamentally, commas are used to split up clauses, which, as I mentioned earlier in reference to subordinate and independent clauses, are the components that make up a sentence. The ability to use commas effectively is essential for your personal statement, as many students who find themselves prone to bad grammar can blame their overuse or underuse of commas as the common culprit. So let's start with the underuse of commas.

Consider the sentence:

"Let's eat grandpa."

Now consider this sentence:

"Let's eat, grandpa."

As you can tell, the first sentence sounds like an invitation for you and another family member to do something absolutely grotesque to your beloved grandpa. On the other hand, the use of the comma in the second sentence ended up saving your grandpa's life, as it was, much to his relief, an invitation for you and him to enjoy a meal together.

Now have a read of this:

"Harry is very clever, he began excelling in chemistry when he was ten years old."

At face value, this sentence might look okay, but it is not. This is what we refer to as a comma splice, which is when a sentence marries two insubordinate (or independent) clauses with a comma, rather than a more appropriate punctuation or conjunction. When a comma is not used in this case, we call it a run-on sentence. Comma splices and run-on sentences are incredibly common, and numerous students make this error in their grammar.

So how can you go about fixing this?

Here are the five remedies:

1. Split the two clauses into two separate sentences.
For example:

"Harry is very clever. He began excelling in chemistry when he was ten years old."

2. Replace the comma with a semicolon.
For example:

"Harry is very clever; he began excelling in chemistry when he was ten years old."

3. Replace the comma with a coordinating conjunction.
For example:

"Harry is very clever, for he began excelling in chemistry when he was ten years old."

4. Replace the comma with a subordinating conjunction.
For example:

"Harry is very clever because he began excelling in chemistry when he was ten years old."

5. Replace the comma with a semicolon and a transitional word or phrase.
For example:

"Harry is very clever; as a result, he began

excelling in chemistry when he was ten years old."

Now let's have a look at the overuse of commas with this example:

"Jimmy had a stomachache, because he drank too much milk."

This is actually not the best use of a comma, as it should read:

"Jimmy had a stomachache because he drank too much milk."

Commas can help the reader to understand the fragmentation of a sentence, but please remember to use them correctly. The examples used demonstrate just how many ways you can use a comma. Therefore, having a firm understanding of correct comma usage is no small achievement. If need be, you can refer back to this Personal Statement Checklist to make sure that you are using your commas and other punctuation in the correct way.

Now on to the next point.

10. Apostrophes

Apostrophes are used to indicate possession or the omission

of letters or numbers. For possessive pronouns such as 'my,' 'mine,' 'his,' 'her' and 'our,' you would write 'yours,' 'hers,' 'its,' 'ours,' and 'theirs' — so you do not need an apostrophe in this case.

When writing about things that belong to more than one person jointly, you should only make the final name possessive with an apostrophe. For example, you would write:

"Matt and Jane's bread."

Conversely, if you are referring to separate things that belong to different people, you should make both names possessive. In the previous example, Matt and Jane both had the same loaf of bread. But now, if Matt and Jane had two separate loaves of bread that belonged to each of them respectively, you would write:

"Matt's and Jane's bread."

Also, it is informal to write 'don't' rather than 'do not' or 'I'll' rather than 'I will.' These are contractions, and they should be not be used in a personal statement.

Finally, when pluralising numbers, you should omit the apostrophe here too.

So this is incorrect:

"The 1930's was a time of economic instability."

But this is correct:

"The 1930s was a time of economic instability."

11. Colons

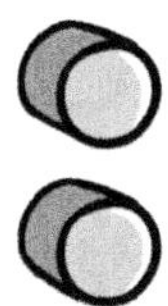

A colon is usually added to a sentence that is already complete. This can be useful when you want to introduce a word, phrase, clause or quotation. The idea behind a colon is that it indicates to the reader that the ensuing words help to explain or add to the words preceding the colon.

For example, have a look at this sentence, and think about why the colon is used incorrectly here:

"People move to California for: the warm weather, the culture, and the food."

This is grammatically incorrect because 'people move to California for' is not a complete sentence. Instead, it should read:

"People move to California for three reasons: the warm weather, the culture, and the food."

Were you to take the phrase 'people move to California for three reasons' on its own, it would be perfectly reasonable to see that as a full sentence and thus a colon is appropriate here.

12. Semicolons

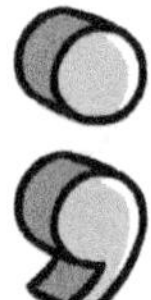

If a colon is used when a complete sentence or independent clause introduces a word, phrase, clause or quotation, a semicolon performs a similar function, except that it is used to join two independent clauses without a coordinating conjunction such as 'and.'

For example:

"We should go to the library to do some homework; the afternoons are pretty quiet there."

A common mistake that students make is thinking that semicolons are interchangeable with commas or full stops. They are not. Rather, they are the 'middle ground,' as they are slightly stronger than commas, but not as conclusive as full stops. Only use a semicolon if you are absolutely sure that it needs to be there.

13. Dashes

It may just be a matter of millimetres, but any eagle-eyed

reader will know the subtle difference between an en dash and an em dash. The en dash (-) is the shorter version of its longer cousin, the em dash (—), which can also be written as two en dashes (--). The en dash is often used to represent time spans or similar differentiation, such as '5-10 hours' or '20-30 percent,' and it is used when words are naturally hyphenated, such as 'editor-in-chief' or 'father-in-law.' The em dash, on the other hand, is more commonly used to signify a break in the sentence or an adjunct to your main point, which can help to improve the fluidity of your writing.

For example:

"There was no arguing with her — she was set in her opinion."

14. Quotation Marks

Using single quotation marks (') (also known as inverted commas) or double quotation marks (") is a matter dictated by the style of English adopted by the university that you are applying for. The US typically opts for double quotation marks while the UK generally prefers single quotation marks. Whichever you choose, it will not make an enormous amount of difference as long as you are consistent throughout your writing. In addition, when you use a quote inside another quote, you should use the opposite style of quotation marks for the nested quotation.

For example:

"Mildred told me that Elaine said, 'I am genuinely happy and in love.'"

15. Exclamation Points

Avoid! There is not much more that needs to be said here. Your personal statement is an important document, and you really must resist the use of exclamation points unless absolutely necessary. When it comes to writing a personal statement, an exclamation point is akin to shouting in order to get your message across in a debate. There is just no need. Rather, you should focus on improving the power and persuasiveness of the words themselves.

16. Question Marks

Once again, use them sparingly. Sometimes students will start a personal statement with a question that they will go on to answer themselves.

For example:

"What is a life of true meaning? In my opinion, a life of true meaning is one in which I can make a difference to people by addressing their mental health issues. It is for this reason that I hope to study psychology."

The name for this style of writing is 'hypophora,' which I will cover later on in this chapter. It is a figure of speech in which a speaker poses a question and then answers it themselves. This can be effective, but as a general limit, try to never use more than one question mark in your personal statement.

17. Parentheses

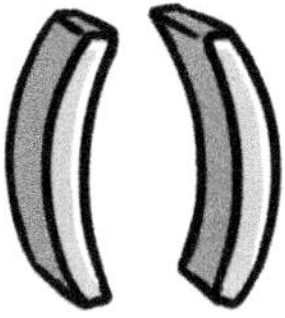

Apart from using parentheses to give further reference to an abbreviation or acronym, such as 'Carnegie Mellon University (CMU),' you should try to completely avoid parentheses or any form of brackets, such as square brackets ([]), curly brackets ({}) or angle brackets (<>).

18. Ellipses

When trying to build a narrative for a storyline, a student might write the following, before going on to the next line:

"All it took was one moment to change my life forever…"

While the use of ellipses here achieves the effect of leaving the reader on a cliffhanger by building suspense, you need to remember that it is a personal statement that you are writing, and not a novel. Please know the difference. Ellipses can be a big risk if you use them in your personal statement, as they can be tricky to master and come across as informal. It is a good idea to remove them from your selection of punctuation when writing.

19. Ampersands

If you have to write the word 'and' in a sentence, never use the curly symbol, known as the 'ampersand,' as a shorter alternative. The only exception to this rule is if you are writing, for example, the name of a company and firm, or some other title that officially includes this symbol, such as:

"Wilson & Co Solicitors."

20. Slashes

You should avoid using slashes as a form of punctuation in a personal statement.

For example, instead of writing:

"Next year, the speech will be given by Mr Smith/ Mr Jones."

You should write:

"Next year, the speech will be given by Mr Smith or Mr Jones."

Or:

"Next year, the speech will be given by Mr Smith and Mr Jones."

21. Capital Letters

We all use capital letters when writing — for example, after a full stop, and when writing people's names, places, times, religions, brands and languages. However, when it comes to writing a personal statement, you should be careful about how you capitalise words in the title of a book, as it is a common mistake that students make.

For example, this is incorrect:

"Around the world in 80 days."

But this is correct:

"Around the World in 80 Days."

When in doubt, just do some research to make sure that you are writing titles and words exactly as they are meant to appear.

22. Numbers

Finally, when writing numbers below 10, you should always stick to writing them in their full words (e.g. one, two, three, four, five, six, seven, eight, nine.) However, once you reach 10, you should write all numbers as numerals (e.g. 10, 11, 12, 13, 14, 15, 16, 17, 18, 19, 20.) The only exception to this rule is if you use a number to start a sentence.

For example, if placed at the beginning of a sentence, then this is incorrect:

"13 years ago, I worked at a dental clinic."

But, this would be correct:

"Thirteen years ago, I worked at a dental clinic."

So now, you have explored two important areas, the Basics and Punctuation. Read on for the next section: Words.

23. Count Nouns and Mass Nouns

A student wrote in their personal statement:

"When I worked at the art gallery, there were

less paintings than I had imagined, but I still endeavoured to make the most of my work experience."

Do you notice anything wrong with this sentence? The word 'less' is used incorrectly here. The phrase 'the number of paintings' is quantifiable because you would actually be able to count them if you wanted to. The correct word here is 'fewer.' The only time that the word 'less' should be used in a similar context is if you are describing something that cannot be counted in discrete amounts, but only measured.

For example:

"While taking blood tests, I was surprised to see that the amount of blood was less than expected."

Blood is a liquid, and it is measured in volume, so 'less' is the correct word to use here.

24. Relative Pronouns

The interchangeable use of the words 'who' and 'that' is a common trap that many students fall into as well.

For example:

"Mr. Rivera was an architect that really liked the Baroque style."

The student is describing a person, and therefore, it should actually read:

"Mr. Rivera was an architect who really liked the Baroque style."

The word 'that' is only appropriate if you are describing an object.

For example:

"His car is the one that makes a loud noise when braking."

These small differences may appear simple, but plenty of students forget to do these final checks in their personal statements. So, if you can, try not to be one of them.

25. Homonyms, Homophones and Homographs.

Homophones and homographs are both types of homonyms. Homophones are words that sound the same but are different in meaning or spelling.

For example:

- Programme v Program
- Peak v Pique v Peek
- Compliment v Complement
- There v They're v Their
- You're v Your
- Alter v Altar
- Allowed v Aloud
- Cite v Sight v Site
- Bear v Bare

- Fair v Fare
- Naval v Navel
- Allowed v Aloud
- Bare v Bear
- Buy v By
- Cell v Sell
- Dew v Due
- Yoke v Yolk
- Principal v Principle

Homographs are words that are spelled the same but differ in meaning or pronunciation. For example, the word 'appropriate' refers to something that is suitable or proper in the circumstances. However, the same word pronounced slightly differently means 'to take something for your own use.'

Other examples include:

- Possess
- Alternate
- Excuse
- Extract

- Second
- Minute
- Light

In personal statements, students unknowingly use the wrong homonym to their detriment. Here are a few common examples from past personal statements:

"My work experience placement at a cosmetic clinic peaked my interest in studying medicine."

"Achieving excellent grades in physics helped to compliment the research that I undertook in the laboratory with my professor."

"It is for this reason that I would like to apply to this program at Oxford."

Each of these sentences ought to say:

"My work experience placement at a cosmetic clinic piqued my interest in studying medicine."

"Achieving excellent grades in physics helped to complement the research that I undertook in the laboratory with my professor."

"It is for this reason that I would like to apply to this programme at Oxford."

In this particular context, it is 'piqued' and not 'peaked.' It is 'complement,' and not 'compliment.' And if you are applying to a British university and you use the word 'program,' you are referring to a series of coded software instructions to control the operation of a computer or other machine. The word that you ought to use is 'programme.' On the other hand, in American English 'program' is preferred. So if you were applying to Harvard University, you ought to write 'program.' As you can see, once again, getting to grips with these finer details can make a tangible difference in allowing you to communicate your ideas with precision, elegance and accuracy.

The Words section was short and sweet, so now let's get onto the next one: Sentences.

26. Sentence Fragments

Earlier on, you learned about how the use of a comma can help to separate clauses, which serves to improve the reading experience. But what happens when a subordinate clause exists in isolation without a corresponding independent clause to complete it within a sentence? The answer: a sentence fragment. This is when an insubordinate clause attempts to masquerade as though it were a full sentence. For example:

"Bradley played football. Because he was good at it."

Or:

"A time of incredible innovation."

Where personal statements are concerned, these are not full sentences at all, and they read poorly. These sentences should read:

"Bradley played football because he was good at it."

And:

"It was a time of incredible innovation."

Sometimes, students start their introduction using a series of sentence fragments to build suspense and a sense of anticipation.

For example:

"Limbs freezing. A moment of trepidation. Heart racing. Nothing could prepare me for the day that I swam across the largest lake in my county for charity."

While this opening is somewhat effective in building suspense, and frankly in just being a little bit 'different' to what most students would write, if you want to be different, you should strive to do it in a way that is impressive and grammatically correct. I advise that you do not just spew out something that gets the admissions tutor's attention for the wrong reason, as this can massively backfire. There are plenty of students who will seek to capture the reader's attention by being needlessly eccentric, but simultaneously risk foregoing the basic tenets of writing, which is ultimately a self-defeating strategy. Once again, do not be that person. Instead, focus on high-quality writing that is honest and authentic, and let the reader be impressed by your brilliant mind, your valuable insights, your deep reflections and your interesting perspectives.

27. Polysyndeton and Asyndeton

Polysyndeton is making a list or series of words, phrases, or clauses that are connected with the repeated use of the same conjunction.

For example:

"I feel prepared to study natural sciences, as I have scored highly in biology and chemistry and physics."

This sentence has a redundant 'and' in it, and it ought to read:

"I feel prepared to study natural sciences, as I have scored highly in biology, chemistry and physics."

On the flip side, asyndeton is the omission of a conjunction such as 'and' in a sentence. For example:

"There is perhaps no subject that I feel better prepared to study, as I am dedicated, focussed, motivated."

This sentence ought to add the conjunction 'and' in order to make sense. It would read:

"There is perhaps no subject that I feel better prepared to study, as I am dedicated, focussed, and motivated."

On occasion, asyndeton can be used to demonstrate a flair for writing with what is called an isocolon. One of the most famous of these is '*veni, vidi, vici*' — which translated from Latin is 'I came, I saw, I conquered.' However, arranging words in this artistic way is a bit of a risk if you do not quite manage to make the impact that you desired. So proceed with caution.

28. Gerunds and Infinitives

A gerund has '-ing' at the end, like 'going.' Meanwhile, an infinitive is a verb that has 'to' at the beginning, like 'to go.' Understanding gerunds and infinitives is largely a matter of practice, as some words are used with the first category while others are used with the latter. Just like learning to play a musical instrument, the more exposed you are to different words, the more comfortable you will become in using them and understanding how they ought to be used.

29. Split Infinitives

While an infinitive is the word 'to' with a verb, a 'split infinitive' separates the word 'to' and the verb with at least one other word, which is usually an adverb.

For example:

"Lisa tried to quickly finish her experiment before the professor arrived."

Writing a sentence like this is not a major issue, but to some writers, it is a tiny faux pas, as it ought to be:

"Lisa tried to finish her experiment quickly before the professor arrived."

30. Incomplete Comparisons

This one is pretty simple, and yet students make the mistake of not completing their comparisons.

For example:

"I hope to join your research lab at Nanjing University, as it is better, newer and more advanced, and I am keen to make an impact in my chosen field."

It is all well and good that this student is so excited about the research lab at Nanjing University, but this sentence begs the question: 'better, newer and more advanced' than what? When you compare one thing to another, please be sure to include what that 'thing' actually is. Sure, the reader may be able to figure out what that 'thing' is, but you should not leave it to them to do the legwork. Be clear, specific and to the point.

31. Dangling Modifiers and Squinting Modifiers

Dangling modifiers are literary mistakes that occur when a descriptive phrase does not apply to the noun that immediately follows it.

For example:

"After declining for months, Michael explored a new method to increase the revenue for our start-up."

This sentence is confusing because the reader is left unsure about what exactly was 'declining for months.' Was it Michael who had been 'declining for months,' or was it the revenue from the start-up that had been 'declining for months?'

In order to address this issue, you will need to amend the sentence structure with Michael as the subject, and perhaps add more specificity with the word 'numbers' to indicate that you are referring to the start-up's revenue, and not Michael.

For example:

"Michael explored a new method to increase our start-up's revenue after our numbers had been declining for months."

This is so much better, and it leaves no doubt in the reader's mind as to what you are trying to communicate and what is actually going on.

A squinting modifier is a word that describes something, but what it is describing is out of place. It is out of place because it could modify the word or phrase that comes before or after it.

For example:

"Jumping up and down quickly entertained him."

This is confusing because the reader is left unsure as to whether the person was 'quickly entertained' by someone 'jumping up and down' or whether the person was 'entertained' by someone 'jumping up and down quickly.'

Dangling modifiers and squinting modifiers are not the end of the world, but if you can avoid them, you certainly should.

32. Periphrasis

This pertains to the use of indirect and circumlocutory writing that uses words to express something that is otherwise expressed by inflexion. Examples of periphrasis are when a student writes 'did go' instead of 'went,' or 'more smart' rather than simply saying 'smarter.' Periphrasis makes for clumsy writing, so it is best that you steer clear of it and double-check your writing to spot it early on.

33. Tautology

A tautology happens when you say the same thing twice over in different words, which is a clear fault of style. It needs to be said that nitpicking tautological statements is the height of being pedantic, and you are unlikely to be flagged for being tautological in your writing. But if you spot tautological statements, it does not hurt to try and straighten them out.

Here are a few examples:

"In my opinion, I think that I will be a great student for this course."

Technically speaking, by saying 'in my opinion,' you are informing the reader about your thoughts, and therefore, the words 'I think' are redundant, repetitive and tautological. Tautology is similar to a literary device called 'pleonasm' in its use of more words than are necessary to convey meaning. This can be used consciously to emphasise a point, such as 'to see with one's eyes.' Nonetheless, it is generally better to avoid these phrases unless you can make it abundantly clear to the reader that they are intentional.

Let's try another example:

"I found the works of the French astrologer, Nostradamus, particularly illuminating, as he was always making predictions about the future."

Once again, I am being very picky here. But, one can only make predictions about the future, and not the past. So writing 'predictions about the future' is technically tautological, even though speaking and writing in this way is generally accepted by most people.

The same applies to the following statements. See if you can spot why each of them is tautological. Some are trickier than others:

"They arrived one after the other in succession."

"She always over exaggerates."

"As I walked to school that day, there was frozen ice everywhere."

"Alice started her talk with a short summary."

"At that moment in time, everything went black."

"I would wake up at 4 a.m. in the morning."

34. Pronoun Disagreement

It is inherent in the name what this actually means, as this is when your pronouns and nouns disagree. As a standard rule, singular pronouns must go with singular nouns, and plural pronouns must go with plural nouns.

For example, this is incorrect:

"Every boy must sign in when they arrive."

'Boy' is singular, and 'they' is plural. The phrasing here ought to be:

"Every boy must sign in when he arrives."

35. Antecedents

An antecedent is a word that comes before a pronoun and helps the reader understand what the pronoun actually means.

For example, read this:

"The doctor found the boy, and he was happy."

Was the doctor happy that he found the boy, or was the boy happy when the doctor found him? Subtle distinctions and tweaks can make a world of difference when you are trying to communicate your points.

36. Prepositions

A preposition is a word or group of words used before a noun, pronoun, or noun phrase that shows direction, time, place, location, or spatial relationships, or introduces an object. Some examples of prepositions are words such as 'in,' 'at,' 'on,' 'of,' and 'to.' When writing, a cardinal rule is to avoid ending a sentence with a preposition. This is not a major issue, but try to address it if you can. A preposition indicates that another word will follow it, so the following example is a grammatical faux pas:

"What reason did he come here for?"

This reads better as:

"For what reason did he come here?"

37. Faulty Parallelism

This error is more common than most people realise. Beyond personal statements, you will see this crop up a lot in CVs and resumes as well. Faulty parallelism occurs when two or more parts of a sentence are similar in meaning but not parallel (or grammatically similar) in form. It often emerges with paired constructions and items in a series.

For example, this is incorrect:

"He wanted to learn more about careers in programming, engineering, biochemist, and research scientist.

However, this is correct:

"He wanted to learn more about careers in programming, engineering, biochemistry, and research science."

Here is another example:

"The key directives of his boss were clear:

1. Meet monthly sales goals.
2. Aggressive marketing techniques.
3. Reporting every day."

This ought to read:

"The key directives of his boss were clear:
1. Meet monthly sales goals.
2. Practise aggressive marketing techniques.
3. Report every day.

You have come a long way in this penultimate chapter of *How to Write an Excellent Personal Statement*. You are now on the homestretch, so keep reading on to make sure that you do not leave any stone unturned. This section is all about the style of the writing that you employ, and what you ought to do to get it right in your personal statement.

38. American English v British English

- Colour or color?
- Organise or organize?
- Centre or center?
- Travelling or traveling?
- Defence or defense?

In truth, the average admissions tutor might not care too much about whether you use American English or British English for your personal statement. However, let's say that you are comfortable writing American English, but applying to the University of Oxford. It is probably a good idea to tweak your text to British English once you are completely done. There is no harm in spending a few minutes doing this. Even if it does not make a huge difference in your application, if you manage to get into Oxford, it may help if you get used to writing British English. So you might as well start now.

39. Colloquialisms and Comedy

No matter how vibrant and creative you are, remember that a personal statement is an important document, so if you decide to be conversational or informal, you are taking a bit of a risk. Also, not all admissions tutors respond well to comedy, puns, satire and sarcasm, and if the joke falls flat, it can be disastrous. If you insist on being comedic, try not to overdo it. Do not neglect the basic, substantive and meaningful points that will make your personal statement actually shine. If you recall from Chapter Four: Structure I, I mentioned the use of paraprosdokians as a means of grabbing the reader's attention from the first line. But, I also mentioned how important it is to reel it in in the ensuing lines. This advice still applies. In essence, comedy or colloquial language should be the icing on what is already a very good cake. Do not forget that your foundations, insights and writing need to be good first, as you cannot dress up something sub-par with gimmicks, charm or comedy. What use is it having fancy icing on a dry and crusty loaf of bread? By getting the basics right and making sure that your foundation is excellent first, if you choose to add onto this with humour, you ensure it will only amplify what was already great to begin with.

40. Euphemisms, Metonymy and Synecdoche

Similar to a colloquialism, a euphemism is a mild or indirect word or expression substituted for one considered to be too harsh or blunt when referring to something unpleasant or embarrassing. While euphemisms help to soften the harshness of things that are unpleasant, if you were writing a personal statement for medicine, and you described a moment when you witnessed a patient die as them 'meeting their maker' or 'kicking the bucket,' this would be inappropriate. Medicine requires an appreciation of the facts, as well as clear and accurate communication. So using the word 'death' is permissible here.

Metonymy involves the substitution of the name of an attribute or adjunct for that of the thing meant — for example, a 'suit' for business executives, or the 'turf' for horse racing. If you are referring to a widely accepted metonym, such as the word 'crown' to refer to the British Royal Family or 'Silicon Valley' to refer to the tech industry, then this is also permissible.

Similar to a metonym, a synecdoche is a literary device in which a part of something represents the whole, or when the whole is used to represent a part. In this case, if you wrote something like 'he had a nice set of wheels' to say that someone had a nice car, it would be inappropriate, as it is too informal for a personal statement.

Use your discretion, and if you are in doubt, simply describe something exactly as it is. There is no need for flowery language if you can opt for a much simpler, clearer and more accurate alternative.

41. Onomatopoeia

Have a read of these first lines of a personal statement:

"Trinnngg-trinnngg! Trinnngg-trinnngg! As I reached for the phone in the early hours of the morning, nothing could prepare me for the solemn news that my grandfather had passed away. That was the defining moment that galvanised me to study nursing."

Clearly, the use of the word 'trinnngg' was designed to mimic the shrill noise of the telephone ringing. This literary device is called 'onomatopoeia,' which is the formation of a word based on the sound it resembles when spoken. Believe it or not, numerous students start off their personal statements with onomatopoeia. Sadly, however, it can sometimes come across as a desperate bid to get the reader's attention. While their intentions are understandable, I strongly advise that you avoid this approach. As I noted earlier on, there is being 'different' in a way that is impressive and authentic, and then there is being different in a way that is contrived, needlessly eccentric, and fundamentally, not providing much real value to your writing.

42. Anastrophe

The next point on the style of your writing is anastrophe. In this case, the traditional sentence structure is reversed, such that the normal structure of 'verb-subject-adjective' becomes 'adjective-verb-subject' or 'adjective-subject-verb.'

For example, rather than saying:

"I was ready to take on the rigours of the science experiment."

A student might say:

"Ready I was to take on the rigours of the science experiment."

This is awkward and unconventional, and you should avoid writing in this manner.

43. Exposition, Imagery and Figurative Language

Let's explore the definitions of these three words, starting with exposition — which is the use of background information, such as historical context, description and characters' backstories within a story or narrative. Imagery is the use of words to create a picture in the mind of the reader. This goes beyond sight alone, as imagery encompasses sounds, smells, tastes and other feelings. Figurative language is the use of non-literal phrases or words to create further meaning in writing or speech.

One of the biggest challenges that students face when writing personal statements is not knowing how to strike the right balance between expository language (i.e. writing exposition and description) and substantive or reflective language. Think about it this way. Let's imagine that you have a personal statement with a limit of 1,000 words. If you use 200 of those words to set the scene or describe your surroundings, while your writing may be beautiful, those descriptions might fail to say anything substantial or significant about your personal skills or insights. They would be somewhat superfluous, and you should rather try to get to your points much sooner. In addition to this, if you find yourself using figurative language, try to ensure that you do not suffocate the reader with all of these fancy literary devices. It can become tiring to read, and at some point, the use of figurative language yields diminishing returns: the more you use it, the less potent the effect will be on the reader.

So only use figurative language sparingly.

The following are all examples of literary devices and figurative language that students use in personal statements:

Similes:

Meaning: 'The comparison of one thing with another thing of a different kind, used to make a description more emphatic or vivid.'

For example:

"When Dr. Ramachandran allowed me to draw blood from the patient for the first time, I knew that I had to be as cool as a cucumber."

Metaphors:
Meaning: 'A form of figurative language used to state that one thing is another thing.'

For example:

"Throughout my academic career, my mother has been my rock."

Or:

"My dad has been such a warrior when I've needed help."

Or:

"When it comes to the sciences, I'm a walking encyclopaedia."

Litotes:
Meaning: 'An understatement in which an affirmative is expressed by the negative of the contrary.'

For example:

"As I explored the many works of Charles Dickens, it became clear that writing those books was no small accomplishment."

Anaphora, Epistrophe and Symploce:
Meaning: 'The repetition of a word or phrase at the beginning of successive phrases, clauses, or sentences. That repetition is intentional and is used to add style and emphasis to text or speech.

For example:

"Purpose is the driver of the greatest of all human feats. Purpose is the best way to inspire others towards a common goal. Purpose is at the crux of why I want to study politics at your institution."

Separate from this, epistrophe is the repetition of a word at the end of successive clauses or sentences, and symploce is the repetition of words or phrases at both the beginning and end of successive clauses or verses, creating a mixture of anaphora and epistrophe.

Other figurative language and literary devices include:

- Chiasmus
- Antimetabole
- Aphorisms
- Hyperbole

- Pathetic Fallacy
- Personification
- Tmesis
- Hypophora
- Idioms
- Symbolism
- Motif
- Juxtaposition
- Allegory

Fundamentally, you have to remember that you are writing a professional document, not an elaborate story. Beautiful and fancy writing does not automatically equate to a stellar personal statement, so try to avoid giving off the impression that you are heading in that direction. Focus on what carries weight through your lived experiences and evidence, and describe these moments in a reflective manner. Exposition, imagery and figurative language can be used to add a little bit of spice to your writing, but just a dash will do — nothing more.

You are now in the final section of the Personal Statement Checklist, and well on your way to addressing the 50 areas that you need to pay attention to in order to do your due diligence when writing a personal statement. This last section focuses on methods by which you can ensure that you are writing as efficiently as possible. This is what I call 'tight writing,' which means that you are communicating your points strongly, but in the fewest words possible.

44. Widows and Orphans

The first strategy to tighten your writing is achieved by targeting paragraphs with widows and orphans. When it comes to keeping to a line count, you can look for paragraphs with just a few words at the end and focus on how you can shorten them to gain an extra line of space. A widow is a lone word or short group of words that appears at the bottom of a paragraph, column or page. An orphan is a similar unwanted word or short group of words that appears at the top of a page.

For example, if you have a look at this text, you will see that the highlighted word 'widows' is on its own line:

"Targeting paragraphs with orphans and widows."

When you have blocks of text stacked above and below each other, a widow or orphan leaves a blank space between the paragraphs, which can needlessly inflate your page count by displacing text onto the succeeding page. To fix this and make your writing tighter, you can try to delete words to pack the text as closely as possible, thereby allowing you to be more economical with the space that you have been given. It is a pretty useful trick when you are struggling to make space in your personal statement.

45. Active Voice

With a view to making your writing tight, you should strive to reduce any 'waffling.' You can usually do this by focussing on active voice, which happens when you make yourself the subject of the sentence.

For example, rather than saying:

"Some interesting books were bought by me."

You would say:

"I bought some interesting books."

Another example is, rather than saying:

"The report was compiled by the actuary."

You would say:

"The actuary compiled the report."

46. Literary Expletives

You can also reduce waffling by getting rid of filler words, otherwise known as literary expletives, and cutting out running starts, where you start a sentence with a string of filler words before 'landing the plane' and actually making your point.

Running starts dilute the quality of your writing because they occupy the places where a reader would normally expect to see a noun or subject of a sentence, thereby leaving readers in suspense about what you are actually trying to say. This slows down the reader's processing speed and makes it a pain to understand your point, which ultimately violates the cardinal rule of writing — which is to make the reader's job as easy as possible. Running starts and filler words make your writing clunky and inelegant, draining a sentence of its true power. You want your writing to be direct, clear and effective, and for that, you need to do your due diligence and get rid of excess text.

For example, this is a bit wordy:

"One thing that I have learned is that..."

You would change it to:

"I learned that..."

In addition, you can remove words such as 'the' and 'that' if you are short of space and need to keep the writing tight.

For example, you could amend this statement:

"The results that we found in our research depended on both the analysis and the style."

You would change it to:

"Our research results depended on both analysis and style."

Do you see how much shorter and more to the point the second statement is? Being selective about the use of 'the' and 'that' can make your writing sharper, and ultimately better.

47. Adverbs

The next strategy is pretty simple, and it is to remove adverbs such as 'really,' 'basically,' 'honestly' and 'truly' from your writing, particularly when you have a tight word count.

48. Conjunctions and Connectives

You may also wish to remove connectives and conjunctions from your writing if you are looking to reduce the word count. In this case, you would target words such as 'furthermore,' 'besides' and 'moreover.'

49. Abbreviations

The next strategy to achieve the goal of tight writing is to contract names and terms into their abbreviation and acronym form, if you are really pressed to reduce your word count.

In this case, you would change:

"European Convention on Human Rights."

To:

"ECHR."

Or:

"The United Nations."

To:

"The UN."

A quick caveat, though — if the abbreviation is too obscure to be known by the average person, then do not use it, and instead write out the full words. Another point — you can also opt to only write the full term with the abbreviation in parentheses the first time that you use it in your personal statement. By doing this, you make the reader aware of what you are referring to. Thereafter, when you use that term throughout the personal statement, you will only refer to it by its abbreviation. For example, you would start by referring to Carnegie Mellon University (CMU) by its full name, and then subsequently refer to it as CMU throughout the statement.

50. Commentary and Repetition

Try to also avoid phrases such as 'like I mentioned earlier' in a personal statement, or repeating points more than once. These phrases give off the impression that you have run out of points, such that you are forced to labour the same ones from the past to keep the reader's attention. They also suggest that you are writing for the sake of filling up empty space.

The final strategy that I recommend to make your writing tighter is to pay close attention to needless commentary and repetition. For example, if you have spoken about an experience and you are really desperate to reduce the clutter, you can target phrases and sentences such as 'which made me feel A, B or C' or 'where I learned D, E or F.' While such statements are enormously valuable due to being reflective, if you are struggling to reduce your word count, portions of these sentences could be the first to go. Your story in and of itself illustrates your point, so you can focus on presenting the facts here, if you really must keep the word count low.

Maximise Your Potential

Ultimately, employing the methods that I have outlined will allow you to check that you are maximising the full potential of your personal statement with succinct, compelling and impactful writing. Please remember that an excellent personal statement is one that conveys substance, reflection, insightfulness and credibility — not just an elaborate and flamboyant spiel of achievements. Always keep that in mind if you find yourself veering off in a new direction or labouring on a point for too long than is necessary. Keep the writing tight and to the point, and do your due diligence.

You have now completed all 50 areas of the Personal Statement Checklist, and you are at the end of this penultimate chapter of *How to Write an Excellent Personal Statement.*

Can you believe it?

The next chapter is the final one of this book. It really has been a pleasure guiding you along, and I can not wait for you to join me for the finale.

FINAL POINTS

After having read the Personal Statement Checklist, go back to your personal statement draft and tick each box to confirm that you are adhering to the correct use of each point.

	Plagiarism
	Spelling
	Flow and Structure
	Fact-Checking
	Tenses
	Grammatical Person
	Formatting

FINAL POINTS

PUNCTUATION

	Full Stops and Periods
	Commas
	Apostrophes
	Colons
	Semicolons
	Dashes
	Quotation Marks
	Parentheses
	Fact-Checking
	Ellipses
	Ampersands and Symbols
	Slashes
	Exclamation Points
	Question Marks
	Capital Letters
	Numbers

FINAL POINTS

	Count Nouns and Mass Nouns
	Relative Pronouns
	Homonyms, Homophones and Homographs

	Sentence Fragments
	Polysyndeton and Asyndeton
	Gerunds and Infinitives
	Split Infinitives
	Incomplete Comparisons
	Dangling Modifiers and Squinting Modifiers
	Periphrasis
	Tautology
	Pronoun Disagreement
	Antecedents
	Prepositions
	Faulty Parallelism

FINAL POINTS

	American English v British English
	Colloquialism and Comedy
	Euphemisms, Metonyms and Synecdoche
	Onomatopoeia
	Anastrophe
	Exposition, Imagery and Figurative Language

	Widows and Orphans
	Active Voice
	Literaty Expletives
	Adverbs
	Conjunctions and Connectives
	Abbreviations
	Commentary and Repetition

Chapter Ten: Completion

Click! You have now submitted your personal statement, and a world of opportunity awaits. The truth is, once you have gone over and over your writing, you need to eventually take a step back and appreciate your hard work. Making the decision to stop working on a personal statement can be tough, because it can feel like there is always more to be improved. However, as I mentioned earlier on, 'a work of art is never completed, only abandoned.' So please bear that in mind. At some point you just need to be comfortable with letting it go and accepting that you have done all that you can to present yourself in your best light. It is normal to look back at your personal statement and feel that it is not truly 'complete,' but you will go crazy if you obsess over it for too long. So just remember that whatever will be, will be. You've done your best.

Now, let it go.

For this last chapter of *How to Write an Excellent Personal Statement*, I will guide you through a personal statement from a student named Dani, who succeeded with her application to study medicine at the prestigious Johns Hopkins University in the United States. If you recall, at the beginning of this book, I compared submitting an application to university to baking a cake, because a variety of ingredients — such as admissions tests, academic performance and interviews — must come together in order to make it a success. Dani's application stands out in light of the fact that her overall grade point average (GPA) for her first undergraduate degree was not exceedingly high. Thus, one can conclude that a mixture of her admissions test score (MCAT) and a brilliant personal statement played a decisive role in getting her over the line.

As you go through Dani's personal statement, try to think about all of the different features, tools and methods that you have explored in this book, which Dani demonstrates in her own writing. By being able to spot these features in someone else's personal statement, you will become better acquainted with the style of academic writing that you will need to incorporate into your own personal statement. Feel free to make notes as you go along too.

So let's begin by having a read of Dani's personal statement. I will pause after each paragraph to evaluate and remark on her writing.

Dani's Personal Statement

Dani writes:

> "The curtains opened, revealing my shadow standing deep into the stage, avoiding the spotlight with uncoordinated, darting motions. I intentionally deviated from the norms of dancing 'full-out' on stage to portray a timidity reminiscent of the stage fright I experienced at my first performance at the age of five. Driven by the crescendo of instrumental music, I effortlessly galloped across the stage into a grand-jeté. This leap defied gravity and the human anatomical confines to symbolize my newfound confidence. Each metatarsal harmoniously absorbed its share of the shock as I juxtaposed the explosive jump with a virtually silent, effortless landing. As the stage lights dimmed, the audience burst into applause, confirming my unorthodox performance was universally well-received. Through movement alone, I communicated and normalized an uplifting story about overcoming self-doubt, a lesson that has carried me on my journey as a pre-medical student."

From the outset, Dani makes it very clear what her narrative is. She is a young woman who was once timid, but who is defying the odds, and overcoming her own self-doubt, in order to achieve the goal of studying medicine. Her vivid description of leaping into the air with a grand-jeté appears to be symbolic of who she is as a person. With this introduction, we can glean a substantial amount about Dani, without her ever having to verbalise those qualities herself. Rather, this opening of her story gives us a flavour of her character.

If you recall from Chapter Four: Structure I, I mentioned that the literary device known as in medias res is an effective way to grab the reader's attention. Dani manages to display this technique rather well as she dives straight into a crucial part of her story, where the stakes are particularly high, as she is performing a tough ballet routine in front of an expectant audience. This makes the reader interested in how the story will develop, and consequently, captures their attention.

Admittedly, Dani uses a fair amount of expository and descriptive language as she sets the scene, but this manages to remain effective because her story is so distinct and specific to her. In fact, it is all about her — but not in a pompous or self-congratulatory way. It is the very definition of 'personal,' as we are getting insights into a specific moment in Dani's life that was poignant and transformative in guiding her path towards medicine. There are no inane or generic platitudes, or remarks about 'wanting to help people,' or overused themes of having wanted to study medicine 'since she was a child.' Dani keeps her story completely authentic to herself, and she shows vulnerability in the process, thereby serving as the ideal springboard to demonstrate how she has developed over time. This makes Dani come across as likeable, but with a quiet and resilient confidence, strength and humility — desirable qualities for any budding doctor.

Now that Dani has made such a powerful and distinctly memorable start, an admissions tutor would have already ticked many boxes in her favour.

Let's see how she fares in the next paragraph.

Dani writes:

> "My family's arduous journey out of poverty after immigrating to the United States did little to blunt the impact of my own personal challenge with self-doubt. It wasn't until my first year at Johns Hopkins (JHU) that I was prompted to adapt to life far from home and earn my place at this elite institution. Following my initial struggle with rigorous chemistry courses, I sought out a research position to supplement my coursework with hands-on biochemistry training. My experience as a student-research-

er provided the necessary mentorship and critical thinking to succeed at JHU. I began my independent research under Dr. Anderson, where I studied the mechanism of action for a calmodulin kinase (CaMKII). CaMKII is vital for the proper function of multiple organ systems, but under oxidative stress, it becomes dysregulated and leads to arrhythmia. I learned that oxidative stress could result from unhealthy lifestyle choices, such as poor diet and alcohol consumption and I became fascinated with the pervasiveness of these choices in promoting illness. Through personalized education, I hope to empower patients to understand their health and optimize their body's function for a longer health span using lifestyle interventions."

Dani's opening sentence of her second paragraph is very satisfying to read. She could easily just have said:

"Years ago, my family moved to the United States as immigrants."

While factually correct, that statement would not have told us anything that specifically pertains to Dani's character.

Instead, Dani writes:

"My family's arduous journey out of poverty after immigrating to the United States did little to blunt the impact of my own personal challenge with self-doubt."

Dani manages to integrate the theme and narrative of self-doubt into this second paragraph, thereby creating a smooth transition and taking the first step towards threading the needle, as I outlined in Chapter Seven: Coherence. Writing 'did little to blunt the challenge' is also beautifully put. Dani could easily have written:

"Years ago, my family moved to the United States as immigrants, but I still struggled with self-doubt."

This version is a tad boring and does not quite make the connection and comparison between the journey out of poverty and Dani's own self-doubt. As you can see, thinking mindfully about how to interweave different themes, and expressing them with creative and elegant writing can really make you stand out for the right reasons, just as Dani has done. Also, if you look closely, you will see that Dani's second paragraph rather neatly demonstrates the R Funnel, which you learned about in Chapter Six: Reflections. In this case, as Dani describes her experiences, it is R Funnel 1 that we see emerging in her writing.

Quickly refresh your memory on what constitutes R Funnel 1:

- **R - Recount**
- **R - Resistance**
- **R - Response**
- **R - Reflection**

Now, have a look at R Funnel 1 in Dani's personal statement:

Recount (R):

"My family's arduous journey out of poverty after immigrating to the United States did little to blunt the impact of my own personal challenge with self-doubt."

Resistance (R):

"It wasn't until my first year at Johns Hopkins (JHU) that I was prompted to adapt to life far from home and earn my place at this elite institution."

Response (R):

"Following my initial struggle with rigorous chemistry courses, I sought out a research position to supplement my coursework with hands-on biochemistry training. My experience as a student-researcher provided the necessary mentorship and critical thinking to succeed at

JHU. I began my independent research under Dr. Anderson, where I studied the mechanism of action for a calmodulin kinase (CaMKII). CaMKII is vital for the proper function of multiple organ systems, but under oxidative stress, it becomes dysregulated and leads to arrhythmia."

Reflection (R):

"I learned that oxidative stress could result from unhealthy lifestyle choices such as poor diet and alcohol consumption and became fascinated with the pervasiveness of these choices in promoting illness. Through personalized education, I hope to empower patients to understand their health and optimize their body's function for a longer health span using lifestyle interventions."

Dani continues to tick a lot of boxes in her second paragraph, particularly as she now starts to demonstrate her academic insights, but not by merely listing accomplishments that can be found on her resume. She sticks to one particular aspect of her studies that interests her, calmodulin kinase (CaMKII), and discusses the findings from her independent research under Dr. Anderson. Crucially, she shares the insights, lessons and reflections that she gained from that research. Dani does not shy away from mentioning that she initially struggled with rigorous chemistry courses, and this works in her favour, because she manages to spin her story as one of triumph and overcoming difficulty with purpose, perseverance and skill.

Dani goes a step further with this sentence:

> *"Through personalized education, I hope to empower patients to understand their health and optimize their body's function for a longer health span using lifestyle interventions."*

She makes clear what her goal would be as a doctor, and considering all that we have learned about her so far — from her family's journey out of poverty to her initial self-doubt — Dani's aspirations seem sincere rather than contrived. Her stories and background provide enormously useful context for why she really wants to become a doctor. We read through, we connect the dots, and we gain an understanding of how Dani has arrived at this particular moment in her life, and where she wants to go. This is what makes Dani's first two paragraphs particularly effective. She manages to turn negatives, such as self-doubt, hardship and struggle, into positives. And she does so without belittling herself or feeling sorry for herself, or fawning over the university to desperately win their sympathy.

So far, Dani's personal statement is heading in the right direction, and with these two paragraphs, she has made a very strong impression. Let's go on to paragraph three to see if she can keep it up.

In her third paragraph, Dani writes:

> "Reframing complex concepts in understandable terms is familiar to me, as I was my family's English translator since our immigration from

> Cuba at the age of six. Despite my father's success as a physician in Cuba, we lived in severe poverty, prompting us to flee as political refugees to Chile. Six years later, we arrived in Miami, where I struggled to learn English after repeatedly moving and adapting to three elementary schools. Once I was ready to begin my role as the family's English translator, I translated passages from the USMLE books for my father before I knew how to perform long division. It was clear to me that our future rested on his performance on these board exams. My job as my family's translator elucidated the role of language in providing people with the tools to become self-sufficient, allowing them to exploit their full potential. I want to serve as a guide for patients as they acquire the knowledge to make informed health decisions."

Dani's third paragraph is rather interesting as it solely focuses on the theme of language being equivalent to power. This works because we learn something more about Dani. Importantly, the skills that she portrays are useful for a medic.

For example:

"Reframing complex concepts in understandable terms."

The ability to explain complex terms to other colleagues and patients in a way that is intelligible and concise is a central pillar of medicine. With this example, Dani impresses upon the admissions tutor that she is highly capable at communicating with others, but she does so with the 'show, don't tell' approach that I mentioned earlier on.

"Repeatedly moving and adapting to three elementary schools."

Having to move schools in what was, back then, a foreign country to Dani would clearly have been a distressing experience for her — not to mention doing so as a child and political refugee. This statement informs us that Dani has already experienced adversity in her life, and yet she has overcome her obstacles. Considering the daily stresses that doctors face in their career, Dani's presentation of herself as a person who possesses resilience and grit is reassuring for any admissions tutor.

"It was clear to me that our future rested on his performance on these board exams."

The fact that Dani, at a young age, took the responsibility of becoming the family translator is an impressive display of her leadership skills and her ability to take initiative. She also mentions that her father was a physician in Cuba, without leveraging her father's background in medicine by making him the focus of her writing, which other students may have been tempted to do. Dani keeps it authentic and personal, and so far, each paragraph has covered its own distinct area, while reinforcing the narrative of overcoming self-doubt and taking action.

In her penultimate paragraph, Dani writes:

"Motivated to address language barriers in a

> healthcare setting, I sought out an opportunity to optimize the outreach efforts of Centro Sol, a JHU Spanish health advocacy and vaccine clinic. I conducted phone interviews with the local Latinx population to improve COVID health literacy, which is how I met Jorge, a Honduran immigrant. With no English proficiency, Jorge received COVID data through local word-of-mouth. Having experienced a language barrier first-hand, I understood how limited Spanish public health information deterred him from voluntarily opting for a vaccine with potential side effects. I urged him to reconsider vaccination from a different lens by addressing the rumors of the side effects. Our shared Latinx experience opened the door to candid conversation and allowed me to deliver valuable information, empowering Jorge to trust in medicine. I want to treat patients who are disproportionately affected by chronic illness by mending their broken trust in medical institutions to correct inequities in healthcare access. As a physician, I hope to alleviate my patients' concerns and promote informed health decisions by disseminating unequivocal scientific data with patience and empathy."

Dani does an excellent job of making the transition from paragraph three to paragraph four, as the former focuses on her role as her family's translator and the latter demonstrates how she used her experiences with her family in a practical setting at the JHU Spanish health advocacy and vaccine clinic.

Dani clearly describes what her role entailed, as she mentions that she conducted phone interviews with the local Latinx population to improve their COVID health literacy. Notably, she manages to tell her story very compellingly through her experiences with Jorge.

Phrases such as 'having experienced a language barrier first-hand' allow Dani to draw parallels between Jorge's struggle and her own, which demonstrates empathy once again. In addition, Dani's efforts to inform Jorge about vaccinations is a demonstrable example of her using her background in science to directly help others. Let's quickly reflect on what Dani wrote at the end of her second paragraph:

"Through personalized education, I hope to empower patients to understand their health and optimize their body's function for a longer health span using lifestyle interventions."

As you can clearly see, Dani reinforces this sentiment with how she helped Jorge, and staying consistent to her original aim makes it feel all the more legitimate and authentic. Similar to how Dani ended her second paragraph, she makes the following statement:

"I want to treat patients who are disproportionately affected by chronic illness by mending their broken trust in medical institutions to correct inequities in healthcare access. As a physician, I hope to alleviate my patients' concerns and promote informed health decisions by disseminating unequivocal scientific data with patience and

empathy."

This is an excellent way to address an issue that has long coloured the healthcare system without being too disparaging and critical. If you are applying to medical school, you need to make clear to the admissions tutor that this is truly what you want to do. Therefore, if you write a wall of text about how much you despise the healthcare system, even if what you are taking umbrage with comes from a place of fact, you run the risk of coming across as whiny and negative. Dani succeeds in raising awareness about the wider issues of distrust in medicine, inequities in healthcare access and the role that language barriers can play in unfairly depriving people in marginalised communities of vital information that may positively impact their health.

So why does Dani's articulation of these issues read so well? It is because she has addressed these issues, but equally mentions what she hopes to do in the role that she would have as a doctor.

For example, consider these phrases that Dani used:

"I understood how limited Spanish public health information..."

"Addressing the rumors of the side effects..."

"Our shared Latinx experience..."

"Opened the door to candid conversation..."

"Empowering Jorge to trust in medicine..."

"Mending their broken trust..."

"Correct inequities..."

"Alleviate my patients' concerns..."

"Promote informed health decisions..."

"With patience and empathy..."

Whether it is completely intentional or not, Dani's words are empowering, constructive, pragmatic and positive — not disdainful. She demonstrates an ability to understand Jorge's circumstances, rather than looking down on him or thinking less of him. Considering the sheer diversity of patients that doctors treat, cultural sensitivity, compassion and understanding are immense advantages that Dani has demonstrated. Overall, Dani has shown excellent storytelling skills, and her narrative has remained consistent and easily understood by the reader. She appears to care about people and their health, and this feeling is largely informed by the fact that she has also faced her own adversities in life. This is why Dani's personal statement for medicine makes her come across as authentic, but equally strong and determined. At this point, any admissions tutor will have been positively persuaded by Dani's first four paragraphs, such that it would require a major faux pas or red flag to derail the excellent impression that Dani has already made.

In her conclusion, Dani writes:

"I approached my journey as a pre-medical

> student with the work ethic and resiliency that my parents ingrained in me, allowing me to transition from political refugee to college graduate. Applying my metabolism research background and communicative dexterity, I plan to simplify complex medical concepts, encouraging patients to actively participate in the prevention and management of their chronic illnesses. Through our similar life experiences, I'm able to empathize with patients like Jorge, allowing me to form trusting connections and prescribe information to overcome skepticism in medicine. I intend to employ my culturally nuanced public health education to connect with a multilingual, diverse patient population and empower patients to procure positive health outcomes. Throughout my life, my role has evolved from translator to Latinx public health advocate, preparing me for my future role as a physician-educator."

As you can tell, Dani's conclusion simply reiterates the main points from her personal statement without introducing a new narrative — as I advised against earlier on. Her opening sentence sounds very conclusive and summarises her entire story:

"I approached my journey as a pre-medical student with the work ethic and resiliency that my parents ingrained in me, allowing me to transition from political refugee to college graduate."

Dani manages to pay homage to her parents and the

lessons that they instilled in her without dwelling on them. In addition, describing her 'transition from political refugee to college graduate' is poignant and inspiring. It draws into focus how far she has come, as she is on the cusp of doing something extraordinary by getting into a top medical school. As we read Dani's conclusion, if there was ever any doubt as to whether she should receive a place at medical school, this juxtaposition between once being a political refugee and studying at medical school is a powerful one that compels us to root for her.

After mentioning her research and work with Jorge, Dani ends her personal statement conclusively and elegantly:

> *"I intend to employ my culturally nuanced public health education to connect with a multilingual, diverse patient population and empower patients to procure positive health outcomes. Throughout my life, my role has evolved from translator to Latinx public health advocate, preparing me for my future role as a physician-educator."*

Similar to how Dani ends the second and penultimate paragraphs, she makes a statement that indicates her aspirations as a physician. This is effective, as her words are forward-facing, positive and determined. Dani presents herself as someone who, despite initially suffering from self-doubt, now believes in herself. As a result, we believe in Dani too.

After going through Dani's personal statement in full, you can understand why she received her offer to study medicine at Johns Hopkins University. And hopefully, her personal statement has proved useful in demonstrating an effective way to present yourself, using your adversity to your advantage.

A World of Opportunity

Earlier on, I mentioned that once you have submitted your personal statement, a world of opportunity awaits. But perhaps I should make a slight correction here. A world of opportunity still awaits, no matter what happens. Never forget that. Competition can be incredibly fierce, and even admissions tutors face a tough task as they struggle to choose one excellent candidate over another with just as many good qualities. No matter where you land, you can always make the most of the situation that you find yourself in. With a positive and forward-looking mindset, perseverance and sometimes a bit of luck and providence, you really can achieve astonishing things. Throughout your academic and professional life, there will always be new challenges and new victories. Your life is not defined by your challenges, and your life is not defined by your victories. Your life is defined by the values, approach and mindset that you keep, irrespective of your victories and challenges.

That is where your true value lies.

Once you have sent your personal statement, all you can do is hope for the best and look forward to the next steps. You have done a fantastic job by reading this book, and hopefully, all of your hard work will lead you to where you want to go.

As a quick summary, you covered in Stage A: Planning:

Chapter 1: Research

Chapter 2: Requirements

Chapter 3: Narrative

Then, in Stage B: Writing, you explored:

Chapter 4: Structure I

Chapter 5: Structure II

Chapter 6: Reflections

Chapter 7: Coherence

Finally, Stage C: Refining included the following chapters:

Chapter 8: Feedback

Chapter 9: Diligence

Chapter 10: Completion

Well done for making it all the way to the end, and thank you so much for reading *How to Write an Excellent Personal Statement.*

Something to Remember

Always keep in mind that every person has innate potential waiting to be harnessed, and how that looks is different from person to person. Whatever happens with your application, always keep hope alive, and know that life finds a way to work  out in the end.

It has been an honour guiding you through this process, and I wish you the best of luck in achieving your goals.

In the next section of this book, I have provided some personal statement samples for you to read, along with my remarks on each one. Have a read, and feel free to refer back to sections of this book when you need to refresh yourself on areas that could help to further sharpen your personal statement.

Stay in Touch

At PlaceCoach, we have already helped thousands of students in their applications to top universities such as Oxford, Cambridge, Harvard, LSE, Princeton, Imperial and Yale, and for a range of courses — such as medicine, law, computer science, dentistry, economics, MBAs, data science and so much more. It would be lovely to hear from you, so feel free to reach out at:

www.placecoach.co.uk

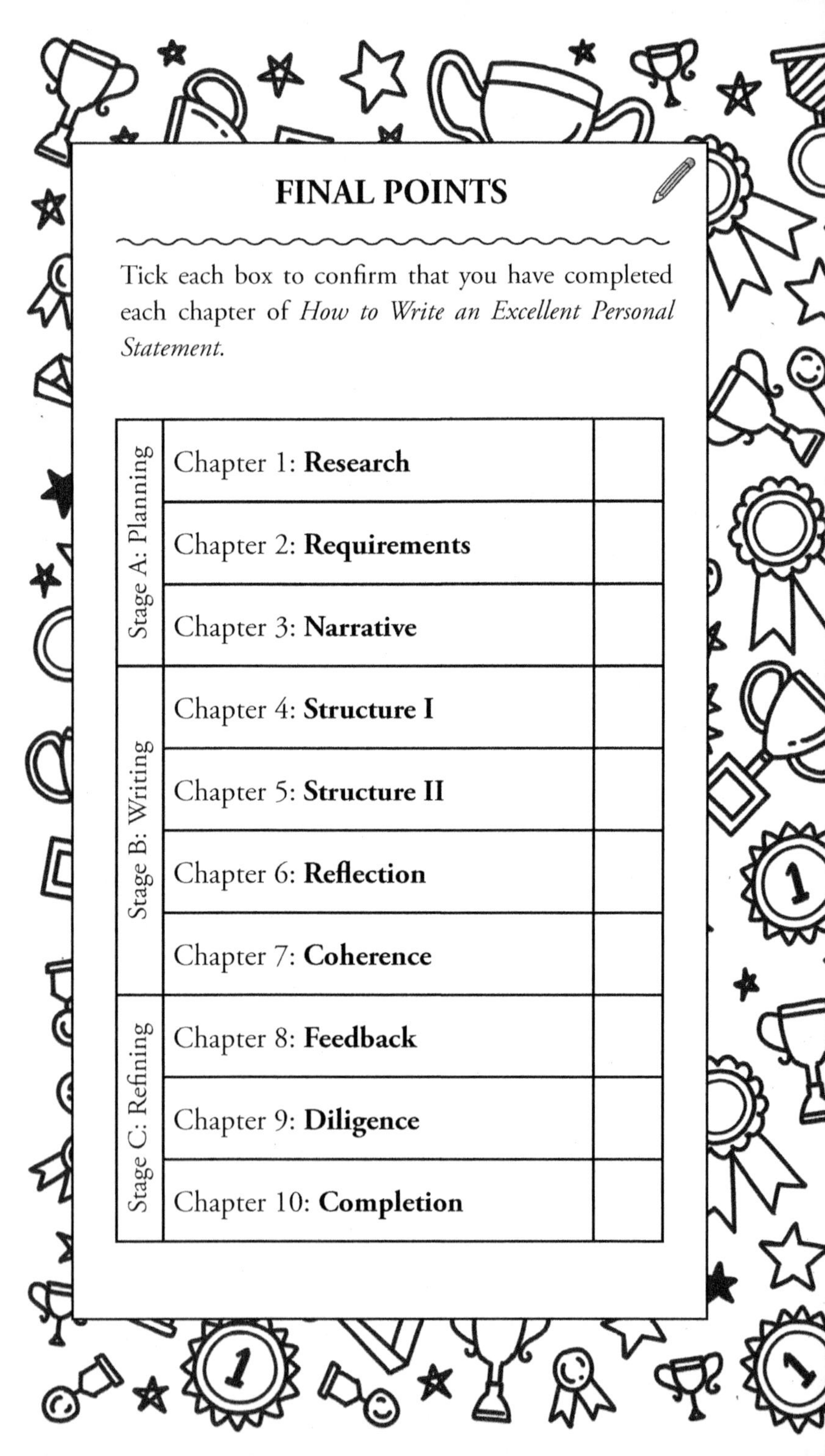

FINAL POINTS

Tick each box to confirm that you have completed each chapter of *How to Write an Excellent Personal Statement.*

Stage A: Planning	Chapter 1: **Research**	
	Chapter 2: **Requirements**	
	Chapter 3: **Narrative**	
Stage B: Writing	Chapter 4: **Structure I**	
	Chapter 5: **Structure II**	
	Chapter 6: **Reflection**	
	Chapter 7: **Coherence**	
Stage C: Refining	Chapter 8: **Feedback**	
	Chapter 9: **Diligence**	
	Chapter 10: **Completion**	

The End

OBRIGADA
Merci
Köszönöm
감사합니다
To
고마워
Дякую
THANK YOU
Dziękuję
תודה
Danke
TAK
gracias
ありがとう
СПАСИБО
GRAZIE
Tack
Շնորհակալություն
D
谢谢
cảm ơn
SHUKRAAN
धन्यवाद
Dank je wel
TEŞEKKÜR EDERIM
TERIMA KASIH
Kiitos
ευχαριστώ
ДЯКУЮ
Дзякуй
ขอบคุณ
DA
شكرا
OBRIGADA
GRACIAS
धन्यवाद
Merci
ありがとう
THANK YOU
Thank you
DANKE
TAK
谢谢
TEŞEK

Thank you for reading.

For more from PlaceCoach, please visit:

www.placecoach.co.uk

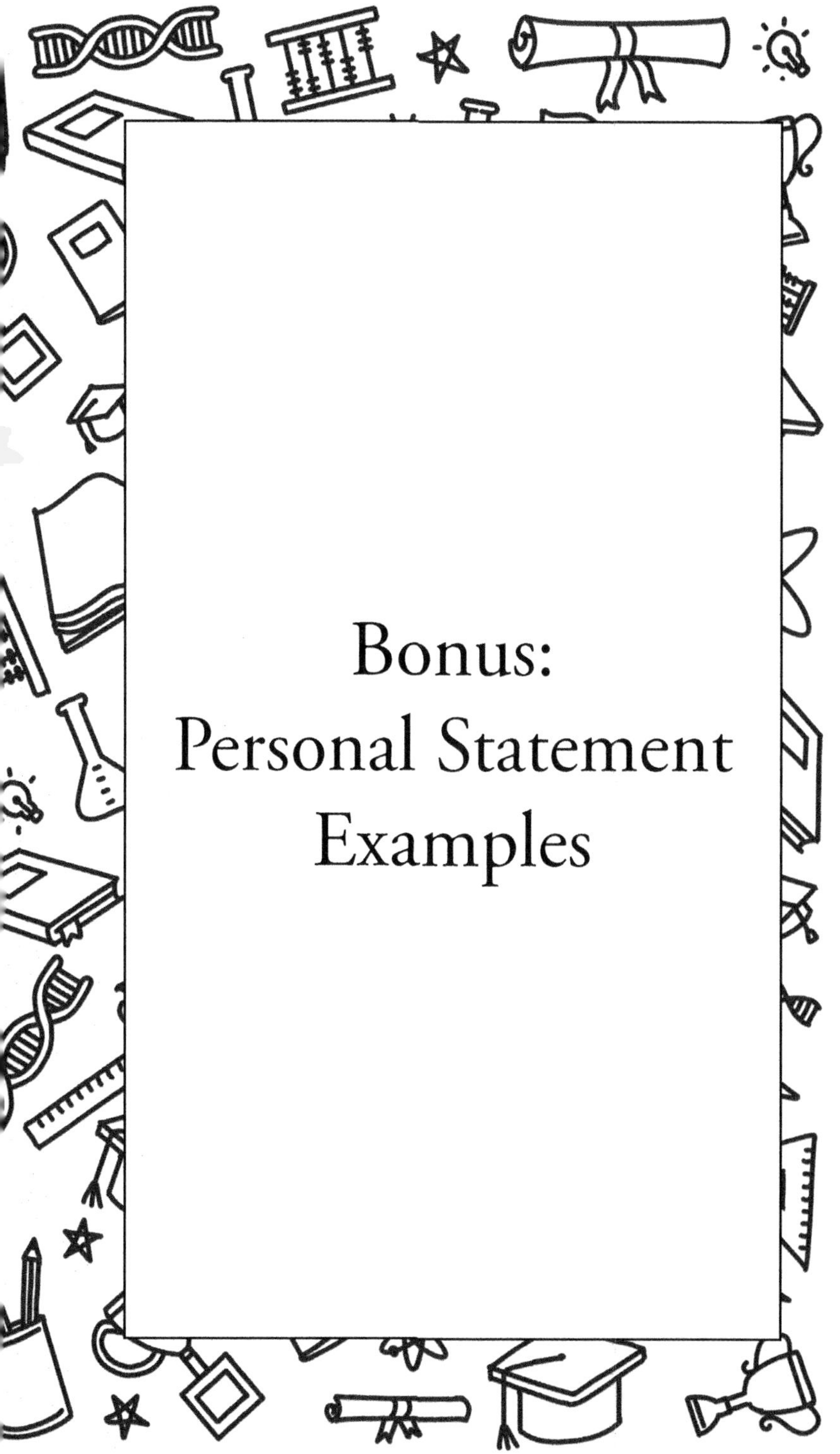

Bonus: Personal Statement Examples

Maebh's Personal Statement

Offer from:

University of Oxford

Subject:

English Language & Literature

Literature is a limitless source of human knowledge; one that is a personal experience to each reader and forever changing as we look back into the past with our own experiences. Looking at Charlotte Brontë's *Jane Eyre* with a focus on mental health and post-colonialism introduced me to the idea of reading older texts with the value of hindsight and a modern outlook. Jean Rhys' novel *Wide Sargasso Sea* seemed to offer one solution to Bertha's silence within Jane Eyre and I found the idea of writing about silenced characters within literature compelling in both its imagination and necessity.

Taking this idea further, I read Carol Ann Duffy's collection, *The World's Wife*, and found the historical grounding of these poems fascinating. Whilst these poems can stand by themselves, research into their context and background and the characters that Duffy was inspired by provides a much clearer analysis of the poems, one that taught me to appreciate the importance of historical and cultural context when reading literature. Duffy provides a voice for women within her collection, mainly using the dramatic monologue form to delve into the thoughts of some of the side-lined women within history. Men are the ones silenced and are presented in a negative light yet, Duffy doesn't instantly present women with redemptive qualities to contrast them, but paints them as multi-faceted creatures; they are presented as human beings, with all the variety of character and behaviour that this implies.

I have always valued literature as a window into societies past, and the influence of context is something that is inextricably linked with the writing of literature. Reading Lorraine Hansberry's *A Raisin In the Sun* introduced me both to American literature, and the context of the 'American Dream' within it. Having chosen to read Fitzgerald's *The Great Gatsby*, I found the disparity between the rich and the poor to be a resonating theme and one that contrasted well with Hansberry's play. Within *A Raisin in the Sun*, the question of wealth is at the forefront and Karl Lindner, as a white man, occupies a place of privilege in comparison to the Younger family. *The Great Gatsby* too shows this inequality with the comparisons between George Wilson and Gatsby himself. I also found form an interesting point of comparison between the texts; both place the reader/audience firmly in the place of a spectator, despite the first person narrative of *The Great Gatsby*. The ambiguity of male characters such as Jay Gatsby and Walter Lee Younger interested me and led me to look at the perception of male characters within these texts as either heroic or flawed characters by comparing the presentation of these characters.

Attending an English masterclass at the University of Cambridge introduced me to deeper and alternative analysis of texts such as *Romeo and Juliet*, which I explored further by watching different Globe productions of the play. As part of the UNIQ summer school at the University of Oxford, I looked into alternative interpretations of *The Tempest* too, exploring ideas such as incest, colonialism and performance in a text in which these subjects didn't seem to be the immediate theme. HE+ extension sessions too introduced me to different aspects of literature in depth.

Outside of reading, I have a great passion for writing, having won a competition run by my college to be published in a poetry collection with a group of young poets for Winchester Poetry Festival; this has opened my mind to the industry surrounding literature and the importance of editing in the creation of it, and led me to become interested in the role of editing and publishing as something I would like to pursue as a career. Reading literature has been something that has shaped my life; I hope that studying it will continue this.

Remarks on Maebh's Personal Statement

From the first line to the last, Maebh showcases beautiful and elegant writing, which is made all the more impressive when one considers how many fascinating insights, observations and perspectives she has. In her personal statement, she mentions Charlotte Brontë's *Jane Eyre*, Jean Rhys' *Wide Sargasso Sea*, Carol Ann Duffy's *The World's Wife*, Lorraine Hansberry's *A Raisin In the Sun* and F. Scott Fitzgerald's *The Great Gatsby*. But rather than merely listing the literary works that she has read, she analyses them deeply and makes comments on issues such as mental health, postcolonialism, inequality, wealth distribution, and the perception of male characters. Maebh covers a range of interesting ideas within her first three paragraphs alone, which is very impressive.

In her fourth paragraph, we read about some of Maebh's activities beyond the curriculum, particularly with the English Masterclass at the University of Cambridge, and the UNIQ summer school at the University of Oxford. Both of these experiences are solid, and they add great value to her overall writing, amplifying her passion and commitment to studying English language and literature. It is also impressive that Maebh has won a writing competition, and she clearly is skilled in this area. Overall, Maebh does an excellent job in expounding upon a range of important topics that she has an interest in, and her passion is palpable.

Ryan's Admissions Essays

Offer from:

Georgetown University

Subject:

Management

"Everyone belongs to many different communities and/or groups defined by (among other things) shared geography, religion, ethnicity, income, cuisine, interest, race, ideology, or intellectual heritage. Choose one of the communities to which you belong, and describe that community and your place within it. (Maximum 1500 characters.)"

Growing up in the small town of Yulee, the community that I had once called home would soon change as I embarked on an intrepid journey by joining the US Air Force. My grandfather was a soldier in Vietnam, and he reminded me that this was a 'rite of passage,' and so, when I first arrived at my new 40-person dormitory at midnight, I contemplated on my bunk what the path ahead would look like.

The next morning, the lights immediately cut on at 5:00 am. One sergeant was yelling, and another was banging on lockers. I sprung out of bed, and was met with planned chaos — a scenario that would soon become the norm, which developed a sense of urgency. All 40 of us had two minutes from dead sleep to get lined up on the wall with our gear ready. Meanwhile, my friend, Rosser, who slept to the left of my bunk had trouble opening the combination lock to his dresser. I helped him to prepare his backpack with the proper inventory items while he was exchanging and revolving numbers through his spinning combo lock. He eventually unlocked it, but we feared that he might not open it in time. Looking back, that first day felt like I was the main character in an intense eight-week action movie. But over time, I learned that I can thrive in adversity and work with all types of people. My military community was a birthplace for friendships and virtues, and I gained an invaluable perspective about service and commitment while growing through my Air Force career.

Remarks on Ryan's Essay

Ryan presents beautiful and vivid writing about his experiences in the US Air Force. He takes the reader on a journey as he describes his grandfather's role as a soldier in the Vietnam War and his first day in the dormitory with his fellow soldiers. It reads somewhat like a novel in some places, and he captures the sense of community within this group, going on to describe it rather poetically when he writes:

"A birthplace for friendships and virtues."

For a standard essay prompt, Ryan writes very well and describes his community in a compelling way that immerses the reader in his personal experience.

Ryan also submitted other essays to Stanford University. Let's see how he fares with those. His next prompt was:

"Some students have a background, identity, interest, or talent that is so meaningful they believe their application would be incomplete without it. If this sounds like you, then please share your story."

I have always been a storyteller. What I realized is that stories have the capacity to take on other forms, images, and outcomes beyond their normal traditions. For example, if I related the background story of my youth as I transformed into adulthood, I would describe a high-school graduate who turned into an American Airman. Yet, beneath the surface, there's always something epic which has more to it — a story, song, or tale that could be crafted so diligently which leads you into this specific world. Although I will not describe those details in this essay, I have created a non-traditional outlet for meaningfully storytelling, parallel worlds, places, or memories.

What had first emerged as a passion evolved into an outlet, which originated when my mom gifted me a bora-bora mural which still covers one of the four walls in my childhood bedroom. An oceanic paradise featuring a tiki hut home, knee-deep water, green background mountains, and a bright sunrise greeted me warmly every time I walked into my room. Powerfully enough, this dreamy childhood mural converged into one of my entrepreneurial niches. The effects of this interior architecture in my own life led me to create similar scenes for others.

I have always prided myself on having an eye for opportunity. And more so, I felt that if I could find a way to infuse the feelings that I experienced from the Bora Bora mural into a product that could be of personal value to others, then somewhat unknowingly, a viable business would soon emerge. I explored the various options available to me that would serve as a platform through which I could bring this idea to fruition, and be commercially successful in the long run. Upon extensive research, I contacted people who could help create this artwork, and upon its completion, I felt ready to share it with potential customers. Within weeks, I was astonished to see my first sale. And thereafter, as I began to create more artwork that sought to capture the essence of my mother's bora-bora mural, I was delighted to see my profits sky-rocket. The success of this project, in my view, is testament to the power of harnessing what is meaningful to us and sharing it with the world.

Just as my mother's Bora Bora mural had a palpable and poignant impact on me, I knew that such a reaction would be reflected in the thousands of people who would buy my artwork in the future. Ultimately, I believe that one of the hallmarks of many of the figures to whom I have once admired is their desire to share the best of the world with others. In this vein of thought, I hope that by applying to Stanford and hopefully being accepted onto the program, I can emulate this same philosophy both in my studies and my future career.

Remarks on Ryan's Essay

Ryan describes in detail how he launched his artwork business, which was inspired by his mother's bora-bora mural. He writes with flair and vivid description and elegantly answers the prompt to share his story. Admittedly, the prompt is somewhat vague and open-ended, but Ryan does a great job in staying focussed on one story and following it through right till the end. He sticks to one narrative, which allows the reader to better follow his story.

Finally, have a read of Ryan's transfer essay. Having already studied at Arizona State University for an online degree in entrepreneurship and management, Ryan answered the prompt for Stanford, which was:

“

Please provide a statement that addresses your reasons for transferring and the objectives you hope to achieve. (650 words)"

As a student at Arizona State University studying technological entrepreneurship and management, I found myself preoccupied due to my other commitments as an active-duty member of the Armed Forces. I have always prided myself on being able to persevere; however, splitting my time between these two pursuits meant that I could not devote time exclusively to one or the other. I had to put my military priorities first. I am getting out of the Air Force in January to concentrate on higher education full-time. I am seeking to transfer so that I can make use of all of the skills I learned at ASU and in the Air Force over the past four years.

I hope to transfer to Stanford in order to contribute marketable ideas and concepts to the community, and to equally benefit from a world-class education that I have no doubt will challenge me at a level ASU did not. While I could explore my academic interests in economic concepts such as industrial organization, big data, and logistics management at ASU, opportunities such as this were limited. The business landscape is constantly evolving, and I found that the degree plan offered at ASU does not reflect this change to the extent that I feel would challenge me intellectually. Stanford's philosophy brings teachers, innovators, and entrepreneurs into collaborative alliances. Given the decidedly entrepreneurial journey that I envision for myself, I believe Stanford can uniquely prepare me to become a technology facilitator and producer. My career goal is to become the CEO of a private defense contractor or commercial business. I plan to utilize

Stanford's unparalleled resources like the research park and StartX for internships and networking.

With the multitude of experiences that I have had, I feel compelled to share my knowledge with classmates and professors. While in the Air Force, I matured through high-pressure and sometimes life-threatening situations, managing immense responsibilities while working on the F-22 Raptor, the United States' most advanced stealth fighter jet. From the age of 18, I was in charge of fixing and maintaining on the ground a supersonic machine that tested the limits of physics in the skies. I have learned the critical teamwork skills and precision necessary to keep fighter jets ready to fly safely, both in the classroom and during extracurricular engagements. As a result, I am confident that I can be depended upon to lead various projects with steadiness and urgency.

In the military sector, it is of paramount importance that technology is kept up to date, and it is clear that the civilian sector could equally benefit from the advances made here. Stanford has been a major research center for the U.S. government in their efforts to improve military defense technology. Through my secret military clearance, I have studied how complex aircraft components and systems are designed, and how they function and malfunction up close. The education offered at Stanford, coupled with my past military experience, will help me to preview new products, machines, and inventions. My early mechanical and engineering insight needs to combine with the higher educational opportunities at Stanford to empower me to translate conceptual ideas into viable enterprises.

It is my plan to learn the entrepreneurial, economic, and

academic perspective, which will help me to organize, strategize, and concentrate all of my previous knowledge into other fields of industry. It is undeniable that technology in recent years has undergone a meteoric rise, and on many occasions, Stanford has been at the helm of the emerging technologies that continue to positively impact people's lives. With this in mind, I feel excited about engaging with like-minded, driven individuals who want to make a difference in the world.

Remarks on Ryan's Transfer Essay

As a member of the US Air Force, Ryan skilfully takes his breadth of experience with high-stakes situations and applies it to his application to study business management at Stanford University, having studied at Arizona State University. His inclusion of life-threatening situations in fighter jets are something that very few people will be able to relate to, and the fact that he was in charge of fixing and maintaining some of these aircraft demonstrates an extremely high level of responsibility and leadership.

Overall, Ryan has a very strong command of writing, and it is a joy to read his stories, each of which is memorable, meaningful and vivid.

Anna's Personal Statement

Offer from:

University of Oxford

Subject:

Philosophy, Politics and Economics

They all act selfishly: corrupt politicians, vulture funds, and the average voter. Although this may be an allegation, it is undeniable that temporal comfort is more often than not chosen over the possibility to provide a better future. I see this in abundance in politics and not seldom economic intentions are behind it. I want to understand such processes by studying how economics and politics influence each other. Are economics the cause for political actions or is it the other way around?

In the first chapter of his book *Der schmale Grat der Hoffnung*, Jean Ziegler uses the process of vulture funds bankrupting entire states as an example of the most powerful people's selfish actions. I found this intriguing in two ways: first, such morally unjustifiable actions anger me; second, from an objective point of view, it is fascinating how different interests clash and that a few influential people have a significant impact on a global level. Globalization has reached an intense form today; economies are so tightly connected that one action leads into numerous others. Ziegler's life inspires me since it resembles my interests and goals. After finishing a bachelor's and master's related to economics, I would like to work in an international political environment, for example as an ambassador, or in a non-governmental organisation.

As an elected municipal youth councillor, I experience political issues livelier than just through the news. Shortly before the German Bundestag elections, the set-up of a panel discussion gave me the opportunity to carry on a conversation with our constituency's candidate of the CDU, Steffen Bilger, now Parliamentary State Secretary, about nationalism, the refugee crisis, and the EU. Although I do not agree with substantial points of the party's agenda, I enjoy hearing a professional perspective. Through evaluating other opinions in addition to gathering facts and figures, I form my opinion. Instituting the Euro in 1999 was a step towards a united Europe, which I support in principle. Reading the third chapter in *Machtbeben* by Dirk Mueller, I reassessed this step. In order to push the European economy through a common currency, the member states have to be on similar levels. Otherwise, the Target2-Balances keep drifting apart. This demonstrates the importance of attuning political decisions to economic facts.

In contrast to politics, in mathematics, there is only right or wrong. The pure logic and absoluteness of numbers form the antipole to the relativeness of politics. Having Mathematics as a main subject for the German Abitur, I enjoy dealing with it on an advanced level. The curriculum is not focused on one aspect but covers a broad area. Consequently, I am comfortable in algebra, geometry, trigonometry, analysis, probability, and statistics, which are crucial skills for studying economics.

My duties as head girl include confidently talking in front of a big audience and conducting meetings. Being elected into the school's committee and the Youth Council, I worked with the school's headmaster and the mayor on several occasions. I can easily transfer these skills and use them for group projects, presentations, and working with professors. For nine years, my participation in an orchestra as the first flute and dancing ballet were great opportunities to meet and work with different types of people.

The award-winning professors, small student teacher ratios, and international reputation are the reasons for choosing the UK as my destination. Due to being in a bilingual class, in which several subjects such as history and politics were taught in English, as well as writing a 30-page long research paper on viticulture in Europe, I am fluent in spoken and written English. As an official proof of my English skills, I scored 115 out of 120 points on the TOEFL iBT in September 2018. With English as a tie point, I am eager to live with inquisitive individuals and study the links between economics and society.

Remarks on Anna's Personal Statement

Anna's personal statement is packed with meaningful experiences and interesting insights — from being an elected municipal youth councillor to her perspectives on the Euro. She delivers her opinions with force from the very first line:

"They all act selfishly: corrupt politicians, vulture funds, and the average voter."

This is an effective opening line, as it grabs the reader's attention and gives us a preview of what the tone of the rest of the personal statement will be. Anna demonstrates extensive academic exploration in her second paragraph by engaging in incisive and reflective discussion about Jean Ziegler's book and how his life has inspired her own aspirations. This is excellent, as she explores topics in a manner that will be expected of her as a future PPE student at Oxford, thereby making it easier for an admissions tutor to imagine her being the right fit for the course. Numerous British prime ministers have studied this course at Oxford, and Anna positions herself as a formidable future leader and change-maker.

Ricky's 'Why Us?' Essay

Offer from:

University of Chicago

Subject:

Economics

"How does the University of Chicago as you know it now satisfy your desire for a particular kind of learning community in the future? Please address with some specificity, your own wishes and how they relate to UChicago."

The University of Chicago. The name alone carried quite a heavy load; a hotspot for innovation, core of university-lead research and a producer of world-changers. You can say this school exceeds my desires for an institution's undergraduate education. As someone who craves entrepreneurship, the opportunities for growth in this area are evident at UChicago. The Booth School of Business exemplifies one of these opportunities for growth. Having access to Booth in my undergraduate education will not only allow me to expand upon my entrepreneurial desire, but will undoubtedly prepare for my track toward becoming a Boothie following undergrad. The countless opportunities for intellectual growth for UChicago students are evident through resources such as the Office of Career Advancement, access to Wisr, and the over 160 research centers, among many others.

Career Advancement holds several professions for UChicago students to immerse themselves into. Among the many pre-professional focuses within this program, I will choose entrepreneurship. This program makes accessibility to well-developed corporations and successful entrepreneurs much easier, offering access to companies such as Grubhub and Venmo. I will have access to Wisr through the Office of Career Advancement. A stand-out attribute of UChicago is its community of alumni; using Wisr will help me collaborate with an alumni mentor who works in my area of interest, connecting me with the community. Also offered through Career Advancement is the ability to work with start-up companies during the academic year. These start-ups will provide the opportunity to intern within an environment enthralled by entrepreneurship, and build relationships with new up-and-coming companies. My career plan in college has always been to form a start-up with other students who share similar interests as me, so having access to a resource like this will help me fulfil that plan.

Continuing research I have started in high school will be possible due to UChicago's abundance of research opportunities. The research I have begun entails analyzing the sensory benefits that slime brings to elementary students with autism. UChicago will allow me to amplify this research, delivering my slime into the hands of more students across the nation. The Human Performance Lab within the Center for Early Childhood Research is where I believe my findings can be applied, specifically, working with Ms. Sian Beilock would be sublime. Ms. Beilock's research of stress' relevance in regards to performance in a classroom setting presents itself as a great opportunity for me to implement a slime. Playing with slime releases endorphins, which in turn, makes for great anxiety and stress relief. By introducing slime into the classrooms that she runs, I can potentially offer another variable for stress relief in younger students.

The student I long to become at my college graduation is a student who took the time to challenge himself with the curriculum offered at his institution, was proactive in establishing connections among people in his career interest, and filled the gaps of his curiosities. By attending the University of Chicago, I know I will exemplify that student come 2026.

Remarks on 'Why Us?' Essay

You may recognise Ricky from earlier on in Chapter Five: Structure II and Chapter Six: Reflections. In a typical personal statement, it is advised that you write about yourself — your insights, reflections, experiences and perspectives. However, in this 'Why Us?' essay, the University of Chicago has given Ricky the opportunity to write about the merits of the university, which he manages to do exceedingly well from start to finish. The opening line is powerful and memorable, and Ricky lists multiple benefits of studying at UChicago, such as the access to well-developed corporations and successful entrepreneurs, the community of alumni and the research opportunities. Overall, Ricky answers the question directly and uses concrete examples to flesh out his responses.

It was also a wise strategy for Ricky to marry the question 'Why Us?' with 'Why Ricky?' because, by mentioning his slime business in paragraph five, he also presents something of value. He demonstrates that while he is eager to study at the University of Chicago, his own research equally brings something to the table:

> *"UChicago will allow me to amplify this research, delivering my slime into the hands of more students across the nation."*

Overall, Ricky's essay answers the question directly, and also presents him in a very favourable light.

Harry's Personal Statement

Offer from:

Imperial College London

Subject:

Medicine

Throughout my teenage years, I was eager to grow older and develop a sense of self. Now at eighteen, I cannot help but feel overwhelmed by multiple responsibilities and ever-present obstacles. I wanted to help people but could not fathom an answer to the question: how? I was made aware that the sense of purpose I sought comes from the service to others, by observing doctors around me. This idea of service is what medicine represents to me. Service is prevalent in all health professions, but with medicine, this act of service is an attempt to balance the ability to heal and the capacity to cause harm. I vehemently believe life in medicine will offer me a sense of fulfilment but not without difficulties. Hard work and resilience serve as sacrifices to uphold medicine's raison d'etre, saving lives.

My study of maths, biology, physics, chemistry, and economics will benefit me in this field. This benefit is independent of the content of these subjects; instead, it is reliant on skills such as critical thinking, abstract reasoning, communication, and cooperation gained through my study of these subjects. Ultimately, it was a broader understanding of the material universe these subjects gave me that I most enjoyed. These skills are integral to succeed in medicine and have been developed, for example, by gaining an in-depth understanding of the human defense system and its susceptibility to different diseases.

I participated in medical seminars and work experiences in hospitals in Nigeria and Ireland, and witnessed the practice of what I learned in class. For instance, learning about the genesis of the Ebola virus during its outbreak in 2014 in Nigeria was enlightening. Watching the practice of vigorous public health in Lagos amidst the panic secured my choice to work in this field. I am an active member of the European Youth Parliament and involved with the Aware and Pieta House Charities. These charities aim to spread awareness of mental health issues and assist sufferers of depression and suicidal distress. These organisations impart positive changes in the lives of people, exemplifying the work I aspire to do as a doctor.

In my final year of secondary school, I had the honour of being appointed senior prefect. My fellow prefects and I were required to be advocates as well as confidants. In this role, I was encouraged to be committed and think of others before myself. I balanced the pressure that came with this role and aimed to set an example for my other schoolmates and support my teachers. I enjoyed many successes, in academics, on the sports field, the stage in drama and debating, and in winning second place while representing Ireland along with my teammates, in the European final of the CanSat competition in 2017. However, these successes were not without setbacks along the way, such as moments of emotional turmoil and not securing a place in medicine last year. These experiences have provided me with the courage to be persistent, determined and to pursue my dreams.

Studying medicine will develop my sense of diligence, integrity, and independence, which facilitate these positive contributions I hope to make. Medicine is a universal language. For example, Henry Marsh's book, *Do No Harm*, which portrays a pragmatic account of his practice as a neurosurgeon, serves as a guide to aspiring neurosurgeons like me, all around the globe. The promise to save lives is entirely independent of location. No matter where I will practice, I aim to uphold this moral code and be a good ambassador of your college. Also, medical journals like The Lancet are informative on the development of medical treatments, and it promotes the Open Science movement. All these affirm my resolution to study medicine. These skills I have worked hard to develop, and experiences, will enable me to make progress in this field and become a neurosurgeon. I am keen to be part of this resilient legacy living in every doctor who fights to change the lives of many, forever.

Remarks on Harry's Personal Statement

Harry makes clear from the start what his narrative is — he wants to develop a sense of self, fulfilment and meaning in his career. He is choosing a career that he is interested in and one in which he will be able to contribute. His paragraph structure is very clear and coherent and closely resembles the six-part structure that I outlined in Chapter Four: Structure I. This makes his writing easy to follow, as we see how his story, thoughts and perspectives have progressed over time. We get the impression that Harry is a student who strongly values service and helping others, and his roles in the European Youth Parliament and as senior prefect attest to this.

Despite his many achievements, Harry does not shy away from mentioning the setback of not getting to study medicine the year before. This works to his advantage, as it demonstrates to the admissions tutor a level of perseverance, grit and dedication to his chosen field that speaks volumes about him. Harry has a range of extracurricular activities, such as sports, drama and debating, and he comes across as a well-rounded student with a clear desire to make a real difference in other people's lives through his professional endeavours.

Dan's Personal Statement

Offer from:

University of Oxford

Subject:

Law

My desire to challenge my analytical skills, and an interest in problem solving, first piqued my curiosity for the subject of law. My investigations into this field have reinforced my belief that this will be a challenging, but enjoyable, area in which to study and ultimately work. In conducting research into the legal profession, I found the arguments against the lack of adequate human rights particularly absorbing. My initial view that the legal system constantly adapted for the better was challenged by Helena Kennedy's *Just Law*, which suggested that civil liberties have actually been lost in recent legislation. I began to appreciate the challenges of maintaining personal freedoms during a climate of fear, and gained a broader understanding of the issues surrounding human rights as a part of law.

Work experience with a solicitor who specialised in wills and probate at Chandler Ray Solicitors provided me with a fascinating insight into one area of law. I demonstrated a capability to listen to and comprehend the facts of a case, often providing a reasoned conclusion. I was also given the opportunity to prepare case folders for barristers at court, giving me an understanding of the detailed preparation that is required for a case. This tested my initiative, as I needed to independently decide which documents were required amongst the large volumes of text available. I followed this up by spending several weeks of the summer holidays in the public galleries at Oxford Crown Court, to see how the documentation compiled by solicitors was used in the courtroom. I challenged myself to follow the evidence presented by opposing barristers and reach a similar conclusion to the judge. When my lack of experience led to an incorrect judgement I found the professionals, when questioned, were enlightening.

My science and maths studies at A-level have developed my ability to learn large quantities of information and apply it to a given scenario, whilst also inspiring some interesting legal debate with my teachers. For example, having learnt how genetic modification is used on plants and animals to improve the human food supply, my research into the arguments regarding whether it is ethically right was intriguing. Keen to learn more about new subjects outside my A-level courses, I took part in an OU YASS foundation course, 'Perspectives on Leonardo da Vinci.' I particularly enjoyed the freedom of independent study. During the summer holidays, I visited the Museo Leonardiano in Vinci, Italy, to learn more about Leonardo's pursuits.

My abilities have been put to the test in several challenging competitions. I was awarded a Silver certificate in the Cambridge Chemistry Challenge this year, and after repeated Gold awards in the UKMT Maths Challenge, an exceptionally high score meant progression into the elite Intermediate Mathematics Olympiad. Theatre is another passion that I have become increasingly involved with — last year I performed the title role in the musical, 'Sweeney Todd'. This experience greatly improved my speaking and listening skills, and my time management abilities. My organisational skills and confidence in public speaking have also led to my selection as deputy head boy this year, a role in which I have already shown reliability and trustworthiness. My responsibility for organising links to local schools led to working with young children and children with special needs, an experience I found very rewarding. It also prompted me to take on the role of 'peer listener' for younger students within my school, which involved listening to the issues facing others, and then helping them to resolve them. These opportunities have provided an interesting alternative to my academic pursuits.

The experiences listed above have convinced me that I not only have the necessary skills to study law, but I am also ready to immerse myself in studying the legal system.

Remarks on Dan's Personal Statement

You may recall an excerpt from Dan's introduction from Chapter Four: Structure I, earlier on in this book. Dan's structure is very easy to follow, and resembles the classic six-part structure that I have advised that you use — except that it mentions work experience before academic insights.

His writing is clear and to the point, and with every concrete experience that he mentions, he manages to do so reflectively. For example, working with a wills and probate solicitor allowed him to demonstrate a 'capability to listen,' and preparing case folders for a barrister in court required that he take initiative by independently deciding which documents were required amongst the large volume of text available to him. With each point that he makes, he ensures that he reminds us what his individual role was, which reduces the risk of his statement coming across as a list of achievements and experiences as you would see on a CV.

Dan also manages to make a connection between having done mostly science A-levels and studying law — a subject that is mostly essay-based. He describes the advantages of knowing how to absorb large quantities of information, and the ethical arguments surrounding genetic modification of plants and animals. Overall, this personal statement is a no-frills, clear and effective piece of writing.

Arjun's Personal Statement

Offer from:

University of Cardiff

Subject:

Dentistry

My initial curiosity for dentistry stemmed from regular visits to my dentist and discussions with her. The blend of precision engineering and artistic flair instantly captured my imagination. I relished the opportunity to investigate dentistry as a vocation through numerous work placements and shadowing experiences, both in the UK and USA. Working as part of a team in a patient based hands-on environment appealed to me immediately. I thoroughly enjoyed working with a diverse array of people and found the combination of science and art in dentistry unlike any other course. I have the patience, determination and enthusiasm that a profession such as dentistry demands, along with the natural creativity and dexterity required to succeed.

Having shadowed General Dental Practitioners for three weeks, my aspiration to pursue dentistry as a career is now greater than ever. I was fortunate to witness a wide range of procedures including fillings, denture construction and root canal treatments. The importance of building a rapport with the patient became apparent early on and in many cases visibly helped alleviate patient anxiety. Clear communication led to a mutual understanding of diagnoses, treatments, patient desires and expectations, with the dentist frequently emphasising the importance of decay prevention. Through these placements I have also obtained a basic understanding of private and NHS dentistry, which will be enhanced further by undertaking work experience with the winner of the 'Private Dentist of the Year' award. Working at a children's nursery, a residential home and a local pharmacy have helped develop my communication skills with people from a wide variety of ages and backgrounds.

Shadowing an orthodontist and oral and maxillofacial surgeons in a local hospital offered me an insight into specialist aspects of dental care. I observed the impact these specialities have on patients' appearance and self-confidence. Exploring some of the dental fields was inspirational, assuring me that I can find a position I will thoroughly enjoy.

At A-Level I have enjoyed studying chemistry and biology, which have provided me with an understanding of anatomy and physiology, which university will enable me to extend. Studying mathematics has also developed my problem solving skills, which are essential for all university students and particularly resonant in the dental field. Alongside juggling the pressure and stress of A-Levels, I mentored younger students, which has developed my organisational and time management skills and increased my ability to work as a role model and mediator for students and teachers.

As a keen sportsman, I haven represented my school at the highest level in badminton and cricket, amongst other sports, demonstrating my ability to work well in a team as well as proving my determination to succeed. Furthermore, through a Community Sports Leadership Award and the Air Training Corps, I have had the opportunity to successfully lead teams. Although my skills in football leave much to the imagination, I am in the process of completing a football refereeing course which offers the opportunity to think quickly and critically in pressured situations; a vital asset in dentistry. Aside from sporting activities, my hand-eye co-ordination and manual dexterity have been enhanced by recently starting to play the guitar, building a model Formula 1 car and constructing a telescope. My interest in astronomy has led me to reflect upon the roles of dentistry in outer space, under the influence of microgravity and how dental problems may be managed in long term space flight.

I am a sociable, enthusiastic and passionate person with a desire to contribute positively to society. Having witnessed only a fraction of what dentistry has to offer, I have discovered a vocation in which I can flourish, through a combination of my enthusiasm and personal attributes.

Remarks on Arjun's Personal Statement

Arjun's personal statement is elegantly written, with no flamboyant description or verbose language. From the beginning, he makes a strong case for himself as a budding dentist by emphasising his work experience and placements. He mentions that he has witnessed a range of dental procedures, such as fillings, denture construction and root canal treatments, but also includes what he learned while undertaking his work experiences. For example, he writes about the importance of building rapport, the value of clear communication when working in teams, and an understanding of private and NHS dentistry, which will prove useful in his future dental career.

The same reflective statements are seen in Arjun's paragraph about his academic background, where he mentions how studying his A-levels strengthened his understanding of anatomy and physiology, and the problem-solving skills that he gained. Throughout his personal statement, Arjun makes an effort to ensure that his experiences are relevant to dentistry, even in his paragraph about extracurricular activities, where he mentions manual dexterity as a benefit of playing the guitar. Arjun's statement carries a lot of weight because it is consistent, reflective, coherent and to the point.

Kwabena's Personal Statement

Offer from:

University of Oxford

Subject:

History and Politics

My experiences growing up in a London council estate have shown me why I need to be a catalyst for change. The turmoil of being mistreated by poorly organised local authorities led me to involve myself in politics so that I may one day be in a position of power in order to change the nature of the welfare state. I also believe that the importance of understanding political history is imperative in order to make meaningful decisions that benefit the policies of the future.

I often wondered why a significant number of people living in a developed nation like Britain were still struggling below the poverty line. Having first watched Ian Hislop's 'Workers or Shirkers' documentary, I was introduced to different attitudes towards helping the poor, mostly focusing on how they were supported by people such as Beatrice Webb and Edwin Chadwick. I then read *The Evolution of the British Welfare State* by historian Derek Fraser, introducing myself to the historical context behind Britain's poverty problem. The welfare state in 1945 aimed to provide 'cradle-to-grave' care for all eligible British citizens following the Second World War. However, researching for my EPQ on Universal Credit made me question how effective it has been in recent years. I explored many horrible accounts of how people in genuine need had been let down by an uncaring and bureaucratic welfare system. An Al-Jazeera TV debate I attended contested that Britain's increasing globalisation over the past century has meant that its institutions and public services now struggle to accommodate the needs of its ever-growing population. With all of this in mind, I concluded that the welfare state is ineffective in bringing people out of poverty, because it is more tailored towards the needs of the previous generation, and not for those of a larger, more diverse 21st-century population.

Wanting to learn more about the history of British poverty, BBC Radio 4's 'In Our Times' podcast showed me how historical attitudes towards poverty were associated with political affiliation. For example, Earl Grey's Whig government sent poor people to live in workhouses under the Poor Law of 1834, seeing poverty as a social disease. In contrast, the Beveridge Report of 1942 proposed the welfare state, as well as free healthcare and the expansion of National Insurance. Through these changes in policy, I saw that during the Industrial Revolution, Britain viewed the working class as victims of their own idleness and used workhouses as a deterrent against unemployment. However, after both World Wars, Britain supported the working-class more as they had suffered the most by contributing to the war effort. J.B Priestley, a gradualist author, furthered my interest in historical attitudes towards poverty through his play *An Inspector Calls*. He showcased how class inequalities in 1912 Britain had resulted in the ill-treatment of the working-class. Priestley wanted a new post-WW2 society that was more hospitable towards the poor as a result of the hardship the world had suffered following the Great Depression of 1929, as well as the chaos of both world wars.

Although I first lacked opportunities and had experienced personal issues during my education, I have always sought to break barriers and make a change in society. Raising £250 for the St. Hilda's East charity and marching against knife crime in East London allowed me to advocate for less advantaged people to fulfil their potential. As well as this, the Amos Bursary scholarship programme has given me a wider scope of the professional world, while also allowing me to reflect on my past to market myself as an open-minded individual with a unique perspective on the world.

Remarks on Kwabena's Personal Statement

Kwabena's personal statement is a riveting read because he focuses on depth and demonstrating academic insights and analysis, rather than just breadth. Since he is a history and politics student at Oxford, this is appropriate, as it is discussions of the kind that he outlines in his personal statement that he will be actively engaging in during tutorials and seminars at Oxford. Kwabena's explorations into the welfare state, poverty and socioeconomic trends throughout British history are illuminating, and he uses credible sources such as his readings of Derek Fraser's book *The Evolution of the British Welfare State* to provide background about how his own ideas have morphed over time. Kwabena also makes a conclusive statement about the welfare state being 'ineffective in bringing people out of poverty' owing to it being 'more tailored to the needs of the previous generation.' The fact that Kwabena is able to take a strong stance on an important point that remains a contentious issue in contemporary debate is a bold step, as he does not sit on the fence.

During parts of his personal statement, Kwabena writes in a manner that more closely resembles an academic essay, as he cites other sources, such as his explorations into government policies of the past, his Extended Project Qualification and even J.B. Priestley's *An Inspector Calls* to provide context for his commentary. This works in his favour because he demonstrates great analytical skills and a robust understanding of the various issues at play.

Overall, Kwabena's personal statement is strong because of its depth and academic exploration. He does not seek to cover as many bases as possible, but rather, picks an issue that is important to him and evaluates it thoroughly.

Oscar's Personal Statement

Offer From:

University of Cambridge

Subject:

Law

The experience I had living in Afghanistan, where laws denied me access to education, was what initially sparked my interest in law. In liberal democratic societies, the free access to education regardless of gender is seen as an inalienable right. This difference between the legal systems' concept of individual rights fascinates me and made me consider what the universal purpose of the law is.

Attempting to deepen my knowledge, I read *The Concept of Law* by H. L. A Hart. Hart argues that there is no necessary connection between law and morality. This argument was convincing as I believe that the law does not hold any such moral authority as unjust laws are possible and there are ethical areas where the law does not have a standpoint. This reflects my experience of living in Afghanistan where the laws enforcing gender discrimination were immoral under a liberal egalitarian moral framework. This led me to the conclusion that a law being identified as law derives from people believing they are obligated to follow it rather than it being inherently moral. I analysed other arguments regarding the connection between law and morality which led me to read *The Controversy Between Professor Hart and Professor Fuller* by G. Breckenridge. Fuller argues that the purpose of the legal system is to uphold 'the inner morality of law,' which I also found to be a compelling argument. The arguments put forward by both Hart and Fuller enhanced my understanding of the controversy surrounding what the purpose of the law is, which is a central topic I would like to further explore.

Having been introduced to the debates surrounding what the law should strive towards, I read *The Rule of Law* by T. Bingham. The book enhanced my understanding of how the rule of law helps reduce inequalities in which individuals would have arbitrary power — the focus of the Belmarsh case, which examined detention of international terror suspects. Could it be argued that due to the increased risk posed by terrorism that the law was justified? After reading Hart's chapter on justice and morality, I concluded that the demands of justice may sometimes be overridden to preserve something of greater value. In this case, national security. The contention surrounding what element of the law should hold precedence interests me greatly and is a debate I look forward to studying at university.

My interest in jurisprudence led me to consider how such principles are put into practice. This inspired me to undertake a placement at Freshfields where I developed an understanding of the legal work that commercial solicitors partake in. I analysed detailed legislation (Bribery Act of 2010) and applied it to the client's case. The clear aim of the act was to establish a strong anti-corruption regime, but I became aware of its shortcomings in poorly defining what 'adequate procedures' entails in practice. This demonstrated to me the discrepancy between the theory of law and the law in practice. The opportunity to study jurisprudence further is an exciting one, as my work experience and my further reading convinced me the philosophy behind laws and debates around the purpose of the law are important contemporary issues that are reflected in everyday life.

At my sixth form's debate club I have been able to examine different perspectives and argue for solutions to complex issues. I also put this into practice as a student leader where I represent different points of view and negotiate a consensus on organising events for the benefit of the community. This ability to readily evaluate and analyse different perspectives and effectively advocate for a solution will allow me to thrive in the study of law.

I now intend to study law at university as studying the fabric of the legal system will provide me with an opportunity to explore and debate contemporary legal issues as well as their role in society, which is a prospect that genuinely excites me.

Remarks on Oscar's Personal Statement

Oscar takes a deep dive into the foundation of our legal systems, having lived in Afghanistan, where he noticed differences in the laws there compared to other countries. The reference to H. L. A Hart and Lon L. Fuller is very appropriate when discussing and critiquing the core purpose of law. It stands to reason that Oscar would be curious about the origins and purpose of law, as he has observed that while liberal democratic societies champion free access to education regardless of gender, not all countries adhere to the same rights. Hart and Fuller espouse opposing views, as is known from the famous 'Hart-Fuller Debate,' and Oscar demonstrates a robust understanding of the conflicting arguments in this area and why they are important.

In his third paragraph, Oscar's description of the 'demands of justice' and elements of the law holding precedence are apt, as they show his understanding that enforcing the law is not always clear-cut and straightforward. His academic explorations come across as authentic, and his placement at Freshfields reaffirms his commitment and passion for law.

Generally, Oscar's personal statement covers many bases and ticks many boxes for a law student. He shows interesting academic insights, concrete experiences and passion.

Chloe's Personal Statement

Offer from:

University of Oxford

Subject:

Human Sciences

Scientific understanding is constantly growing, revealing answers to questions we have asked for hundreds of years. Research is integral to developing this understanding, whether by analysing microbes in a lab or observing human interactions. I aspire to contribute to this research and development to create real solutions for problems faced today. My interest was piqued by a podcast by geneticist Adam Rutherford and mathematician Hannah Fry. One episode explored the controversy of ancestry DNA tests and what they truly reveal. Genetic markers in DNA are identified and compared with those of others who have had their genome sequenced, the majority of whom are of European descent. I learned that these tests are not representative of all ethnicities, and that I had been mistaken in thinking that DNA samples trace our direct ancestors.

To expand my knowledge of what DNA reveals, I read Rutherford's book: *A Brief History of Everyone Who Ever Lived*. He mentions the discovery of Homo floresiensis remains in 2003, explaining how skeletal remains provide evidence for evolution and how we categorise our ancestors into different species. It led me to do further reading to learn why the discovery caused controversy. The bones found were small in skull size and stature. One theory suggests this was a helpful adaptation for island living; others suggest it is evidence of a pathological condition, like microcephaly. Multiple fossils of similar size were found, and it is improbable that they all suffered from microcephaly, hence why the island dwarfism theory is more compelling to me. Before reading this, I had never considered how we understood so much about our ancestors and their existence. It demonstrated the complexity of human evolution and how we evolved from our ancestors. It also showed the importance of an interdisciplinary approach; combining biology, geography and anthropology to link the fossils and the environment to explain the findings. Independent exploration into this discovery was riveting and gave me a real insight into evolution, and I am eager to broaden my understanding of this topic.

During the summer, I participated in several summer schools. The Sutton Trust Summer School involved subject lectures in biology and psychology. In a practical microbiology session, we learnt about culturing bacteria, using different agar to culture different bacteria. These lectures were a good insight into researching in microbiology and an exciting opportunity to develop my knowledge of practical methods. Another involved lectures on social and cultural anthropology, specifically on research in the field and reflecting on how public spaces are used by the community. This introduction to anthropological research methods and how ethnographers work showed me how research varies and how knowledge is gained in different disciplines. A further biology summer school involved conducting a virtual investigation with cell culture models to investigate potential anti-cancer drugs and conclude which should be recommended for clinical trials. Writing a lab report on the methods and results was a chance to develop analytical and research skills. I also wrote a discussion paper, learned how to cite references, and reflected on what I could improve after comparison with other research papers.

Outside of my studies, I am a keen participant in debate club. I am open minded, working with my peers to have friendly debates despite conflicting views. One of my favourite debates, surrounding the issue of cultural appropriation, allowed me to consider others' experiences and the differences between appreciation and appropriation. Exposure to, and discussion of, a variety of opinions is a valuable experience as it allows me to reflect on my views and why I have them.

Remarks on Chloe's Personal Statement

Chloe's personal statement packs a punch because it shows depth of thought and a genuine curiosity for various topics relating to human sciences. Her remarks about DNA, ancestry and island dwarfism are very interesting and revealing, and Chloe meanders through each of the topics that she covers with great ease and a robust understanding of the key issues. She is very reflective in statements such as this:

> *"I learned that these tests are not representative of all ethnicities, and that I had been mistaken in thinking that DNA samples trace our direct ancestors."*

This is very encouraging, as it shows that Chloe is inquisitive and is open to challenging her previously held beliefs and understanding.

Chloe builds upon her academic exploration in the latter half of her personal statement with strong supercurricular experiences, such as the lectures at summer schools. She learns key skills, such as research methods and writing lab reports, which she will be expected to continue to use once she becomes a student at Oxford. By demonstrating a degree of proficiency in those areas, as well as the right mindset to study human sciences, Chloe positions herself as the ideal student.

Henry's Personal Statement

Offer from:

University of Cambridge

Subject:

Veterinary Medicine

'Man's best friend' is a commonly used phrase that sums up much of our history and relationships with animals. These relationships, including those between other species, fascinate me greatly and it is by becoming a vet that I wish to contribute further towards the care and study of our animal companions. We value them as we value our family, therefore I wish to protect my clients' emotional well-being by providing essential care for their pets. I have seen some of the qualities vets must possess in order to carry out the multitude of tasks that benefit animals and indirectly their human companions. Determination and tenacity coupled with the belief that their actions are beneficial are vital to one's success as a vet.

My work experience has further taught me these values. During my two weeks of work experience at the local vets, in addition to the six months when I helped out each week after school, I have seen the rewards of rescuing an animal. One case I remember is the process of rescuing a stray dog that had suffered a broken pelvis and long term dislocated hip. The affection she showed towards everyone, despite the undoubtedly excruciating pain she must have felt, made me so pleased to see her well and adopted into a safe home. I also worked for two weeks on a livestock farm with pigs, sheep, cows and poultry including the weekly chicken slaughter, the weaning of lambs and piglets from their mothers and the process of tagging new calves. All this has taught me how the commercial side of our relationship with animals differs from the way we treat a family pet. I helped raise a litter of guide dog puppies and have had a weekend job at a stable yard since September. I benefit from all my animal related work experience, whether learning new things about vet practices and farms, such as animal husbandry, or reading about an animal orientated lifestyle in the books of James Herriot and

Monty Roberts.

Having so far revelled in my subjects at A level, I attained over 90% in the four courses I am taking to A2 and 100% in four of my module exams; I relish the prospect of further intensive study in the subjects I enjoy. The biological and chemical processes of life intrigue me so I am keen to learn more about how they can, together, achieve life. I extend my attention beyond just the obligatory studies of my subjects by taking part in further challenges. I have gained three gold and two silver awards in the UKMT Maths Challenge, including progressing on to the Olympiad round. Recently, I achieved a gold award in the Cambridge Chemistry Challenge; so with these achievements, as well as my inclusion in Mensa, I harbour great satisfaction in my academic ability. With school I went on the French exchange, through which I met many new people and was able to experience a different culture as well as share my own with others. I frequently volunteer to help at school events and in the past year have taken part in science fairs to teach primary school children all about the subjects I enjoy, sold the school to prospective students at the open evening and ran the BBQ at a recent school fund raiser.

Outside of lessons I am a keen sportsman, playing squash and football regularly. Since May, I have set up and run a 6-a-side team in a local league, where I keep the accounts and organise the team sheet, as well as playing for another 5-a-side team. I have completed my Bronze Duke of Edinburgh award and am half way to achieving my Gold. Expeditions to the Lake District and Snowdonia have provided a fantastic opportunity to develop team and organisational skills especially on the former when we coped with unexpected challenging circumstances.

To conclude, I have great ambition to succeed in the challenge of becoming a vet and playing a major role in the community, helping animals and their owners to have a better quality of life. I aspire to develop exciting new techniques in medicine, like Noel Fitzpatrick, which might spill over into human health care.

Remarks on Henry's Personal Statement

Henry's personal statement has a structure that is easy to follow. He establishes his narrative clearly in his introduction as one of compassion and care. He remarks on the widely-known description for dogs as 'man's best friend,' but does so broadly, in reference to the relationship with animals and humans.

Henry dives straight into his extensive work experience for his second paragraph. This works well because veterinary medicine is a subject within which practical work is a constant necessity. It makes sense that he reassures the admissions tutor that he has a strong background here.

With each experience, Henry writes reflectively. For example:

"All this has taught me how the commercial side of our relationship with animals differs from the way we treat a family pet."

Henry has done exceedingly well academically, having attained full marks in four of his modules. While listing academic results in a personal statement is not encouraged, Henry's remarkable grades are worthy of highlighting. He also has a wealth of extracurricular activities that portray him as a highly intelligent and well-rounded student.

Chelsie's Personal Statement

Offer from:

King's College London

Subject:

MA in Medical Ethics and Law

My reasoning for wanting to study this MA encompasses four main areas: my academic interest, volunteering experiences in the medical field, my future career aspirations, and knowledge gained at the Department of Health during a summer internship.

Throughout my undergraduate degree in law, I have studied a variety of modules that have enabled me to engage with interesting legal and ethical dilemmas, such as assisted dying, the moral duty to save lives, and mental capacity. Because of this interest in legal and ethical issues, I tailored the third year of my degree to focus more on medical and science-based topics. My dissertation focuses on exploring the ethical challenges posed by germline genome editing and considering whether the technology should be used and what constraints may be required if its use is to be permissible. I am taking a module on mental health and mental capacity law. One of my tutors on this module, Isra Black, is an alumnus of the MA. I have had a very enlightening, in depth conversation with him about modules, course structure, teaching and the university, which left me with a clear understanding of what this course entails and a keenness to study it. This MA will provide an opportunity to learn new things as well as fulfilling my academic interests by revisiting topics from my undergraduate degree and exploring them further at a higher level.

In addition to my academic interests, I undertake medically related roles that I balance alongside my final year of undergraduate study. I am a volunteer for a language and speech therapy charity that provides support to individuals with aphasia and work as a hospital assistant at York Hospital, which involves aiding nurses and providing care to patients. The ability to study moral issues that arise in medical practice, such as those covered on the 'Moral Theory and Medical Ethics' module, will be directly applicable to the work I do and my future career aspirations. I am exploring pursuing a graduate medicine degree and a subsequent career in the medical profession. Developing a deeper understanding of the law surrounding the medical field will enable me to put the knowledge gained from the course into practice and be better informed to help patients, and to empathise with the staff I work with.

During the summer of 2019, I interned at the Ministry of Justice in London, which enabled me to spend time shadowing fellow civil servants at the Department of Health. Discussing upcoming policy with communication and policy leads exposed me to some of the issues that the National Health Service is facing, such as limited funding and staff shortages. Studying and debating the allocation of resources and medical dilemmas on this course will allow me to link the insights gained at the Department of Health with the academic study that underpins the policy decisions to consolidate my comprehension of this area.

In summary, the completion of this MA will provide the appropriate step required to enter into the medical field, enabling me to further pursue and develop and my knowledge of this area. I would relish the opportunity to conduct further study into my academic areas of interest that I can use to enhance my patient care and performance when working within the medical profession.

Remarks on Chelsie's Personal Statement

Chelsie's personal statement has a robust structure and is elegantly written. She outlines her reasons for wanting to study the MA at King's College London right from the beginning, as she cites her academic interest, volunteering experiences in the medical field, future career aspirations, and knowledge gained at the Department of Health as the core pillars. By making this clear in her introduction, she makes her personal statement easy to follow.

Chelsie comes from a legal background, but ethical debates surrounding her areas of study, such as 'assisted dying, the moral duty to save lives, and mental capacity,' prompted her to tailor her third year more toward medical and scientific topics. She strengthens her personal statement by expounding on her dissertation, which focussed on genome editing, and how the decision to take a module on mental health and mental capacity law provided support for her dedication to medical ethics and law.

Chelsie's mentioning of Isra Black — an alumnus of the MA that she applied for — was a positive addition to her personal statement because an admissions tutor might perceive Chelsie more favourably upon learning that she has engaged with a person they may personally know. It highlights a connection and commonality that would otherwise have not been known. Chelsie also takes a specific interest in the module, 'Moral Theory and Medical Ethics,' which is excellent, as it demonstrates that she has undertaken research that is specific to King's College London, rather than generic. She also has solid work experience and summarises her points succinctly in her conclusion. Overall, this is a strong personal statement, and Chelsie presents herself in a positive way.

Martin's Personal Statement

Offer from:

University of Birmingham

Subject:

Medicine

I was once struck by three words on a poster. The caption, 'Enable – don't disable' hit a chord because it mirrored my beliefs. My long term aim is to make a difference, by enabling the less fortunate, sick and disabled to lead more productive and rewarding lives through medical intervention.

When I became involved at a centre for children with autistic spectrum disorders, the experience proved invaluable in offering me an insight into their lives. I developed the patience, sensitivity and empathy required to care for vulnerable children and to assist with the individualised support programmes necessary to help maximise the progress a child with autism can make. I have gained first-hand knowledge of patient care within different areas of health care. Becoming a voluntary assistant in a nursing home brought me into close contact with the elderly, many of whom had dementia. I was surprised by patients with acute short term memory problems who had no trouble recalling the distant past. But, by reading various books and articles in medical journals, I now have a deeper understanding of the illness. Working with the elderly is extremely rewarding and it has greatly enhanced my listening skills. I have matured a great deal by helping at a local hospice and I will continue by assisting with the provision of palliative care of patients once a week during the next six months.

I was privileged to have shadowed doctors at an NHS GP surgery and a private health clinic. This enabled me to appreciate the varied nature of general medical practice, the importance of effective doctor-patient communication, and the role of primary healthcare within the wider NHS. Further time spent in an A&E department unveiled the importance of teamwork and the multi-disciplinary approach to patient care. While there I witnessed the resuscitation of a patient who had suffered a myocardial infarction. The relentless way with which the team administered CPR successfully was admirable, yet I appreciate that on occasions, despite the tireless efforts of the team, patients do not survive.

I fully realise that to aspire to a career in medicine requires a fastidious approach to everything that I do. I possess an enquiring and logical mind and excel when confronted by significant challenges, however, I also believe in the need to remain humble, to act sensitively towards the feelings of others and to be prepared to always give more than I take. My role in a team was essential when I took part in a debating competition, which covered topical issues within politics, such as ethical questions regarding euthanasia and organ donation. This experience was transformative and helped to strengthen my communication skills and confidence in presenting my ideas to others.

I am an ambassador for a local charity where I have participated in campaigns about issues such as fair trade. As a keen sportsman, I took my school football team to the County Cup four times, and to further enhance my team building and interpersonal skills I participated in the Duke of Edinburgh Award Scheme. During a busy schedule, I play the piano or become involved in my other interests: creative writing, poetry, painting and chess. I am also an avid writer, and was short-listed to the final ten contestants for a nationwide competition. I was also appointed as a mentor to my peers and lower year students in mathematics and chemistry and I have gained a silver award in the Biology Olympiad and for Mathematics.

I eagerly anticipate being able to combine my innate concern for the well-being of others, my good communication and organisational skills and my conscientious attitude towards academic work to pursue a career in medicine.

Remarks on Martin's Personal Statement

Martin's personal statement makes a strong impression due to his focus on work experience within medicine. Martin also demonstrates curiosity and a willingness to learn about areas that are obscure to him. For example:

> *"I was surprised by patients with acute short term memory problems who had no trouble recalling the distant past. But, by reading various books and articles in medical journals, I now have a deeper understanding of the illness."*

It is reassuring to know that Martin took the time to learn more about the debilitating illnesses of the patients in the care home. Thereafter, as he mentions his work experience at a GP surgery, Martin includes several reflective statements about how he has learned about teamwork, effective doctor-patient communication, and the role of primary healthcare within the NHS.

Martin's extracurricular activities are extensive — from high-level sports to the Biology Olympiad. These are all commendable and they add colour to his character. His conclusion is short and to the point, as he merely reiterates his original goal to use his skills in a manner that helps other patients through healthcare.

Phoebe's Personal Statement

Offer from:

University of Manchester

Subject:

Psychology

Having experienced personal mental health issues, I chose to take psychology at A-level, partially to help me gain a better understanding of myself but also due to its importance and relevance that it has in everyday life. I very quickly found it to be a fascinating subject which I have thoroughly enjoyed studying, and I have found my personal situation has given me a valuable insight and deeper understanding of some of the topics. I quickly came to realise that this was a subject I wanted to continue to study beyond A-level with a view to using my personal experience to help others, both academically and professionally.

As with my other A-level subjects, I have committed myself to my studies of psychology. I have built on the study skills I started to develop for my GCSEs to develop a disciplined and effective study and revision procedure which has allowed me to stay on top of my coursework and also given me time to undertake personal further research into some of the aspects of the subject that have been of particular interest, such as schizophrenia. I enjoy finding out how the biology of the brain is related to the onset of psychological disorder. As well as watching a range of TV programs (both documentaries and dramas portraying mental health issues), I have taken advantage of the wide range of material available on the internet, including videos and podcasts. Using the internet as a resource has also allowed me to develop skills such as assessing resource quality.

Outside of my core A-level subjects which include geography and maths, I have also elected to undertake an EPQ to help develop my research skills. The topic for my EPQ had to be independent of my A-level subjects, yet I still wanted to study something aligned to my interest in psychology. I chose to research the effects of captivity on the mental well-being of animals and have drawn on personal research from the internet, international zoos, vets and students of this subject.

Although my study schedule is demanding, I still recognise the importance of making time for extra-curricular activities, as I am very creative and enjoy expressing myself in different ways. I enjoy playing the flute and piano, currently working towards my Grade 8 flute and Grade 4 piano, and committed to repeat the distinction or merit passes I have achieved in previous exams. My music has given me a great number of opportunities, including the chance to play flute with the National Children's Orchestra of Great Britain. I am also a keen hockey player of high ability and play for my school and my local club's Ladies' First Team. I have been fortunate to have had the chance to travel to some interesting destinations with my family and have enjoyed and learned much from my travel experiences. A recent trip to the Dominican Republic and the chance to see the real country beyond the holiday resorts gave me a fascinating insight and first-hand knowledge which I applied to my A-level to further my geographical knowledge.

I have undertaken two work experience placements. The first was when I was selected to assist teachers in running a remote Outward Bound type activity course which saw me working with and supporting the staff in delivering a range of active training to 200 Year 7 pupils over the course of a week. For my formal work experience placement over the summer, I was unable to secure a placement relating to psychology as I had hoped for, but instead chose to work in a charity shop for a week. I have been appointed by my school as a School Ambassador which sees me representing the school to parents and children and assisting staff with open days and similar presentations. I have also undertaken the 4-week National Citizen Service (NCS) course which allowed me to develop valuable skills such as first aid, while strengthening my teamwork and communication skills. During NCS, my group raised over £1000 for charity. I am very proud of this achievement as I know that I have helped people in need.

Remarks on Phoebe's Personal Statement

Phoebe is open and honest about having experienced personal mental health issues, and from the beginning of the personal statement, the reader gathers that Phoebe is curious about herself and the importance of mental health in a wider context.

Phoebe mentions schizophrenia and how the biology of the brain is related to the onset of psychological disorder, which demonstrates a genuine interest in understanding how and why psychological disorders arise. When writing about the effects of captivity on the mental well-being of animals, Phoebe introduces an illuminating topic to the reader, as most students might solely have chosen to write about psychology as it pertains to humans, not animals. This topic is not expounded upon further, but is a valuable resource for Phoebe to develop in an interview.

Phoebe's range of extracurricular activities are impressive — from musical talents to hockey-playing at her local club. Her work experience with other pupils is valuable to mention in this personal statement, as it may have improved her communication skills, which are important in her field. Phoebe is honest about not being able to secure work experience related to psychology, but manages to demonstrate transferable skills. She generally presents herself very well.

Alec's Personal Statement

Offer from:

University of Cambridge

Subject:

History and Economics

My passion for history was sparked by my interest in global politics and foreign affairs. I am particularly interested in the transition from authoritarian dictatorships to stable democracies and the effect on the people caught up in it. Most importantly, the nature of history satisfies my curiosity about the events that have shaped the world today and I enjoy discovering details of the human factors at play.

I completed an independent research project on the role of Anthony Eden in the Suez Crisis following Nasser's nationalisation of the canal. This event was unique in its significance not only in the context of Britain's colonial demise, but also in the wider context of the Cold War. My study of Eden's correspondence with Eisenhower revealed Eden's increasingly paranoid thinking and exposed a critical breakdown in communication during the height of the crisis. The Suez crisis can broadly be viewed as a clash between the new, post-war, world order and the pre-war generation running the country. However, I concluded that the assertion that the crisis was the fault of Eden's paranoia alone was unfounded; factors such as Nasser's provocative belligerence should also be taken into account. This project also shed light on Britain's current global position and helped to explain her foreign policy.

The Cold War's impact on the Suez Crisis encouraged me to explore the collapse of the USSR focussing on the GDR's transition from police state to secure democracy and the consequent impacts on the East German people. The symbolic power of the Berlin Wall carried immense weight and I discovered that long after it had been torn down, Berliners experienced, 'die Mauer im Kopf.' Moreover, an established suspicion of neighbours, borne of the fact that one in seven East Germans were paid Stasi informants, contributed to an uneasy transition from a divided to a nominally united Germany. Timothy Garton Ash's *The Magic Lantern* elucidated several prominent trends in the process of democratisation, describing The GDR's transition as a 'refolution.' Crucially, I learned the importance of detachment when evaluating historical events that evoke a visceral emotional reaction, such as the fall of the Berlin Wall. My study of this period has been particularly useful in my analysis of events in Belarus, thus demonstrating the role of history in the present.

A school university preparation programme on social relations in Early Modern England emphasised how little I knew about the day to day lives of the people we were taught about in our A-Level courses. Studying the extent to which kin or neighbourliness were more important to those living in this period, I learned that this question relied on unquantifiable emotions and that semantic differences between anachronistic terms such as 'family,' could fatally undermine an historian's judgement. Refuting JA Sharpe's view that an increasingly litigious society was indicative of the strength of neighbourliness, I argued that the period saw a retreat into insular households. Furthermore, I encountered the challenge of structural bias in attempting to judge the role of gender in a period where historians are starved of sources from a female perspective.

As school captain I have developed a range of skills, not least the ability to organise and motivate a large team and articulate convincing arguments. Outside the classroom, I enjoy representing my school in both cricket and rugby. I take an avid interest in global current affairs, reading widely on foreign policy and global politics. I coach at my local cricket club and for the school rugby team. I volunteered at a food bank during the height of the coronavirus pandemic and am working towards completing my gold Duke of Edinburgh's Award. I am interested in learning more about the historical factors that have shaped our present geopolitical reality and in honing my historical research and critical reasoning skills.

Remarks on Alec's Personal Statement

Alec's personal statement is highly reflective, analytical and insightful, which makes it a pleasant read. He starts off his statement by defining what his specific interest is:

> *"...The transition from authoritarian dictatorships to stable democracies, and the effect on the people caught up in it."*

This sets his narrative, and we see his explorations match this narrative throughout the essay. His commentary on Anthony Eden's role in the Suez Crisis is interesting due to the stances that he takes and his analysis. For example, he describes the Suez Crisis as 'a clash between the new, post-war, world order and the pre-war generation running the country,' but concludes that the assertion that 'the crisis was the fault of Eden's paranoia alone was unfounded' and that Nasser's provocative belligerence should also be taken into account. It is interesting to actually read Alec's opinions on the issue, rather than him merely describing the Suez Crisis without much critical thinking and discussion of the key issues at play. This same level of analysis is seen in his ensuing commentary about the Berlin Wall. Alec's remarks on early modern England are equally insightful, and this curiosity and depth of thought remains a strength throughout his personal statement.

Clive's Personal Statement

Offer from:

London School of Economics

Subject:

Law

A society without laws is like a body without a skeleton. The diverse scope of law and its potency to shape people's lives particularly appeals to me. I found the issues concerning the retreat from human rights rather absorbing and I sought to understand the power of legal intervention in maintaining the rules on which society is governed. I was enlightened by Helena Kennedy's *Just Law*, which portrayed the erosion of civil liberties as commonplace in the legal system. Further reading of Aung San Suu Kyi's *Freedom from Fear* brought to light the ruthless consequences of human rights infringement on innocent people. The ability to apply my analytical and problem-solving skills to communicate and develop cogent arguments drives my interest in the wider law.

Spending time at a criminal law firm provided me with practical experience of sorting legal documents, reading cases and recognising similarities between them. My listening and reasoning abilities proved invaluable when given the opportunity to shadow barristers in court. The meticulous way in which cases were prepared and delivered was a great lesson. During an assault trial, I found dissecting arguments, evaluating accounts and evidence exciting in order to reach the final verdict. Several weeks at a Magistrates' Court, brought a range of interesting legal cases and on one occasion I seized the opportunity to discuss the points of a civil dispute with a judge after the hearings. Further exposure to serious cases at the Royal Courts of Justice emphasised the emotional detachment required in the legal profession. My work experience has reinforced my confidence that law will be a fascinating and evolving field to study and work in.

Studying A-Level physics and maths has greatly strengthened my ability to learn and process large volumes of text without compromising attention to detail. In long Physics questions, applying this information to different scenarios required accurate and critical observation under time constraints. As head maths mentor, I enjoyed communicating these skills to fellow peers and this helped me to improve my own lateral thinking. Issues concerning designer babies in Biology to the synthesis of energy in chemistry sparked numerous legal debates and my essay on green chemistry won an award. Reading *The Economist* and *The Guardian* continues to provide groundwork for understanding global issues. As the a volunteer for a local charity, I enjoyed raising awareness on pertinent issues, such as animal rights through public speaking at events and conferences. For three consecutive tenures, I was elected chairman of the school council, a role in which I showed responsibility and trustworthiness, as I served the community and sought to address their needs and concerns. I admire the collaborative efforts that can make a difference in school communities and the nation as a whole.

Last year, I took part in a public speaking competition with my observations on how our identities change as we mature into adulthood and I was delighted to be featured in my school's magazine. I also established a podcast where I discuss a variety of topics, such as bullying and youth crime. As a keen sportsman, I represented my school's lacrosse team — a sport that serves as a much needed catharsis during extremely busy periods of study. I also enjoy sculpting, poetry, playing the cello, and rugby. During a year's voluntary work, I was privileged to work with special needs children and this tested my ability to empathise and communicate with others. I pride myself on my empathy, which I hope to infuse into the field of law, and I am eager to do so upon graduation.

My experiences and skills attest to my aspiration to study the challenging, enjoyable subject of law and ultimately to work in the legal system.

Remarks on Clive's Personal Statement

Clive's personal statement reads well due to its simplicity and robust structure. The first line of his personal statement is a general statement, but it gives indication of the important role that law plays within society:

"A society without laws is like a body without a skeleton."

Thereafter, Clive's commentary on civil liberties and human rights abuses are both powerful and relevant to his interests, and serves to reinforce his opening line pertaining to the fundamental need for laws in a functioning society. Clive visited the Royal Courts of Justice and a Magistrate's Court, which is commendable. However, his strengths emerge when he writes reflectively about what those experiences meant to him:

"During an assault trial, I found dissecting arguments, evaluating accounts and evidence exciting in order to reach the final verdict."

Beyond his academic undertakings, Clive has also been very vocal in his school community, having taken part in public speaking competitions and established a podcast. These all present him as a confident and passionate person.

Angela's Personal Statement

Offer from:

School of Oriental and African Studies

Subject:

Law and Social Anthropology

Non-Western and Western societies vary in gender roles and socially constructed ideology. Yet, patriarchy is prominent in the United Kingdom and Ghana, restricting some women to the domestic sphere which limits them in the workplace and politics. This course especially explores gender. This is a social construct I am curious to learn greater context about, as laws, norms and values are built on a consensus. However, throughout history women have remained disadvantaged.

My self-interest in true crime created even more awareness of how law and society interlink. Through watching documentaries, I observed a pattern. Gender related laws are passed after an unfortunate ordeal, because of public campaigning and societies changes in perception and outlook. Jane Clough was a victim of domestic violence and 'Jane's Law' created pivotal outcomes for defendants since they are given a second opportunity to be vocal about why they believe their perpetrator should not be granted bail. The legislation for domestic violence requires funding, policies and mandatory police training to approach the delicate subject for successful change.

My study of sociology at A-level has introduced me to the concept of the 'dark figure of crime' relating to the domestic and sexual violence not recorded and the significance of socialisation. Education of culturally and socially constructed gender expectations gives rise to pressure on how to behave. Furthermore, our criminal justice system and societal norms are as complicit as each other in protecting women through ineffective laws and the difference in socialisation of the sexes. Studying religious studies has enabled me to focus on moral dilemmas and made me consider how the effectiveness of laws can be unachievable due to social problems. Discussing controversial issues in class emphasised how universal laws for the public are a flaw of the criminal justice system. Watching 'The Innocence Files' documentary investigating America's infamously harsh court system, enabled me to compare the development of legislation to improve human rights in the UK and the problems facing our penal system. I understood how ineffective capital punishment was and is as a deterrent, creating miscarriages of justice, especially in cases where compassion and leniency was vital for unbiased sentencing rather than portraying a message to society.

I practised and learnt the effectiveness of critical thinking and research skills by undertaking 'The BMJ' human resources virtual work experience, where I was tasked to provide a solution for a disciplinary hearing. This taught me the importance of being well informed and balanced in order to provide a fair judgement. Additional Springpod virtual law work experience enhanced my interest in learning about the many laws which govern society, such as employment law. As a member of the Debate Club in secondary school, I obtained collaborative skills and an ability to remain open-minded to others' opinions and to compromise within a team. I was also a library monitor which taught me key organisational and communication skills when assisting individuals. Volunteering at school open days has been a chance to effectively represent the student body. Reading a range of media has made me more socially aware of the need to accurately record the effects of events on society.

I express my creativity as an avid writer and reader of poetry. Researching my Extended Project Qualification enabled me to view the progression in policing, as a result of new definitions of crime emphasising society's continuous changes.

I am enjoying the task of writing a well-informed, balanced dissertation with a concise well-argued conclusion.

I am committed to deepening my perspective on effective legal processes as a solution to societal issues. My initiative as an individual to immerse myself fully in my studies portrays how I will go above and beyond for this degree at your academic institution.

Remarks on Angela's Personal Statement

Angela starts off her personal statement with commentary on the prevalence of patriarchy and its impact on women in the workplace and politics:

> *"Yet, patriarchy is prominent in the United Kingdom and Ghana, restricting some women to the domestic sphere which limits them in the workplace and politics."*

She explains why these issues are important, as laws, norms and values are built on consensus, and also emphasises why the course she is applying to would be of particular interest to her, owing to its focus on gender issues. This is an effective way to make her look like a more favourable candidate for this course, as she has a specific interest in the SOAS curriculum.

Throughout the rest of her personal statement, Angela remains reflective and insightful, as she not only describes her experience but mentions what she learned from each — such as the BMJ human resources virtual work experience and the debate club at school. Overall, her writing is very good.

John's Personal Statement

Offer from:

London School of Economics

Subject:

Law

For me, studying the Law LLB will be enjoyable, as it will be constantly challenging, deeply intriguing and highly rewarding at the end of the process. I am really inspired and motivated by the opportunities that the law course will provide. For example, the LLB covers a range of different types of law, which would enable me to work in an array of legal establishments. This is beneficial as it widens my choice of careers, giving me the flexibility to experience different sectors of law before specialising in one area.

Studying at undergraduate level would be suited to me as I already have background knowledge in law, including recent changes to the public legal system of the country, for example, the impact of the Constitutional Reform Act of 2005 in the United Kingdom. This was because the act removed the judicial powers of the Lords and transferred them to the Supreme Court of the United Kingdom, which guarantees a fair and impartial trial for all cases tried in the court — that being the fundamental idea behind the legal system.

Criminal Law will be an interesting module of the LLB for me. I would like to become a barrister for a big, successful city law firm, so I would relish the opportunity to investigate, learn and read around this aspect of law. I also have an interest in International Law, recognising the problems that arise. For example, if two people in a marital partnership were living in two countries were to divorce, which country's judiciary would they use? I hope to investigate similar problems and solutions to further my knowledge.

Aside from my growing knowledge in law, I believe I have the skills to study it, which I have developed through my A-Level subjects. For example, English language requires me to analyse a group of texts and then classify them based on certain rules, such as purpose, audience and mode of transmission. I must then apply my subject knowledge when analysing the text to discover its pragmatic and hidden features. History and religious studies are also great foundations in preparation to study law, as they require deductive skills. In History, I formulate an argument and a conclusion based on a range of sometimes fallible sources. In R. E., I have to understand the meaning behind philosophers' viewpoints to understand the concept of an argument. These skills will help while studying law, allowing me to pick out relevant information in legal documents, ignoring less essential detail such as repetitive disclaimers. By sorting out what can be applied to the case given, I feel I can progress through the law course, with credit given to the skills I have learnt during my studies at A-Level. It has also taught me the 'creative power of thinking,' to think clearly, carefully and independently. I have kept a consistently high initiative, which will help me with research and analysis assignments during the LLB. These skills, shown in my consistently high school reports and grades, will help me throughout the three year course.

During my time at St Mary's College, I have been involved in lots of extra-curricular activities that have developed my skills and character. In sixth form, I have been involved in the school newspaper, *The Messenger*, firstly as a writer, and as the editor this year, where I am responsible for recruiting and managing a team of writers, assigning articles which suit their writing style and interests. I have developed leadership skills, as I have to be a good communicator and listener to get pupils writing for the paper, yet I have to be firm on those who do not finish articles on time. By striking a balance, I can be a good editor and colleague to work with. This will help me in university life, in aspects such as group seminars and other activities such as managing societies.

I am aware that law is a challenging course that will push me to my limits. However, my desire to achieve will always be at the forefront of my motivation, and this will help me overcome the challenges of the course.

Remarks on John's Personal Statement

John demonstrates a curiosity about law with his commentary on the Constitutional Reform Act of 2005 and the way that it removed judicial powers of the Lords and transferred them to the Supreme Court of the United Kingdom. He taps into one of the core pillars of the legal system — a fair and impartial trial — showing that he understands why this subject is important.

John's strengths emerge in his reflective writing about his A-levels, where he mentions the value that each subject has brought to his learning. As a law student, analysis of texts is a regular practice, and therefore, mentioning how his English literature A-level helped him in this regard is appropriate. Similarly, his reference to the benefits of deductive skills from having studied religious studies and history are equally relevant for a law student. Beyond the classroom, John has also been proactive with his school newspaper, and he is not shy about writing about the scope of responsibilities that he had in this capacity. This demonstrates leadership, organisational skills and a sense of purpose, which stand him in good stead as a future law student.

Esther's Personal Statement

Offer from:

University of Manchester

Subject:

Modern History with Economics

The current curriculum is not inclusive. It fails to depict all the sides of British history, the good and the deplorable. During lockdown, I founded a campaign called 'Black History Matters' on social media, which educated people on key overlooked Black British figures such as Harold Moody. I was invited by Warwick University to be a keynote speaker for a webinar called 'The UK Curriculum: Our Fight for Education Equality,' where I spoke about the importance of the inclusion of different perspectives and narratives in the UK curriculum and the small steps that can be taken to ensure this. For a few years, I have been investing in looking beyond the perspectives presented to me in my curriculum and unearthing different viewpoints. Studying economics and history would allow me to explore the symbiotic relationship between the two, giving me the knowledge to analyse past events and use economic theories and concepts to infer about the future. I am particularly interested in the rise of the British Empire and the impact of colonialism and imperialism on the African economies and policies used to combat postcolonial issues. In order to maintain a favourable macroeconomic environment in this situation, investments in agriculture and technology may prove essential to promote longer-term growth.

The interplay of trade, exploration and competition for scarce resources is a powerful force in history and current economic interactions, crystallised in the rise of colonial empires. Interested in issues of colonialism and the historical and economical effects, I decided to attend lectures examining aspects of the Empire that are often misinterpreted, including 'The Indian Uprising of 1857-8' by Dr Sean Lang and 'The Ending of Slavery in the Nineteenth-Century World' by Professor Adam Smith during a history study day at University

College, Oxford. These lectures reinforced my interest in Modern History and in how 19th century colonialism and British imperialism affected global areas such as West Africa, Australia, and India. This led me to read *A Fistful of Shells* by Toby Green, which explores the commercial ties Africa had with Europe before colonialism. My interest in the economic forces that have shaped history has led me to read books such as *Thinking Fast and Slow* by Daniel Kahneman, which highlights human cognitive biases and susceptibility to 'nudges.' I pursued this further by undertaking a University of Toronto online course entitled 'Behavioural Economics in Action,' which elucidates how governments can exploit these weaknesses and utilise them to influence human behaviour.

Many historical events have an economic base, for example, the French Revolution where the agrarian crisis of 1788-89 generated discontent and rage caused by food shortages. The Revolution highlighted the unfair tax system under the Ancien Regime, and the outcome of the unrest in France was the establishment of a uniform tax system, which was based mostly on an individual's income. Also, my work experiences at Deloitte UK and PwC have increased my commercial awareness and helped me to understand how taxes and other economic policies can affect businesses and clients. From this, I gained insights into how large firms adapt to economic occurrences such as the recession and infer from historical events (2008 credit crunch) to adapt their strategies and to maintain a high level of efficiency.

My positions as president of my school's Afro-Caribbean Society, head of the gospel choir and a school monitor (prefect) have helped me develop my interpersonal skills, as my roles have entailed events management, team-building, public speaking and balancing extracurricular activities and academic commitments. In the future, I would like to work in the finance and technology sector and studying economics and history will give me an excellent foundation. I am excited about deepening and exploring my interests further at university.

Remarks on Esther's Personal Statement

Esther's personal statement stands out because it focuses on a specific critique, being personal, and showing deep reflection on important issues. The first line of her personal statement clearly indicates the observations that Esther will make in the rest of her statement.

"The current curriculum is not inclusive. It fails to depict all the sides of British history, the good and the deplorable."

By taking a very specific stance in a key area of interest, Esther makes her writing come across as very compelling to read. She is eager to examine the history of the British Empire and the impact of colonialism and imperialism on economics in Africa, as well as Australia and India. The reference to Daniel Kahneman's *Thinking Fast and Slow* is interesting because it demonstrates that Esther is keen to understand cognitive biases as a tool for understanding why people think the way that they do, which is a key skill. Her description of the 'symbiotic' relationship between history and economics is apt, and uncovering the economic origins of the French Revolution further supports this stance.

Will's Personal Statement

Offer from:

University of St Andrews

Subject:

Medicine

The opportunity for endless research due to the ever-changing knowledge from medical breakthroughs suggests that medicine is a vast and dynamic subject, something which deeply motivates me. The complexity and the personal impact of patient care and support learnt through work experience placements strengthened my desire to delve deeper into this occupation.

Visiting different wards and clinics at Addenbrooke's Hospital gave me an insight into the skills and roles of a doctor. Witnessing interactions with patients during their time of anxiety, be it consultation or a major operation, taught me the importance of regular and effective patient-doctor communication. This was demonstrated during a kidney biopsy when the doctor's compassionate approach toward the distressed patient as he guided him through the relatively painful process showed how kindness in a medical setting could go a long way. The placement also gave me an opportunity to come across rare conditions such as Behcet's disease, where the cause is yet to be known. This suggests that there is the potential to explore and find cures through further advancements in the field of medicine.

Volunteering at a care home with elderly patients with dementia and Alzheimer's gave me an insight into how nurses deal with agitated patients. This experience demonstrated that as a healthcare professional, human empathy is crucial, highlighting to me that medicine is as much an art form as a science-based profession. Shadowing a pharmacist and volunteering at a pharmacy has helped me appreciate the roles of the multidisciplinary team within the NHS. The role of allied health professionals helps build a culture of appreciation and respect, which is an important aspect of the values of the NHS. The unfortunate emergence of a global pandemic fuelled my desire to help patients by becoming a vaccine volunteer. This experience has taught me crucial skills in dealing with high-pressure situations, which mirrors a doctor's duty of making logical decisions in an intense environment during rigorous patient consultations.

The book, *A Beautiful Mind*, inspired me to write an extended project qualification titled, 'How much of a threat does cannabis use in adolescence pose compared to the genetic risks for the development of schizophrenia?' By analysing the literature and extracting information, I was able to understand the fundamentals of medical research, creatively think in relation to the structure of the essay and use my critical judgement with advice from my supervisor to make logical decisions. In the future, I hope to conduct primary research into the neurology of the endocannabinoid system to gain a deeper understanding of the complexities of mental illnesses.

Beyond academia, I have achieved a merit in Grade 8 keyboard; I play cricket and regularly meditate. This is important as time-management of activities whilst prioritising the importance of work will help reduce the stress of a doctor's intense schedule. In addition, organising a charity event to raise awareness for a rare genetic disorder, being a school prefect and managing the distribution of food at a temple have all helped me to develop my personal and interpersonal skills whilst improving my teamwork and leadership skills. Through my experience at a hospital and in healthcare, I have realised that these skills are needed throughout the NHS to improve a patient's quality of life. As biology captain in charge of innovation, trying to create the best resources for struggling students taught me a data-driven approach to problem-solving. By shadowing doctors on a ward round, I learned that this chain of thought is a crucial skill used in medicine.

Through varying encounters, my critical thinking, compassion and leadership skills have developed and have given me the tenacity to succeed in this demanding career. The combination of logistics and the humanity of medicine propel me to pursue this incredible career as a doctor.

Remarks on Will's Personal Statement

With an abundance of work experience, Will has a lot of material to work with in this personal statement, and he uses this to his advantage. The work experience placements that he mentions are visiting different wards and clinics in Addenbrooke's Hospital, volunteering at a care home with elderly patients with dementia and Alzheimer's, shadowing a pharmacist and volunteering at a pharmacy. It is encouraging to see how reflective Will is about each of these work experience placements, as he shares the lessons learned and the insights that he had, rather than merely producing a list of what he did. For example, he mentions 'the importance of regular and effective patient-doctor communication,' which is very appropriate within medicine. From his voluntary role at the care home, he learned about empathy, and at the pharmacy, he learned the importance of multidisciplinary teams within the NHS. All of these are highly sought-after qualities for a budding medic, and Will's charity event and prefect role also demonstrate the impact that he has had within his school community.

Abigail's Personal Statement

Offer from:

Middlesex University

Subject:

Law

My interest in Law developed after reading the case of Stephen Lawrence, where recognition of institutional racism became widespread. I believe that law is a set of rules which a designated country recognises as a regulator for all its people's behaviour including those of different ethnic backgrounds. However, certain laws which are put in place such as Section 60 of the Criminal Justice and Public Order Act 1994 exemplifies how those in power can abuse the system since, the 'Stop and Search' process mainly targets black people, who are nine times more likely to be stopped, compared to their white counterparts in the UK today. Hence my commitment to studying law at university, as I will ensure that equality for all people will be my main concern.

In order to enhance my understanding of law, I have been fortunate enough to gain work experience at the law firm, Hogan Lovells. As a result of undertaking this internship, I discovered other types of law such as corporate law, which has been of interest to me. My time spent at Hogan Lovells put me in contact with a range of lawyers and I have been mentored by them. Through my work at Hogan Lovells, I have been able to grasp how intricate the work of a lawyer is on a daily basis. The lawyer whom I received mentoring from enhanced my understanding of corporate law, together with law in general. It highlighted how lawyers have to anticipate the needs of their clients. From this work experience, I have gained and developed vital skills such as time management, along with being able to work under pressure.

Studying government and politics at A-Level has given me further understanding of the current political state of a country and its governance. The current political climate of mistrust from the public, with members of the cabinet and prime minister himself scrutinised by the media, links back to the topic of 'The Prime Minister and the Cabinet,' which I studied in Unit 2. This has helped me develop skills such as wider reading and research, which I know are essential for law. A-Level French has given me the opportunity to deepen my understanding of language learning, but also discover French culture and customs. France is now a multicultural society, but has its legal system followed this evolution, one may ask? Are immigrants living in the suburbs (La Banlieue) treated the same as the middle class (La classe moyenne)? Watching 'Les Intouchables' gave me a greater insight into the class and social fracture in France. I understand that within the legal practice, you are expected to work with people from different backgrounds.

During my time at Our Lady's, I actively participated within the school community where I once was a school council representative. I was able to make changes such as making suggestions on celebrations to be more recognised such as Black History Month, and performed a spoken word about Black History Month that year. Celebrating the importance of Black History also gave me the chance to improve my public speaking skills and is useful within legal practice.

I am also a Youth Board Member of the Envision Community Apprentice Programme, a charity whose aims are to help young people and their level of employment through tackling real-life social problems. Throughout this period, I learned the value of selflessness and helping others combat real-life social problems such as body image. I was required to work in a team in order to achieve this goal, which was a success. I also worked part-time as a store associate in TkMaxx for eight hours a week. This has given me the experience of being in a working environment and forming working relationships with a range of people. Overall these are skills which I know will be useful in my pursuit of a career in Law and equip me in my next step of education.

Remarks on Abigail's Personal Statement

Abigail makes clear the origin of her interest in law with the case of Stephen Lawrence. While accepting the reality of how law works, she argues that those who enforce the law in the United Kingdom do so in such a manner that discriminates. This becomes her narrative from the beginning, and is confirmed by the final sentence of her introduction, when she writes:

> *"Hence my commitment to studying Law at university, as I will ensure that equality for all people will be my main concern."*

Abigail's work experience at Hogan Lovells is a great addition to this personal statement, and the main takeaways that she has from this internship are learning about corporate law, understanding the intricacies of law, anticipating the needs of a client, promoting effective time management and working under pressure. On the heels of having studied government and politics at A-level, Abigail explores the 'climate of mistrust' within politics, and extends this sentiment to French politics too. She has also participated in her school community, which is commendable, in addition to her work as a Youth Board Member of the Envision Community Apprentice Programme. Abigail covers a lot of ground with this personal statement and writes well.

Daniel's Personal Statement

Offer from:

University of Oxford

Subject:

History and Politics

I hope to develop my knowledge of how political communities function, through studying History and Politics. I have attended a number of lectures on different topics at various universities, including on Brexit. Professor David Reynold's lecture on Brexit and history discussed how the presentation of ideas and language used is important, highlighting the connotations of the word 'leave,' which I had not considered. These included freedom and change, which may come across as a more persuasive argument to a voter who feels disenfranchised, wishes to reject the current norm, or who hopes to hark back to a past Britain. David Harvey's *A Brief History Of Neoliberalism* similarly highlights how neoliberal values for example focus strongly on freedom of choice for the individual, yet in reality this ideal is undermined by the fact that increasingly neoliberal regimes seem to be 'undemocratic.'

Reading the news (including different newspapers with wide-ranging views), following journalists on Twitter and watching shows like Question Time have given me a more informed view of the world, allowing me to engage using different mediums with politics to formulate my viewpoint. I am interested in how social media has brought more people into the political debate, allowing the public to digest politics in a more open yet casual way, and enabling politicians to utilise this within campaigns by spreading their key messages in an easily consumable way. Examples such as Boris Johnson's repeated use of the same few short memorable soundbites on Twitter can be contextualised within neoliberal thinking — a focus on the individual rather than on the collective means people engage with individual issues more openly. To frame this within David Harvey's thinking, by doing this the people are almost allowing themselves to be dominated by the 1% as part of the veil of rhetoric constructed by neoliberalism.

Another personal interest of mine is the development of the Holocaust, in particular how historians can have vastly differing interpretations of events and the factors that can lead to one. Here I encountered schools of thought (intentionalism and functionalism), useful tools to look for near-consensus among a body of similar historians, but these can miss the complexities of individual arguments. While both Longerich and Fleming could be classed as intentionalists, Fleming argues that direct intent for extermination was prevalent from 1933 in language, while Longerich argues that this meaning only developed in the 1940s as part of transition to further radicalisation. On the other hand, Cesarani felt Jewish policy was unclear and language creates the illusion of order. I gained a more developed understanding of the strengths and limitations of texts by reading other historians' reviews, such as Jonathan Steinberg, highlighting that Cesarani did not utilise German language material in his research.

In school, I led a Blood Brothers Drama workshop for GCSE students where I explained the play's historical context, highlighting the importance of events within theatrical writing and exemplifying the impact of Thatcher's policies, part of neoliberal growth more globally. Participating in the Student Debate Society has developed my ability to respond quickly to other viewpoints without prompt, and to focus on the value of the idea rather than on the individual arguing it. The most thought-provoking debate was on whether to have a second Brexit referendum, particularly as the idea of democracy can be utilised by both sides, making it a nebulous concept. After my degree, I am considering a career in government to make a positive societal change. What I want to offer is a student willing to engage in debate who is open to new ways of thinking.

Remarks on Daniel's Personal Statement

Daniel's personal statement is excellent. He has an academic writing style and focuses almost exclusively on emphasising his intellectual perspectives and ideas. Daniel states that he is interested in the role that social media plays in bringing people into political discourse, particularly as it is so ubiquitous to users. He also explores how social media helps politicians within their campaigns reach out to people online. This is an interesting subject to discuss, as it is topical and relevant in modern politics within an increasingly connected society.

Daniel's commentary on neoliberalism is explained well, and throughout his personal statement, he draws from multiple sources and thinkers, such as Longerich and Fleming, which provides credibility.

Daniel's contribution to the Blood Brothers drama workshop is an interesting supercurricular activity that relates to his chosen subject, thereby demonstrating his wider interest in his field. It is also encouraging to read that he has participated in the Student Debate Society, which certainly helped to improve his communication skills and understand the viewpoints of others.

Overall, Daniel's personal statement presents his intellectual insights in various areas, and he explores his ideas with great analysis and evidence.

Bill's Personal Statement

Offer from:

University of Leicester

Subject:

Engineering

One's first flight is often a very memorable moment: the growl of the engine as the plane hurls down a runway and rises above the clouds — likewise, my passion for engineering flew high. The marvel of flight and the computational systems used in aiding its possibility reveals to me the ways in which, through engineering, the impossible can become possible. I believe I will be able to make a consequential impact in future innovations that take the world to new heights. From the motors in a small hand-held fan to the massive GE90 Engine, engineering has been woven into the fabrics of our everyday lives and the genius of inventors and innovators before us inspires me to seek higher education, and to be among those who make our world an easier place to live in.

Physics details the world from a fundamental level. Through studies in A-Level physics, fields such as electricity have expanded my interest in the inner workings of software, as I have learned about the foundations from which more complex systems are developed — systems ultimately powering our commercial aircraft, among other devices that I would love the chance to explore. This led me to investigate the case of the Boeing 737 Max which had a multitude of software problems which led to the unfortunate crashes of two planes. The extensive research gone into identifying and fixing the problem with the MCAT software has been fascinating to keep up with, and prompted me to partake in an online research project, through which, I was able to develop my critical thinking skills as well as research techniques that I am ready to utilise while on the course, ultimately achieving a certificate for the project. Such situations demonstrate the diversity of engineering away from the physical manufacturing of machines, which itself, I found to be just as important through my A-Level maths course — maths being the language through which the sciences function and cooperate. In particular, learning the mechanics division of the course whilst studying kinematics and its links to the physics topic of materials, showed me the ways in which the design of the products can be optimised to complement the system as a whole, so that it can function more effectively. It helped to explain how the larger fan blades on the new Boeing 777X allow it to have better energy efficiency than its predecessors when I decided to watch its first test flight on the 25th of January. In A-Level chemistry I have come to learn the significance of a powerful and capable electrochemical battery, whether it powers the motion of a vehicle or a mobile's operating system, and I realised how the energy source for a system brings all components together to create a functioning product and how it drives both the software and the physical machine.

As they say, two minds are better than one. Through participation in social action projects like #CombatLoneliness in my town, I am no stranger to the importance of teamwork when coming up with solutions to problems. No engineering feat has been achieved alone and I am aware that, on this course, teamwork is likely to play a big part in my success. I am always up to the challenge, whether leading a team or acting as support. As demonstrated during my NCS team-building exercises, I make sure my contributions are valuable and productive. In addition, I take care of my health and well-being by engaging in workouts that help to keep me fit for practical work. The discipline it requires has enabled me to develop drive and motivation for other activities I partake in and allows me to practice time management. Studying at university will grant me the ability to mature these skills as well as gain new ones while on my course. I approach tasks with positivity, and a level head. By completing my chosen course at university level, I will establish the next step in my journey to being among those that change our world for the better.

Remarks on Bill's Personal Statement

Bill presents himself as ambitious, reflective and passionate, and his descriptive language helps to communicate his points rather memorably. For example:

"The growl of the engine as the plane hurls down a runway."

"Engineering has been woven into the fabrics of our everyday lives."

Notwithstanding the descriptive language, Bill manages to infuse a great amount of reflection into his writing too, which allows the reader to get insights into how he thinks and how he has developed intellectually:

"I realised how the energy source for a system brings all components together to create a functioning product."

Bill portrays himself as someone who can strike the right balance between leadership and being a team player. These skills are essential within his field, and Bill provides evidence of his competence through his extracurricular activities.

Katie's Personal Statement

Offer from:

Nottingham Trent University

Subject:

MA in Journalism

As a university graduate and aspiring writer, I am thrilled to discover this MA course. I am yet to find another institution that offers anything as exciting, specialised, or relevant to me and my goals. My ambition to pursue a career in journalism is rooted in my desire to challenge societal problems that are also deeply embedded in my personal life, such as the fight for gender equality. My aim is to write articles that are empowering, not detrimental. There are not enough writers, like that of 'Lalalaletmeexplain' in OK! Magazine, who create educational and inspiring content, and I would like to build upon this to shift the editorial narrative from harmful to helpful. The increase in online media consumption means that it is a journalist's responsibility to safeguard the reader as well as entertain them.

In 2020, I created my own online blog, www.thingsmumdidnt-tellme.com, to influence this positive change in media content. My articles cover topics such as dating, sexual health, and mental wellness. My website continues to play an imperative role in building my editorial confidence and teaching me about audience engagement. As a result of my blog, I was appointed by Meg Matthews to write a piece for her renowned website, www.megsmenopause.com, called 'Living with a Menopausal Mum.' Seeing my article published on such a large and educational platform is thrilling and certifies that journalism is the career path I wish to take. Both editorial examples demonstrate my versatile capacity to innovate my own material or write for a brief. I strengthened this ability during my time at the University of Kent by writing essays for English literature that had to adhere to a strict criterion, whilst also producing portfolios for creative writing that required originality over rules.

However, I now wish to develop my talents and skillset at Nottingham Trent University. The course modules that NTU offers, such as 'Journalism, Ethics and Society,' are particularly appealing to me; I believe that the role of the journalist needs to be undertaken with careful moral consideration which I am keen to practise. For example, the UK is currently facing a petrol crisis, and this is largely due to the amount of alarmist reports that have circulated in the media, therefore having a damaging effect on key public resources such as our ambulance service. By considering the greater welfare of society as opposed to audience engagement via shock tactics, situations such as these can be avoided. Furthermore, visual presentation is just as important as the written word in journalism, as it is used to aid and convey the correct message. During my final year as an undergraduate, my work was noted as 'visually arresting' in examiner feedback, and it was my aesthetic experimentation that awarded me an invitation to read and display my material at the Datableeder Poetry Event in 2018.

Going forward, I am keen to learn how to use Photoshop and InDesign at NTU to build upon my visual skillset further. I consider that NTU's MA course in Magazine Journalism would be invaluable in assisting me on my path to an exciting and rewarding career as a journalist. Not only would the professional facilities, including one of the UK's largest student newsrooms, equip me well for the industry and the world of employment post-graduation, but I would also like to fully immerse myself in the extra-curricular opportunities that NTU advertises. For example, I believe I would thrive in the NTU Pride society as someone who is a part of (and advocates strongly for) the LGBTQ+ community. I would also love the opportunity to write for the university magazine, *PLATFORM*, on topics such as mental health, whereby I am certain I can support the well-being of other students during their studies. Overall, I am extremely excited at the prospect of immersing myself into NTU's culture as a dedicated and enthusiastic student, making the most of everything that the university has to offer.

Remarks on Katie's Personal Statement

Katie does an excellent job of demonstrating both her passion for journalism and the wider issues surrounding this field. In her introduction, she makes clear what her narrative is and why she wants to study journalism:

"My ambition to pursue a career in journalism is rooted in my desire to challenge societal problems that are also deeply embedded in my personal life, such as the fight for gender equality."

She also refers to the growth of online consumption of media, which is a pertinent topic within journalism and the dissemination of information. With each of the points that Katie makes, she presents her own opinions and reflections, which adds value to her writing. For example:

"I believe that the role of the journalist needs to be undertaken with careful moral consideration."

Katie tailors her writing to her chosen university, and shows enthusiasm in the activities and projects that she hopes to take part in if admitted. This achieves the desired effect of making her appear enthusiastic and determined as a student.

Ethan's Personal Statement

Offer from:

University of Glasgow

Subject:

Medicine

Since reading the *How my Body Works* series as a child, I have been fascinated by anatomy and the way in which intricate systems can work together so cohesively. Whilst studying human biology, I became increasingly interested in the pathology of common diseases and illnesses, and how we are able to treat them with modern medicine. I believe there is nothing better than being able to improve a person's life, no matter the size of the change, which is why I have always been drawn to a career in medicine, as I know it will combine my love of science with the skills required to make a difference.

Shadowing a plastic surgeon for a week in a secondary care position provided an insight into the demands and challenges facing NHS workers, such as long hours and staff shortages. Whilst observing a consultation with a patient who underwent a rhinectomy due to substance abuse, I witnessed the qualities required to succeed as a doctor along with the importance of a multi-disciplinary approach to care. The consultant emphasised the importance of being non-judgemental as a doctor whilst showing empathy and following an ethical code. I have developed such skills whilst working for Relationships Scotland as I am often the first contact for many clients who find it difficult to discuss their situation and may become emotional. Such a role has also improved my organisational skills and ability to work as part of a multi-disciplinary team. Dialogue with medical students gave me an insight into the challenges that may arise during patient care. Volunteering with Citizens Advice gave me experience facing many of these challenges, such as language barriers, intoxication or anger towards oneself, making me an ideal candidate for a career in medicine. Helping vulnerable members of society has taught me how to approach delicate subjects with empathy, whilst teaching music at a sensory impairment school allowed me to appreciate the importance of individualised care and the personal reward of helping someone reach their goal.

My love of science saw me undertake a four-week research placement at The University of Glasgow, studying the optimal environmental conditions for stomatal regulation in various plants. This required setting up various experiments and recording my findings in an academic report. This provided an understanding of lab-based skills and scientific research, whilst involving patience and attention to detail, which are key qualities of a doctor. Studying law has given me the ability to consider the moral and ethical ramifications of an action and solve problems logically and concisely. Solicitors and doctors are very alike, with both having the ability to effect positive change in the lives' of others, and both being bound by a strict code of conduct. Further reading introduced me to difficult legal, ethical and moral aspects of practising medicine such as consent, clinical negligence and end of life care.

Keeping up with the workload of my degree, working part-time, volunteering and maintaining a social life and hobbies, such as cycling, photography, piano and leading the Mock Trial Society, required learning how to best manage my time and prioritise. This allowed me to unwind from my studies and is a key attribute required when studying and practising medicine. Holding a committee position in the Mock Trial Society involves taking on a leadership role in raising awareness of the society, engaging new members and planning careers and social events.

My goal is to make a positive change in people's lives. I have the skills, the personality and the academic ability and drive required to succeed. My love of science combined with my excellent communication and interpersonal skills, empathetic persona and maturity make me an ideal candidate for the challenges of studying and practising medicine.

Remarks on Ethan's Personal Statement

Having secured his first degree in law from the University of Dundee, Ethan's transition to medicine in this personal statement reads well due to its reflective language. For every experience, Ethan does not fail to include the insights that he gained along the way. Shadowing the plastic surgeon and witnessing the rhinectomy taught him the importance of taking a multidisciplinary approach to medicine, being nonjudgmental, demonstrating empathy and following an ethical code.

Thereafter, Ethan writes about his experiences at Relationships Scotland, which improved his organisational skills and ability to communicate with others in difficult situations. Each of these skills is necessary for any budding doctor, and Ethan appears to have been mindful about prioritising the attributes that portray his most meritorious traits, as well as those required in medicine. This is an effective strategy. With each line, the admissions tutor is reassured that Ethan has the qualities required to excel as a doctor.

Considering that Ethan is applying to the University of Glasgow, mentioning the research placement on stomatal regulation is a good idea, as it demonstrates specificity to that university. He also accrued valuable lab-based skills, which is another strong point. Finally, Ethan's reference to the transferable skills from law is excellent, as he manages to bridge the gap between two fields that may otherwise have appeared irreconcilable.

Sergiou's Personal Statement

Offer from:

University of Oxford

Subject:

Philosophy, Politics and Economics

I am deeply involved in politics at different levels and want to be equipped with the knowledge to change the society in which we live, advocating for a political system that is fair and in which all people can thrive. Ultimately, it would be my dream to be able to see my currently nascent ideas fully enacted. My application comes from a unique position, as I am somewhat running my life and aspirations against the clock of my own biology: since childhood I have had to deal with a very serious illness prompting me to grasp and fully exploit every opportunity. My limited progress in primary school instilled a desire and work ethic to push beyond the bounds set by others. This determination still burns brightly in me: I want to channel my enthusiasm through academia providing enhanced depth and credibility to my ideas.

I co-founded the Barts' YES Forum by contacting and persuading the CEO of the Royal London Hospital to create a facilitator for youth voices across the Trust. I have also designed and established a mentoring scheme for young people suffering from long-term illnesses. Through this scheme, I met a vast variety of people; I have therefore seen how effective activism can yield practical results and developed the skills to lobby fund managers and politicians successfully. As a member of the NHS Youth Forum, I have been chosen as a representative in the government's NHS Long Term Health Plan. Standing as a member of the Youth Parliament for Enfield, I understand the impact of political decisions at a practical level. Currently I am campaigning in Parliament for my motion 'Put an End to Knife Crime,' as well as drafting the Youth Violence Commission, alongside Vicky Foxcroft MP. I fully intend to use a gap year to fulfil my commitment to these current projects. I have been awarded: Young Entrepreneur of the Year 2016, MUN Best Speaker in

Human Rights Committee and an international Emmy award for the BBC documentary 'Same But Different.'

The theoretical aspect of Theatre Studies has complemented my work with Chickenshed and the National Youth Theatre. When helping to build a community school in Ecuador and teaching in Tamil Nadu, I appreciated the wealth of knowledge that can be gained from communication with people from different life experiences. When volunteering in Ecuador, I considered thoughts from economists such as Dambiso Moyo, that foreign aid can cripple a nation's independence and achievements, but felt that voluntary work is vital to establish basic infrastructure in underdeveloped countries, despite agreeing with Moyo that equality of opportunity is more important than equality of resources.

Considering my recent projects, I was intrigued by the ideas of John Rawls, Robert Nozick and Ronald Dworkin, particularly their views of 'arbitrary traits.' I believe that, as far as possible, such traits should not adversely affect an individual's contribution to society. The question becomes what role the state has in ensuring that these traits are not limitations on citizens' negative freedom. I strive to revise the contemporary belief of 'compensating for arbitrary disadvantages' simply through pecuniary means. In this I believe that compensation is a necessary but insufficient condition of people with disadvantages being able to compete on an equal footing. Starkly against this, the old Victorian philosophy which posited that disabled people are impotent is superannuated; we need a rigorous theory on which the rights, obligations and responsibilities that are evoked from the facts of arbitrary traits are coherently conceptualised and acted upon. I strongly believe that a harmonious whole can only be achieved with a complete reappraisal of this theory, resulting in the positive enactment of contributions that everyone can make, regardless of physical 'arbitrary traits.'

I feel I have the necessary attributes, perspective and experience to make a valuable contribution to university life.

Remarks on Sergiou's Personal Statement

Sergiou starts off his personal statement with two sentences that represent his overarching goals and ambitions — namely advocating for a fair political system 'in which people can thrive.' He also mentions issues regarding his health, which add greater context and understanding of his circumstances and his drive to succeed. Where Sergiou thrives is in the multitude of experiences and projects that he has undertaken, such as co-founding the Barts YES Forum, designing and establishing a mentoring scheme for young people suffering from long-term illnesses, being a member of the NHS Youth Forum and the Youth Parliament, and campaigning alongside a member of Parliament for his motion 'Put an End to Knife Crime.' Sergiou's experiences attest to the genuine passion and determination that he has to make a meaningful difference in society. In addition, his insights from his voluntary work in Ecuador are eye-opening, particularly with regard to him echoing Damiso's view that foreign aid can 'cripple a nation's independence and achievement.' His reference to the ideas of Rawls, Nozick and Dworkin is apt for his chosen course, and his intellectual explorations are explained well.

Lamar's Personal Statement

Offer from:

University of Warwick

Subject:

Politics and International Relations

Voters, dishonest politicians, and venture capitalists have all contributed to the spread of the dangerous illness of selfishness. Atomistic views have historically ruled society because they are believed by those who are more concerned with their own interests than those who practise collectivism. This tendency can still be seen today when people with poor moral character hold positions of authority. Having said that, I am certain that the world requires new leaders, and I am confident that I can help spark that transformation. It is critical that I obtain a degree in politics and economics in order to better understand how our current leaders make decisions, identify systemic flaws, and work for systemic improvement that narrows the wealth-poverty divide.

The world's inequalities have increased my understanding of how society works. As a result of this, I decided to read *The Creature from Jekyll Island.* The Federal Reserve, considered a dictatorial tool that promotes war, is central to the book's argument, which demands its abolition. It claims that if the Federal Reserve had not existed, conflicts such as World War II would have been less damaging. As a result, my political views shifted, and I sought a platform to openly express them, so I attended the 'Congress to Campus' event at the US Embassy. I took advantage of the opportunity and spoke with two former members of congress. This event taught me the importance of free expression and why talking to individuals who disagree with you can help you learn more and understand different perspectives.

This drive for social justice influenced my A-level choices. My political science classes have taught me about the effects of political power. For example, the Conservative Party may advocate for higher taxes, whereas the Labour Party advocates for lower income taxes. People who support the opposition suffer if the other party wins. This demonstrates how the election system is based on a winner-take-all system, as those who do not vote lose their right to express themselves and are forgotten. I found this troubling since it generates political ambiguity, making it difficult to decide where I stand politically. However, there remains comfort in the unknown. Studying economics allows me to focus on society through a detailed lens while providing relief from the uncertainties in politics. For instance, I can see how higher taxes harm those with lower incomes more than those with higher incomes, or how increasing migration from foreign nations harms the economy. This increased focus helps determine the veracity of my political convictions. On the other hand, English literature has allowed me to express myself creatively. This was stressed in my comparative paper for Small Island and Translations, which wrote about the effects of Imperial Britain. These literary texts have given me the opportunity to express my personal thoughts on the British Empire and how it affected me as a black man.

I have had various job opportunities, including a PwC internship where I developed a plan to reduce the UK's carbon impact with others and presented it to PwC directors. I cherish the knowledge I have received because I hope to build long-term projects to increase the level of living in low-income communities in the future. Additionally, I submitted an essay about black masculinity, a topic that is significant to me since, as a young man, I felt compelled to adhere to this white normative idea of what a man is, which forced me to rethink what a black man is. The essay's mature themes assisted my success in the Cambridge University essay competition and helped me earn the Jack Petchey Award. It also revealed my interest in pursuing a doctorate in a field with a similar theme.

My academic background has well prepared me for a career in politics and economics. Politics and economics use logical and practical methods, whereas English literature develops analytical, persuasive, and essay-writing skills that I believe are necessary for the course. My current perspectives on the two disciplines may shift, but I am confident that my skills and extensive academic background will enable me to pursue new intellectual interests.

Remarks on Lamar's Personal Statement

Lamar delivers a powerful essay that showcases well-reasoned and deeply explored arguments and observations about political issues such as the Federal Reserve, the UK's two-party system, imperialism, his identity as a black man and black masculinity on a societal level. His opening line is attention-grabbing:

"Voters, dishonest politicians, and venture capitalists have all contributed to the spread of the dangerous illness of selfishness."

The reader is curious to learn more about what he thinks. With each point that Lamar makes, he uses evidence and keeps his writing style reflective and analytical, which makes it a compelling read that allows us to get deeper insights into his mindset. It is also impressive that Lamar had success in the Cambridge writing competition and with the Jack Petchey Award. He is undoubtedly a formidable individual.

Sam's Statement of Purpose

Offer from:

University College London

Subject:

Master's in Law (LLM)

The UCL LLM is one of the best, with the Faculty of Laws ranking in the top 10 law schools globally. The UCL LLM stands out because of its significant module range and specialisms. I am interested in pursuing the general LLM, so that I can focus on both domestic and international law. My interest is the human security intersection of humanity and the accountability of governments. My area of interest is equally divided between domestic and international law: national security, administrative and constitutional law, with global security concerns, including armed conflict, dispute settlement, and mass atrocities. I would base my research essay specifically on the overlap of domestic national security law with international legal obligations, following on from my dissertation on MI5's engagement in criminality, focusing on safeguarding from abuse and oversight.

For the general LLM, I am particularly interested in the following modules: 'International Criminal Law,' 'International Human Rights Law,' 'Judicial Review,' and 'Aspects of National Security Law.' Other modules I find very interesting include: 'Use of Force,' 'International Humanitarian Law' and 'Policy of International Courts and Tribunals,' 'Judges, Courts and Judicial Decision-making.'

Whilst reading for my LLB, I have often desired to explore areas of law in much greater depth and complexities than are on offer at undergraduate level. The academic standards and rigour of the UCL LLM inherently entails very advanced discussions on practically and conceptually complex, contentious issues of law, supported and promoted through the demanding, immersive learning environment.

UCL equips students with the highest levels of analysis and

arguments needed for legal practice. Reading for the LLM would enhance all of my legal skills required for a successful career as a barrister, e.g. critical thinking, legal analysis, legal research, argument formation, written communication, and a thorough knowledge of the subject. On a career progression, an LLM from a university as acclaimed as UCL would improve my chances of obtaining Bar Practice Course scholarships and eventual pupillage at a leading public law firm or international chambers. A solicitor-advocate and barrister I speak to regularly — partners at Mishcon de Reya and Quinn Emanuel, respectively — are alumni of the UCL LLM and described their time at UCL as having had a substantial role in their evident successes.

I am currently in the final year of my LLB Law degree, expected to achieve a high first-class, deemed in the top 5% of my cohort in light of my extenuating circumstances. I have been awarded a First Class during each year of my degree. My written work in the past 15 months has all been awarded Firsts (frequently graded 75% or above). Given my record of high-quality work, especially during such family crises, I believe I am a strong candidate for the intense studies at UCL.

Alongside my studies, I am the Treasurer of the University of Reading Law Society where I set up a fund for disadvantaged students, and I have worked at a litigation funding firm, Asertis, since July 2020 where I assisted on projects alongside top legal experts in their fields, including world-record-breaking multi-billion pound international litigation. My studies are accompanied by ongoing participation in the internal Osbourne Clarke moot, where my research, presentation skills, and argument development were acknowledged. This also included extended mediation training sessions from Resolve Mediation, negotiations training, and a client interview training session and subsequent competition by Kennedy's Law, during which my presentation, confidence and legal knowledge and analysis received positive feedback. I am in discussions for an internship at Mishcon de Reya and another firm.

I would continue pursuing extracurricular activities at UCL and mini-pupillages. The Public International Law Pro Bono Project for LLM and PhD students is particularly exciting, especially accompanying my intended PIL and human rights modules.

Remarks on Sam's Statement of Purpose

Sam's statement of purpose reveals many aspects of his character and his interests, and is informative and comprehensive. He makes clear the modules that he is most interested in and the areas of interest that he wants to explore at University College London. It is evident that Sam has performed brilliantly in his undergraduate law degree at the University of Reading, as he has achieved a string of first-class marks in his exams and is in the top five percent of his cohort. He also demonstrates solid experience outside of the classroom, as he was the treasurer of the University of Reading Law Society, worked at a litigation funding firm, and participated in the Osbourne Clarke moot. Sam has shown a specific interest in UCL by mentioning the Public International Law Pro Bono Project for LLM and PhD students, which helps to show his eagerness to study at UCL specifically. Overall, Sam's academic attainments and his diversity of projects contribute to the strength of his statement of purpose.

Chantel's Personal Statement

Offer from:

University of Westminster

Subject:

Psychology

At a time when one of the biggest killers of young men in the UK is suicide and it has been reported that one in five teenage girls around the age of 15 self-harm due to mental torment, I believe that having access to qualified clinical psychologists is more important than ever. I find the study of human behaviour fascinating. The opportunity to analyse the reasons for peoples' actions and the biological and environmental factors which may influence their mind intrigues me. I am eager to expand and deepen my knowledge and understanding of psychology, rooted in research and a strong evidence base.

My study of A-level psychology has enabled me to develop the ability to conceptualise and grasp complex ideas. For example, many Freudian theories such as the theory of personality were quite difficult for me to comprehend at first. However, I found that by applying the theories within the context of case studies, I was able to better understand the concepts. In addition to this, I have developed the ability to write well-structured essays that are concise and present all of my thoughts in a logical and sequential manner. A-level biology has taught me to appreciate the structure and complexity of the human body and how various parts and body systems work together to achieve a goal. I have always been fascinated by all of the thousands of biological processes occurring in the body at one moment that we are unaware of and I would love to look in depth at the structure and chemistry of the brain at degree level. This is a topic we briefly began to explore in A-level psychology, regarding the biological approach to behaviour, but I am keen to learn about this topic in more depth.

Recently, I completed a work experience placement at Homerton University Hospital. My duties included assisting patients in the 'step-down unit' of the hospital, where patients who had just come out of theatre were held for recovery. Whilst there, I tended to patients, made sure that the effects of the anaesthetic had worn off and ensured that they were fully conscious before they were discharged or shifted to other wards. I checked their blood pressure, oxygen levels and heart rate at regular intervals and engaged in general conversation with them to ensure their mental well-being as well as their physical well-being. This experience showed me that I would love to work with members of the public as I enjoy social interaction with different types of people from different demographic groups.

In secondary school, I was a prefect. This role allowed me to work amongst my peers to ensure that a calm, safe and welcoming environment was maintained around the school. It showed me that I enjoy working with others as a team to achieve a common goal, but also if need be, I can work as an individual to accomplish any task or goal. This opportunity also allowed me to develop leadership skills as sometimes I had to assign and manage tasks for the other prefects. This role permitted me to explore my flexibility in the way I am able to work and it also allowed me to challenge myself, which is something I enjoy. I am also currently acting as a peer mentor to an AS student, assisting in helping to improve their understanding of chemistry and biology. I found this experience very rewarding as it has helped me to develop my communication skills and assess the needs of the individual that I am working with on a one on one basis. This is a skill that I believe would be highly beneficial in a professional setting.

I enjoy being a listener and confidant to my friends and family.

I would like to further utilise my compassionate and caring nature to help the vulnerable and improve their well-being. I am eager to embark on the challenge of successfully completing a degree in psychology. I know this endeavour will take hard work and perseverance and I am prepared to fully apply myself to the goal of expanding my knowledge and eventually becoming a skilled clinical psychologist.

Remarks on Chantel's Personal Statement

Chantel's opening line about the prevalence of suicide and self-harm among young people in the UK is poignant and underscores the motivations behind her desire to study psychology. Her second paragraph takes on a standard structure that is easy to follow as she expounds upon how her A-levels in psychology and biology have provided useful skills for her onward learning and development. For example, for the former subject, she writes:

> *"I have developed the ability to write well-structured essays that are concise and present all of my thoughts in a logical and sequential manner."*

This is a strong reflective statement, particularly as the act of presenting one's thoughts in a logical and sequential manner will be important for her future career as a psychologist.

Chantel's description of her work experience placement at Homerton Hospital is also reflective, as she not only describes her action, such as tending to patients, but also how working with members of the public and interacting with people from different demographics appeals to her. She presents herself compellingly and comes across well.

Thea's Personal Statement

Offer from:

King's College London

Subject:

Spanish & French

Throughout my studies, I have developed a passion for not only learning the French language but also learning about French culture and history and its global impact. I would love the opportunity to improve my French language skills as well as learn a new language so that I have the ability to communicate with so many more people in their own language when I travel the world. During my education, opportunities to visit other countries or experience other cultures have been limited due to either financial barriers or the COVID-19 pandemic. For some, this might have caused them to lose interest but for me, it has only made me more determined to have these experiences. I became particularly drawn to learning Italian and more about its culture when learning that Italy has more UNESCO world heritage sites than any other country, due to its tremendous cultural history.

I have recently become especially interested in French law. I have thoroughly enjoyed researching and learning about the role of the French feminist and lawyer Gisèle Halimi in the legalisation of abortion in France. Her fight for equality began at the age of 12 when she starved herself for eight days in order to achieve the right to be able to choose to read. This desire to choose never faltered throughout her life and in 1971, she cofounded the movement 'Choisir' alongside Simone de Beauvoir. Over the course of the next few years, Halimi fought for the rights of women all over France to choose, and represented a 16-year-old girl in court when she was charged for an illegal abortion after being raped. The young girl was acquitted and this trial, known famously as the Bobigny trial, changed the perspectives of people all over France. In my opinion, if it weren't for Halimi winning this trial then the legalisation of abortion in France would have happened much later than 1975 as Halimi forced people to consider that if women didn't have the right to choose what happens to their own bodies then there was no way that they could have any real social standing. My interest in French law led to choosing it as the topic for my A-Level Independent Research Project, developing my critical analysis, evaluation and academic research skills.

I participated in the Scholars Programme which introduced me to writing essays at degree level as well as giving me the skills to be able to research unfamiliar and complex topics and write in a succinct manner. I was awarded a 2.1 for this assignment and gained an insight in to the commitment needed to achieve success at degree level. I also completed a TEFL qualification within school. Over the course of the two days, I learnt about how to teach in a language that students are unfamiliar with through using target language and how useful body language, facial expressions and objects are when teaching a language. This course makes me an ideal candidate for a languages degree, as it enhanced my knowledge of how a language is learnt from a different perspective; a language has to be broken down with various grammar points and key repetition. I believe this will help me when learning a new language as I will be able to see where the language is similar to English and French and where it is different. Furthermore, I will employ a variety of different approaches to best improve my French and to learn Italian. In addition, having this qualification means that I will have more opportunities when travelling the francophone world since I would love to work in a school with young people and teach them English. I also have a part time job working as a waitress which has increased my confidence in speaking to new people, helped me learn how to stay calm in stressful situations and how to balance my education and a part-time job.

I believe I already have many of the skills required for me to make university a successful experience and am excited to be given the opportunity to improve my language and communication skills whilst simultaneously broadening my horizons.

Remarks on Thea's Personal Statement

Thea demonstrates a passion for French language, culture, history and law, which is most palpable when she describes the role of the French feminist and lawyer Gisèle Halimi in the legalisation of abortion in France. This part is very thorough and descriptive, but she also provides her own reflections on the issue, as she concludes with Halimi's role in the debate on abortion, writing that it would have been legalised in France much later than 1975.

The Scholars Programme that Thea took part in provided a great amount of value for her long-term education, as she learned how to write essays at a degree level. In addition, the TEFL qualification is an asset to any student looking to study a foreign language as a degree, and Thea goes into detail about the importance of body language, facial expressions and objects when teaching a language.

Thea also manages to include transferable skills from working as a waitress, such as the confidence to speak to new people and stay calm in stressful situations, which is commendable.

Her conclusion is short and to the point, and it reiterates her commitment to studying for her chosen degree at a higher level.

Gresa's Personal Statement

Offer from:

University College London

Subject:

Politics and International Relations

Studying history is an insight into how our modern-day institutions, customs, and values have evolved to be what they are today. I grew up listening to my family's experiences during the Kosovo War and hearing the newest developments surrounding the struggle for statehood. My personal understanding of the conflict has been enriched by watching the documentary *Lufta ne Kosove* which argued that the war was an inevitable reaction to the pre-existing ethnic tensions in the region of Kosovo, escalated by the Yugoslav Wars in the 90s. I found the documentary's arguments were validated by the book written by Serbian human rights activist, S. Biserko, in *Yugoslavia's Implosion*. This issue remains prevalent today; the 2021 Human Rights Helsinki Report found that there was explicit racism toward Albanians in the north of Serbia. Linking historical conflicts to modern-day political issues is a key reason why I want to study these subjects together.

I believe that revolutions occur when underlying long-term social change pushes a society into a state of instability, where even a minor disturbance could trigger a revolution, an idea explored in J. Goldstone's *A Very Short Introduction*. For example, decades of famine, the flaws of newly implemented parliamentarianism, and the incomplete emancipation of the serfs were all long-run causes of the 1905 Russian Revolution; similarly, the oppressive nature of being a puppet state within the Soviet bloc created the conditions for revolution in Hungary in 1956. However, it took short-term shocks to turn instability into revolt — defeat in the Russo-Japanese War or the encouragement provided by the Poznan protests were the triggers for those respective revolutions.

The internet's response to the murder of George Floyd resulted in an overwhelming rise in debate about racialised police violence. I am interested in the argument that the criminal justice system in the US today serves as a prolonging of the institutional suffering of Black Americans even after slavery, a view also found in the documentary '13th.' The most interesting part of my personal research, however, involved discovering neo-fascist counter-reactions to the Black Lives Matter movement online. This provoked me to read *Fascists Among Us* by J. Sparrow, which documented the modern radicalisation of far-right groups. The deployment of propaganda to reinforce political agendas was something I also explored during a Cambridge summer course: 'Heritage and Politics.' Having watched Tommy Robinson's address to the Oxford Union from 2015, I was able to draw a contrast between neo-fascism in the US and the exclusionary policies of the English Defence League. Far-right thinking in the US can be viewed as a reactionary movement of individualistic concerns directed against marginalised groups, whereas it is clear that the EDL possesses an anti-immigration lens of nationalism. Even though I did not agree with many of Robinson's ideas, I was fascinated by his ability to articulate a radical argument so deftly. History and politics both involve the manipulation of facts to influence opinion, a key reason for why I find the study of both so intriguing.

Clifford Chance's two-year ACCESS programme gave me an insight into the legal and corporate aspect of modern politics. Discussing issues such as ESG responsibilities that companies may have helped me understand current affairs better. I work as a tutor and volunteered at my local library, both of which have given me the necessary organisational skills needed to be a better student. Experiences like interviewing Baroness Garden and leading the politics society at college deepened my interest in both history and politics as it has given me an insight into how historical and political theory is applied in real life. I look forward to the challenges of university life and aspire to make the most of every opportunity.

Remarks on Gresa's Personal Statement

Gresa's personal statement is deeply reflective, analytical, personal and excellently written. It ticks multiple boxes, and she makes a very strong impression on the reader. The first line from her introduction defines the rest of her essay:

"Studying history is an insight into how our modern-day institutions, customs, and values have evolved to be what they are today."

She draws from her own experiences of listening to her family talk about the Kosovo War and Kosovo's struggle for statehood. She mentions the documentary *Lufta ne Kosove* and the book *Yugoslavia's Implosion* as guiding her opinions on the subject. By examining the impact that historical conflicts can have on modern-day political issues, Gresa seeks clarity on issues that continue to affect millions of people.

Her commentaries on the instability leading to revolutions, including the Russian Revolution and the 1956 revolution in Hungary, are very apt. Beyond this, Gresa's interest in the US criminal justice system and the analysis of neofascism is insightful, and her comparisons between far-right thinking in the US and that of the UK is interesting too. Gresa's personal statement is packed with rich analysis and intellectual insights that present her in a very positive light for her chosen programme.

Molly's Personal Statement

Offer from:

University of Oxford

Subject:

Experimental Psychology

I enjoy all of my A-levels but it was at an open day that I had an epiphany and knew that I wanted to explore the neuroscience behind the alpha-band activity over the visual cortex in the brain's right hemisphere. I had already looked at the brain in my biology A-level and became drawn further into the complexity of such a fundamental part of the body.

Reading *Unthinkable: An extraordinary journey through the world's strangest brains* by Helen Thomson opened my eyes to rare brain disorders and how the brain can shape lives in unexpected yet incredible ways. Thomson describes a woman who has a disorder where she feels permanently lost. As I read about the doctor's attempt to diagnose the condition through a concept called 'network theory,' I realised the intricacy of the human brain and the fascinating way scientists are able to treat such conditions. The author also explores schizophrenia, one of the most complex of all human disorders, and one that I hope to study in more detail at university. Its strong genetic component and environmental triggers made me think about how the external world influences the brain. Thomson's book led me to read *The Brain. The Story of You* by David Eagleman, and *A Mind of its Own. How Your Brain Distorts and Deceives* by Cordelia Fine.

When I visited 'Smoke and Mirrors: The Psychology of Magic' at the Wellcome Collection, finding out from experimental psychologists about the power of suggestion made me wonder if it's ever ethically justifiable to deceive someone. The process and results of the experiment were fascinating as people were shown to be dangerously compliant when tricked into believing a brain scanner could read or influence their thoughts. This reminds me of Milgram's obedience experiment which investigated the conflict between obedience to authority and personal conscience. I would love to study cognitive science as learning more about the brain and behaviour can help discover and treat neurological disorders, which is something I am committed to.

I have completed an EPQ asking, 'what are the most commonly used recreational drugs in the UK and how detrimental are they to the brains and behaviour of young adolescent individuals?' I looked at the impact of these drugs socially and biologically and was intrigued by the brain's protective response to cocaine. Experiments show that cocaine susceptible neurons and their synaptic connections change shape when first exposed to the drug, through a molecular pathway regulated by the gene integrin beta1. Scientists discovered that if they blocked the pathway and prevented this cell-shape change, mice became three times more sensitive to the effects of cocaine. Research websites such as psychologytoday.com and sciencedaily.com have bolstered my interest in these subjects. Learning about new ways to provide visual signals to the blind through stimulating the optic nerve is an exciting prospect as it reflects the advanced neurotechnology the future holds and its potential to change lives.

Work experience at the Francis Crick Institute in the stem cell research department gave me valuable time working in a lab and stimulated an interest in practical scientific research. Working at Matrix Law Chambers and a bank's legal department gave me an insight into what it means to be part of a team in a professional workplace, but only confirmed my choice to explore a career in neuroscience and psychology. I would love to gain a more detailed understanding of the inner workings of the brain and a path towards a career in these fields. It is astounding that humans have made so much progress in understanding the universe, yet we still know very little about our brains. I am eager to work alongside experts in such a rapidly developing field. I hope that my school work, internships, outside interests and further reading show I have the resilience, hard work and analytical skills to thrive on these demanding courses.

Remarks on Molly's Personal Statement

Molly's personal statement makes a strong impression due to its specificity and depth. She has clearly been engaged in a great amount of reading about how the brain works, and we see that from the start with her comments on the books *Unthinkable: An Extraordinary Journey Through the World's Strangest Brains*, *The Brain: The Story of You*, and *A Mind of its Own: How Your Brain Distorts and Deceives*. Her curiosity developed as he visited 'Smoke and Mirrors: the Psychology of Magic' at the Wellcome Collection, where she questioned the ethics of deception. This was interesting, as it demonstrated Molly's own insights on a fascinating topic, rather than merely stating what she did.

Following this, Molly's extended project qualification on recreational drugs was also insightful, as well as her commentary about new ways to provide visual signals to the blind. The work experience placement at the Francis Crick Institute in the stem cell research department was strong, and Molly succeeds in demonstrating transferable skills from the legal field. She cites teamwork as a skill learned from those experiences, and describes how they reaffirmed her commitment to neuroscience. Molly demonstrates curiosity and passion for her subject and makes a great impression.

Zane's Personal Statement

Offer from:

University of Oxford

Subject:

Economics and Finance

Understanding and applying economics means tackling crucial topics that affect everyone. How can we utilise resources and circumstances to maximise prosperity? The focus of economics, which is to solve real-world issues such as this, informed my decision to study A-level economics. This has enriched my curiosity by developing my understanding of the significance of financial markets. As a result, I wish to further my knowledge by pursuing a degree in economics.

I explored my interest in economics by reading Marshall's *Prisoners of Geography*, which analyses how the physical geography of economic superpowers shapes their success. For example, Russia's ability to export goods has always been held back by its lack of control over a warm-water port. By contrast, the US has always benefited from having an easy-to-navigate landscape and access to two major oceans for trade. Another book that has cultivated my interest in economics is Kate Raworth's *Doughnut Economics*, which presented a new economic model geared towards sustainable development by limiting GDP growth. The book essentially argued that the solution to improving economic welfare was not endless GDP growth. Although I am not convinced of the effectiveness of this new economic model, I enjoyed how it has challenged and added to my understanding of economics.

A-Level geography has enhanced my understanding of economics because of the overlap between geography and economics. Covering topics such as globalisation has given me a strong appreciation for the real-world implications of economics. Geography has also helped prepare me for undergraduate economics by improving my ability to analyse and interpret quantitative data, using methods such as chi-squared and standard deviation. I found these tools very useful in my coursework on Oxford's housing crisis, arguably the most significant example of a market failure in my local community. I enjoyed conducting this fieldwork investigation because it allowed me to research a topic that relates to my enthusiasm for economics, an experience I hope to replicate when studying economics at the university.

I have completed 'The Business of Logistics,' an online course offered by the Chartered Institute of Logistics. The course gave insights into various tactics that firms such as Coca-Cola, DHL and Amazon use to maximise efficiency. The course required me to write multiple reports on case studies and presentations on what I learned, which allowed me to develop my evaluative and presentation skills. The second was an accountancy and finance course provided by Springpod. This course covered various types of job roles available in the finance industry and the functions of those roles. These courses have improved my problem-solving skills because they required me to research case studies and use my knowledge to think of solutions to finance-related issues that applied to the firms in the case study. Both of these online courses have fostered my interest in the financial sector and as a result, I would like to pursue a career in financial economics.

I have developed communication skills and the ability to work well in a team by playing for my school's basketball team. I also volunteer for a charity called the Parasol Project which organises activities for children during the school holidays. My responsibilities were to lead sports-related activities for the children. As a result, I have gained leadership and communication skills. I believe that all of these skills will contribute to my success in university life and pursuing an economics degree.

In conclusion, I believe I will be able to thrive in pursuing an economics course because of my ardent passion for the subject and ability to apply the subject to the real world.

Remarks on Zane's Personal Statement

Right from the beginning of Zane's personal statement, it is clear that his academic background has played an important role in guiding his understanding of ideas. This includes Zane's A-levels in economics and geography, as well as the books that he has read. His reference to Tim Marshall's *Prisoners of Geography* is interesting to read. However, his answer is enhanced by the second book that he mentions, Kate Raworth's *Doughnut Economics*, as he reflectively explains how the ideas mentioned in the book challenged those that he previously held:

> *"Although I am not convinced of the effectiveness of this new economic model, I enjoyed how it has challenged and added to my understanding of economics."*

It is refreshing to see that Zane has approached Raworth's book with an open mind, despite not fully championing the ideas that are presented there. Of Zane's extracurricular activities, the Parasol Project is the most unique, and he is reflective insofar as the leadership and communication skills that he learned there.

Florence's Personal Statement

Offer from:

King's College London

Subject:

Medicine

Three years ago, one of my classmates developed a rare, aggressive form of leukaemia (T-ALL), and had to be withdrawn from school due to the severity of the diagnosis. A GoFundMe was set up to help raise funds for a ground-breaking new treatment that only three other people had received prior. Although family and friends helped to raise over £500,000 for the treatment, he sadly passed away in 2021. The severity of the disease and the bravery he showed whilst in the hospital made me appreciate the privilege it is to be trusted with providing care to individuals in their most critical moments. This inspired me to pursue a career in medicine so that I can also contribute to delivering life-changing care and have a positive, long-lasting impact on society.

To gain further insight into the workings of a healthcare environment, I spent two weeks shadowing the lead dentist at a dental surgery. The clinical experience was invaluable as I was able to interact with many different patients and further develop my understanding of how clinicians convey compassion and build rapport within their surgery. I also had the chance to observe the administrative aspect of healthcare, which is just as crucial as the clinical side, and observe how essential it is in keeping the practice running smoothly and maintaining a comprehensive service for patients.

As an avid, A-level chemist and biologist, the sciences have allowed me to further hone my problem-solving skills and develop my ability to extract relevant information and apply it to the situation at hand. Similarly, doctors present this skill during consultations with patients by dissecting the relevant information to provide an accurate diagnosis. However, my study of sociology has equipped me with a key understanding of a variety of communities and cultures. Clinicians interact with people from a wide range of backgrounds and social groups, and understanding those communities can help lead to a better quality of care as well as health outcomes. For this reason, understanding the 'why' and 'how' behind each patient as an individual is an essential piece of the puzzle; something that is well displayed in community medicine.

Aside from the sixth form, I enjoy keeping up with medical news by reading scientific journals such as *The New Scientist*. The medical field is constantly evolving and therefore staying up to date with new research and treatments is critical. Reading *The New Scientist* has also significantly improved my ability to efficiently read and dissect academic articles. Comprehension skills are an essential part of medicine as both a student and clinician.

During the summer I spent time reading *This Is Going To Hurt*, an autobiography documenting the life of a junior doctor. This allowed me to appreciate the time, effort and dedication required daily by doctors as well as the more difficult aspects of the career, such as long hours and losing patients while remaining empathetic and professional. The author also addressed the importance of managing stress. To do this, I enjoy taking time out by going for walks, listening to music or watching anime. This allows me to strategise and outline plans to ensure I stay organised.

Attending a lecture on The Power of Community by UCL's Global Health lecturer provided me with further insight on how having an impact on health as a doctor is more than just being able to recite information from a textbook, and on the importance of interpersonal skills within a multidisciplinary team. I have the privilege of developing my interpersonal skills when acting as a guide for new cohorts joining the school, working with staff and other students to help them assimilate, something I hope to continue at university.

While I am aware that medicine is not the fantasy it is often portrayed to be, I hope that through my journey towards becoming a doctor I can further develop the skills that I have laid a foundation on and make a difference in this rewarding field.

Remarks on Florence's Personal Statement

Florence's personal statement is beautifully written. The language is simple and easy to understand, and her structure is very sound. Invoking my advice from Chapter Seven: Coherence, Florence's personal statement threads the needle very well.

Her introduction is poignant, and the passing of her classmate despite raising £500,000 for his treatment underscores the ephemerality of life and the limitations of doctors. Florence demonstrates pragmatism and an understanding of the drawbacks of medicine through her experiences, and affirms this in her conclusion:

"While I am aware that medicine is not the fantasy it is often portrayed to be..."

This makes Florence come across as more credible, as she is not under any illusions as to the difficulties that doctors face. From her academic insights to her work experience and projects, Florence ticks multiple boxes and clearly has what it takes to excel as a medical student and future doctor.

Grant's Personal Statement

Offer from:

University of Warwick

Subject:

Politics and International Relations

My interest in studying Politics stems from my Jamaican heritage, which led me to research the country's colonial history. The *Catch a Fire* documentary on the Morant Bay rebellion of 1865, exposed me to the activism of Paul Bogle, who rioted against social injustice and colonial misrule within the country. Jamaica's long-standing experience of oppression influenced political philosophers like the Pan-Africanist Marcus Garvey. Reading his book, *Philosophies and Opinions of Marcus Garvey*, I was introduced to his Black nationalist viewpoints where he created a semi-monolithic image of Blackness in his 'Black Diaspora.' However, Garvey's inclination to separatism challenges Jamaica's multiculturalist motto, 'out of many, one people.' Bogle's political reforms, compared to Garvey's belief of Black Capitalism, highlights a shift of priorities over time to create a better Jamaica. I believe that Michael Manley's socialist democratic approach gave the country the most political freedom, as he restored social hope through a national minimum wage and his Project Land Lease to maximise agriculture within the country. I hope to improve my understanding of policies by analysing their social and economic impact at university.

My most recent visit to Jamaica in 2020 gave me a visual of the consequences of the nation's international relations. An article by Ruben Gonzalez-Vicente provided an analysis of Caribbean development, dependency and post-colonial conditions. This directly affects Jamaica's plan to become a republic by 2025 as it starts a fight for dominance over its territory and state. *World Systems Analysis* by Wallerstein introduced me to the trend of underdeveloped periphery states being dominated economically by more industrialised states. The Dependency Theory also suggests that developing countries will continue to be seen as weak by more developed nations, regardless of their economic progress. This made me question whether the Windrush scandal would have still occurred if Jamaica had been a more developed country. In an essay for 'Thinking Black,' I concluded that Jamaica's dependency perpetuates a lack of geopolitical respect, sustained by the Hierarchy of Race, and that it is only through breaking dependency that Jamaica can realise its full potential and gain the necessary geopolitical power to prevent social crises like Windrush due to the inextricable link between race and economics.

After attending SOAS' Anthropology summer school, I was introduced to the influence of borders and how they can be racially and ethnically subjective. The Rwanda plan showcased the desire to exclude certain ethnic minorities from entering the country, with parties like Reform UK reinforcing a negative image of immigration and endorsing Euroscepticism. As a 'multicultural society', the UK is seen as a melting pot of cultures, however, some cultures have 'melted' more than others. I discussed this very issue on the BAME podcast I run in my school, where we explored the concept of identity. I highlighted how as a black male in the UK, I often feel disconnected from British culture. The campaign group EQUAL introduced me to 'THE GANG Matrix.' This was a reaction to the London riots to identify the level of those deemed as threats to society. It was revealed in 2018 that 80% of names belonged to people of BAME backgrounds. The perception created has made me question whether equality in the UK will ever be achieved with the influence of anti-immigration campaigns. However, the myth of Black criminality has drawn attention to the Black British experience and the effect of stereotypes placed upon certain races, genders and ages is a vital step to achieving an equitable society.

I have expanded my political and professional potential as an Amos Bursary Scholar, which has helped me to gain mentorship from Wes Streeting and work experience in his office.

Remarks on Grant's Personal Statement

Grant's personal statement is a compelling read because he makes it personal to him and it is highly specific, while equally referencing multiple credible sources and interesting arguments. He is thorough in his description of Bogle's political reforms in Jamaica and his comparison of them to Garvey's views, which he describes as a 'shift of priorities.' His analysis brings real value to the writing, as it is not merely describing other people's ideas, but rather joining the dots and seeking to evaluate the wider issues at play. He makes multiple enquiries and commentaries about important issues such as the Windrush scandal, black capitalism and republicanism in Jamaica, which provides depth and richness to his writing.

Grant also illustrates a nuanced way of thinking when he writes:

> *"The UK is seen as a melting pot of cultures, however, some cultures have 'melted' more than others."*

This phrase is memorable, and it captures his opinions about multiculturalism in the UK rather succinctly and elegantly. In addition to this, Grant's passion for this topic was demonstrable by his BAME podcast, and being recognised as an Amos Bursary Scholar is highly commendable. Overall, Grant has written a superb personal statement.

Bart's Personal Statement

Offer from:

University of Oxford

Subject:

Law

My enthusiasm for law stems from the way in which it has the power to automatically bind one to society. Hobbes theorises that acceptance into society involves a social contract; one automatically cedes an element of their sovereignty to a higher authority, thus is obligated to follow established rules. My interest lies in how such rules, which ultimately dictate every aspect of an individual's choices, are formulated to reflect a reasonable, just and universal standard, and specifically what defines such a standard, thus upholding a system of accountability which is respected within society.

Reading 'United Biscuits (1991)' at BCLP to evaluate the VAT status of Jaffa Cakes, I initially questioned how law could induce such extensive analysis into an ordinary household good. However, given the appearance of Jaffa cakes and studying the complexity of confectionery in Tax Law, I understood that interpretation intertwined with rationality emerges in determining whether consumers should pay tax on them. Although the judge concluded that Jaffa cakes have characteristics of both cakes and biscuits within the VAT Act 1983, on the point of size, I believe they failed to also consider the size of cupcakes, which, despite being similar to that of biscuits, are not identified as such. They also provided a weak case considering marketing, given that the location of a product on display does not necessarily have any bearing on its nature; it is ultimately a retailer's decision as to where they choose to market their goods. From this experience, I precisely realised the depth of law and its relevance to everyday life, even in the simplest sense. Such meticulous, intricate thinking is integral in challenging perceptions to develop just laws.

My A-Level curriculum enabled me to form differing interpretations of law, for instance economics introduced me to competition law, through which I conducted further research into collusion, finding that the CMA can fine up to 10% of an annual undertaking's turnover. This solidified my outlook of law as limiting exploitation of different classes. A Cambridge lecture on judicial review introduced me to ultra vires in constitutional law, through which I consolidated an understanding via Brexit developments. R (Miller) v The Prime Minister is a clear example of the extension of power beyond limits, against the electorate in favour of Parliament. Hence, I desire to study whether law enables society to function with stability or whether it is simply a social construct that legitimises a permanent hierarchy.

Richard Susskind's *Tomorrow's Lawyers* suggests the dwindling of human involvement in future legal services amidst growth of AI in the legal sector. However, I believe this to be unconvincing as client rapport and commercial awareness, ineffectively exhibited by AI, will constantly remain integral. Attending 'Pathways to Law' lectures at LSE built my knowledge of Tort Law and Contracts and working in the Abu Dhabi office of White & Case allowed me to witness the practical implications of such law through creating resources for infrastructure contractors regarding arbitration and dispute resolution. Participating in the K+ Summer School exposed me to concepts in International Law, such as transitional justice. Extending my research, I wrote an essay supporting the use of IGOs for establishing sustainable peace in post-conflict states versus local attempts at peace-building, given their non-corrupt status and ability to create stable judicial institutions, namely the ICC. Furthermore, writing a legal essay advising parties in a property dispute allowed me to scrutinise each element of the Theft Act, through which I assimilated the cruciality of precise definitions for valid fulfilment of an offence.

Alongside studies, I have maintained a part-time job which has taught me time-management and the ability to balance multiple priorities — highly advantageous for the successful study of law as an academic discipline.

Remarks on Bart's Personal Statement

Bart's personal statement is elegantly written, both in terms of the language used and the substance of the writing itself. Bart's opening is clear:

> *"My enthusiasm for law stems from the way in which it has the power to automatically bind one to society."*

He does an excellent job of examining the relationship between the laws that we must all adhere to and the idea of ceding our sovereignty to a faceless authority. In the process, Bart draws reference to Thomas Hobbes' theory of a social contract, which is a central pillar in understanding where law derives its authority.

Bart's analysis and commentary about the legal case 'United Biscuits (1991)' is deeply illuminating and interesting to read. He demonstrates a nuanced understanding of whether a jaffa cake should be described as a cake or a biscuit, with a perspective that is useful for any law student. He also goes on to mention the concept of ultra vires in constitutional law, as well as offer his opinions on the role that artificial intelligence might play in future legal services. He shows a well-rounded understanding of various facets of law, and writes with aplomb.

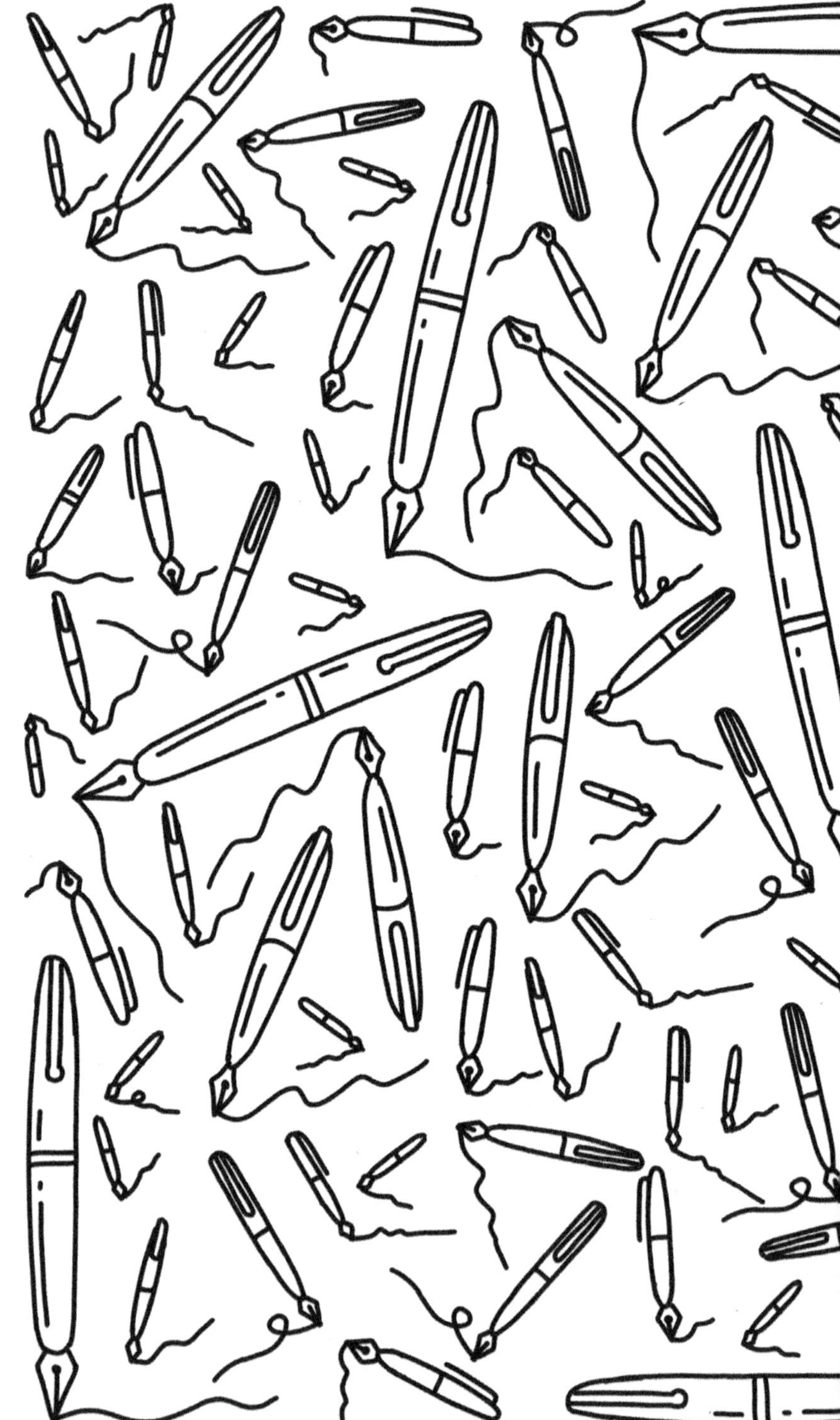

Acknowledgements

Joi Massat
Shanna Siega-Alinson
Layla Shaheen
M. K. Williams
Rob Dircks
Chris Holmwood
David Greenhalgh
Shenley Brook End School
Royal Latin School
Stowe School
Claire Turner
Rosemary Kaye
Jayne Davis
Fifi Hallberg
Evan De Wet
The Hutchins Family
Christian Neale
Kwabena Osei
Demi Kuyoro
Mark Wood
Usama Nazir
Charles Mance
Hayley Louise White
Katie White
Molly Cohen
Yvonne Field
Jason Skyrme
Phoebe Jones
Maebh Howell
Sam Flannery
Elaine Brown
Valerie Washington
A. J. Whittaker
Ryan O'Neill
Greg Centineo
Ricky Waite
Daniela Barata Herrera
Daniel Ingle
Henry Miller
Theo Sergiou
Xin Yue
Abigail Wonga
Anna Steinbrich
Esther Akinn
Harry Oke Osanyintolu
Bill Kemawor
Nina Gamgort
Cari Fletcher
Chloe Pomfret
Alec Hodgson
Thea Leighton
Ethan Mcilwaine
Harry Carlile
Mia Jarvis
Arjun Patel
Brielle Ruggs
Chelsie Angeles
Angela Aggrey
Daniel Dipper
Tahmid Choudhury

Our Services

Gold Package

With our basic service, the 'Gold Package,' we will provide **feedback** on your personal statement or other application document, such as a statement of purpose, motivational letter or Common App essay.

- Feedback
- Unlimited Revisions

Word Count: Up to 1,000
Delivery Time: 2 days

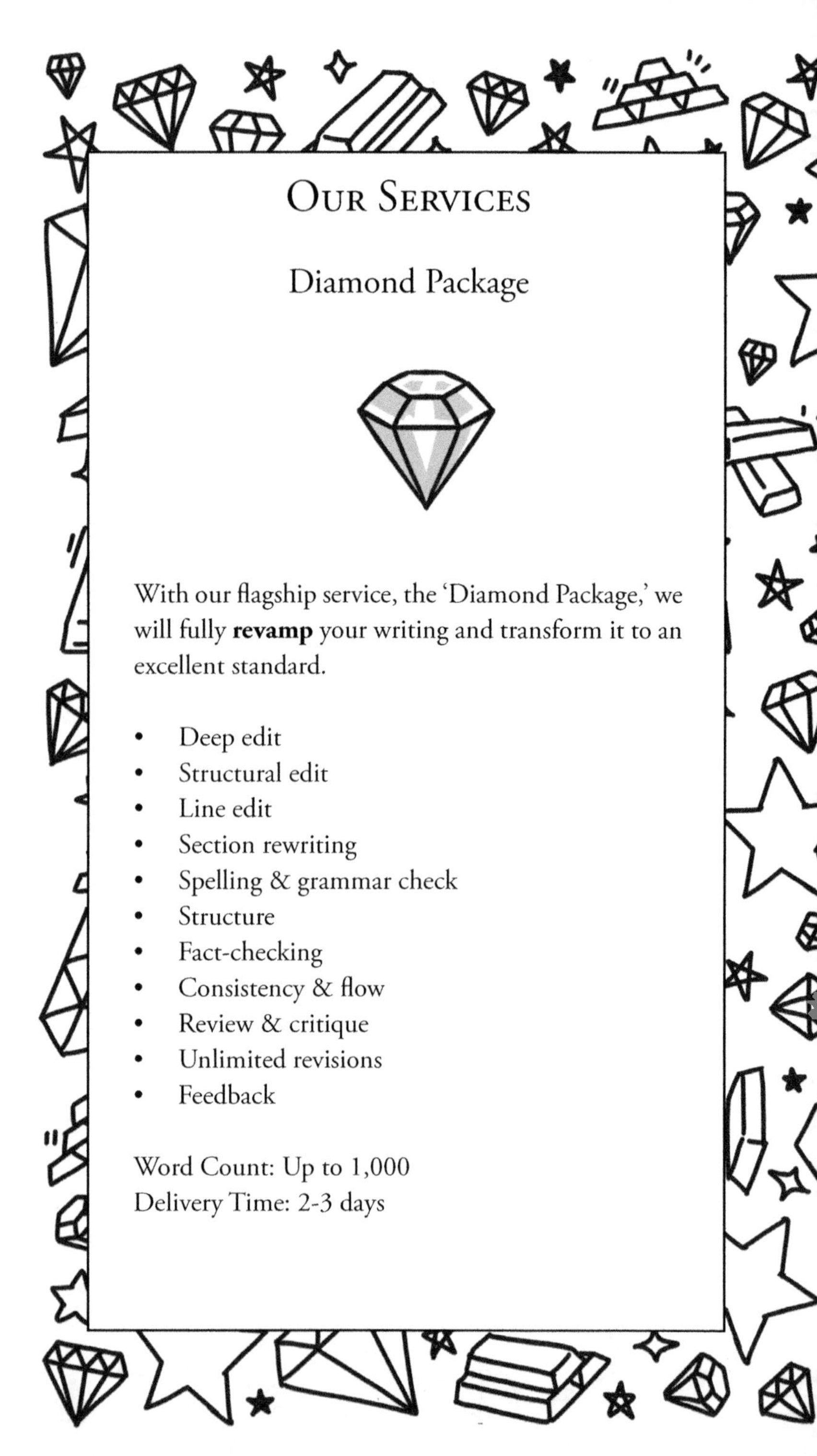

Our Services

Diamond Package

With our flagship service, the 'Diamond Package,' we will fully **revamp** your writing and transform it to an excellent standard.

- Deep edit
- Structural edit
- Line edit
- Section rewriting
- Spelling & grammar check
- Structure
- Fact-checking
- Consistency & flow
- Review & critique
- Unlimited revisions
- Feedback

Word Count: Up to 1,000
Delivery Time: 2-3 days

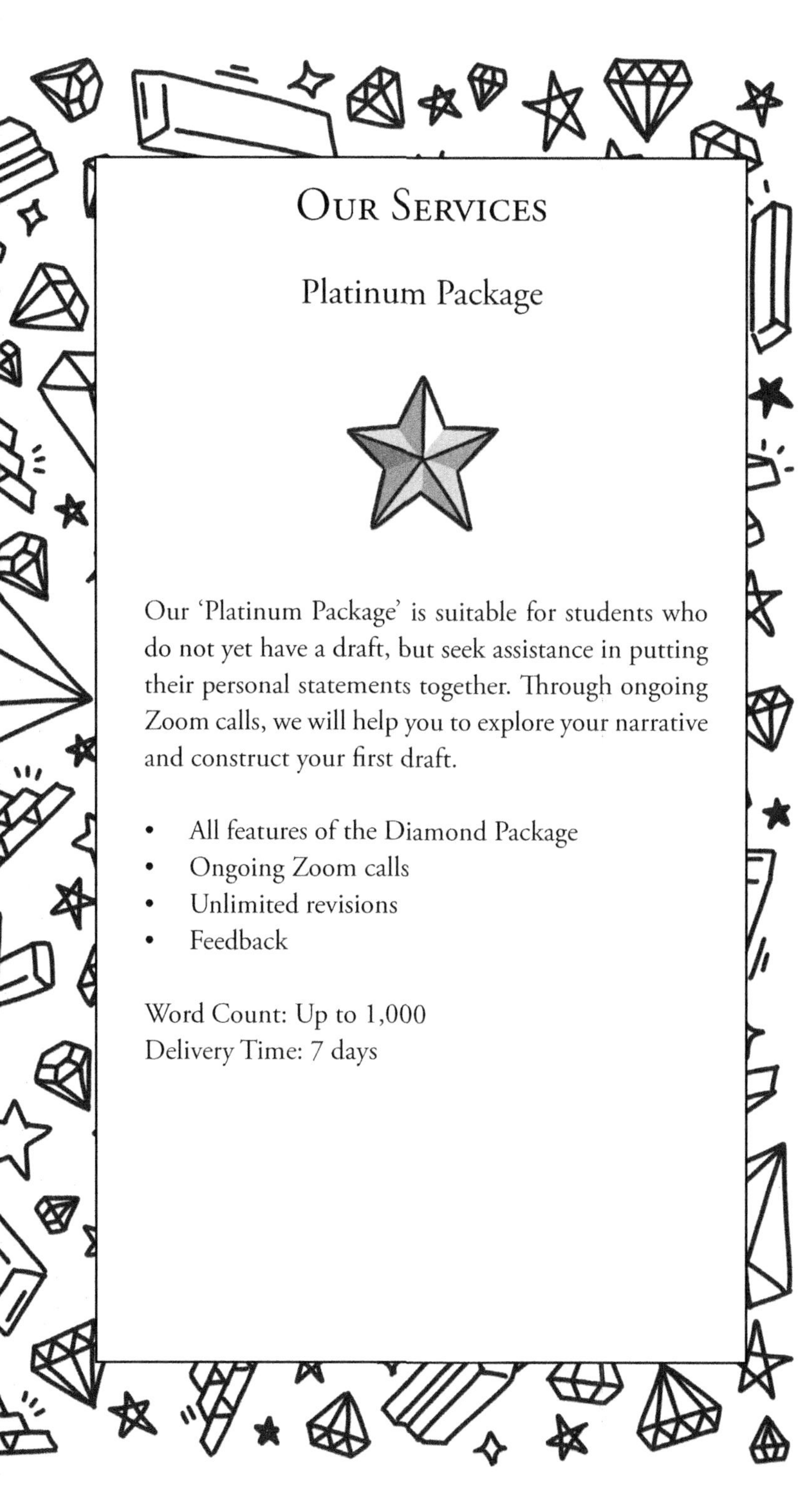

Our Services

Platinum Package

Our 'Platinum Package' is suitable for students who do not yet have a draft, but seek assistance in putting their personal statements together. Through ongoing Zoom calls, we will help you to explore your narrative and construct your first draft.

- All features of the Diamond Package
- Ongoing Zoom calls
- Unlimited revisions
- Feedback

Word Count: Up to 1,000
Delivery Time: 7 days

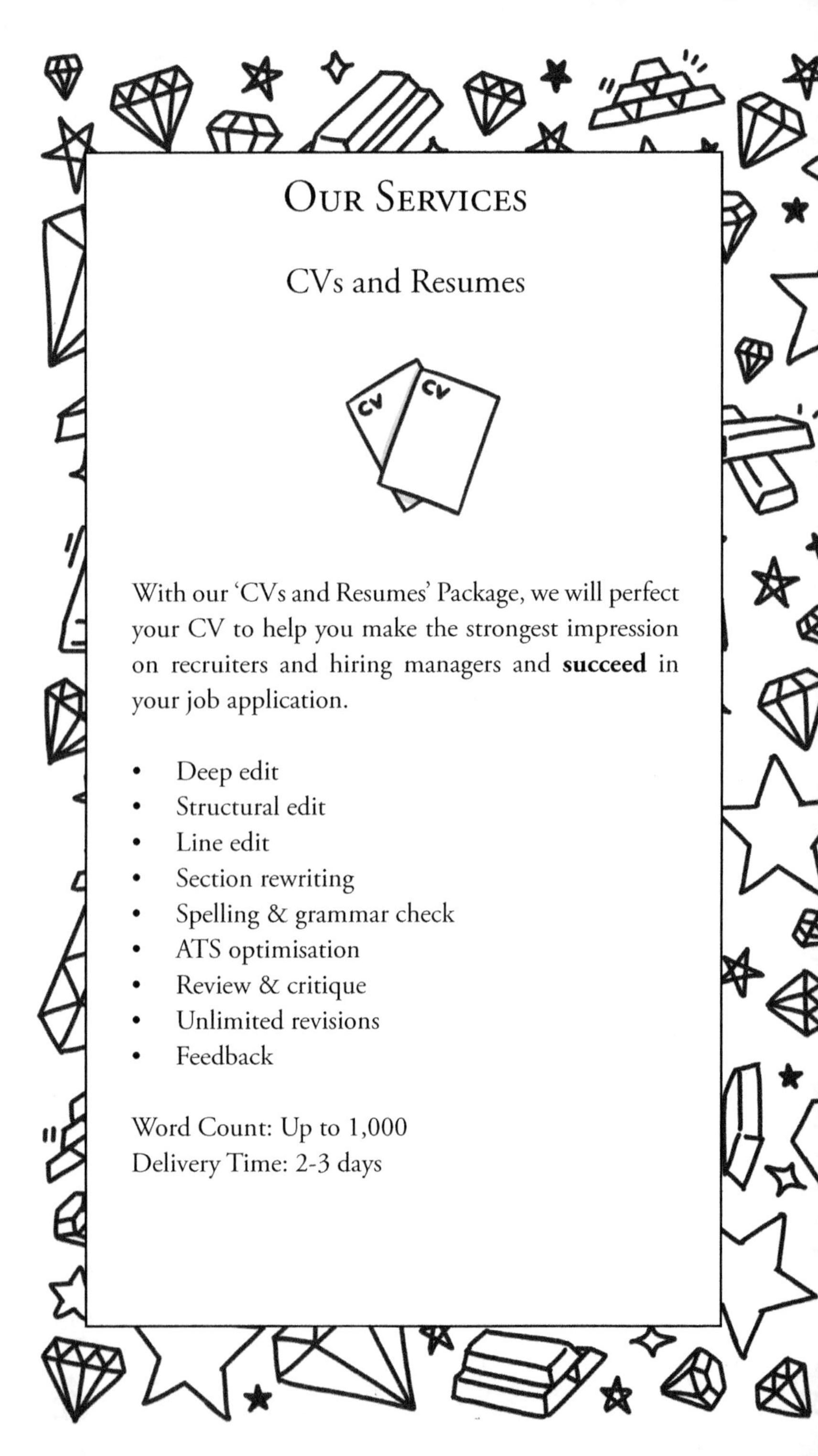

Our Services

CVs and Resumes

With our 'CVs and Resumes' Package, we will perfect your CV to help you make the strongest impression on recruiters and hiring managers and **succeed** in your job application.

- Deep edit
- Structural edit
- Line edit
- Section rewriting
- Spelling & grammar check
- ATS optimisation
- Review & critique
- Unlimited revisions
- Feedback

Word Count: Up to 1,000
Delivery Time: 2-3 days

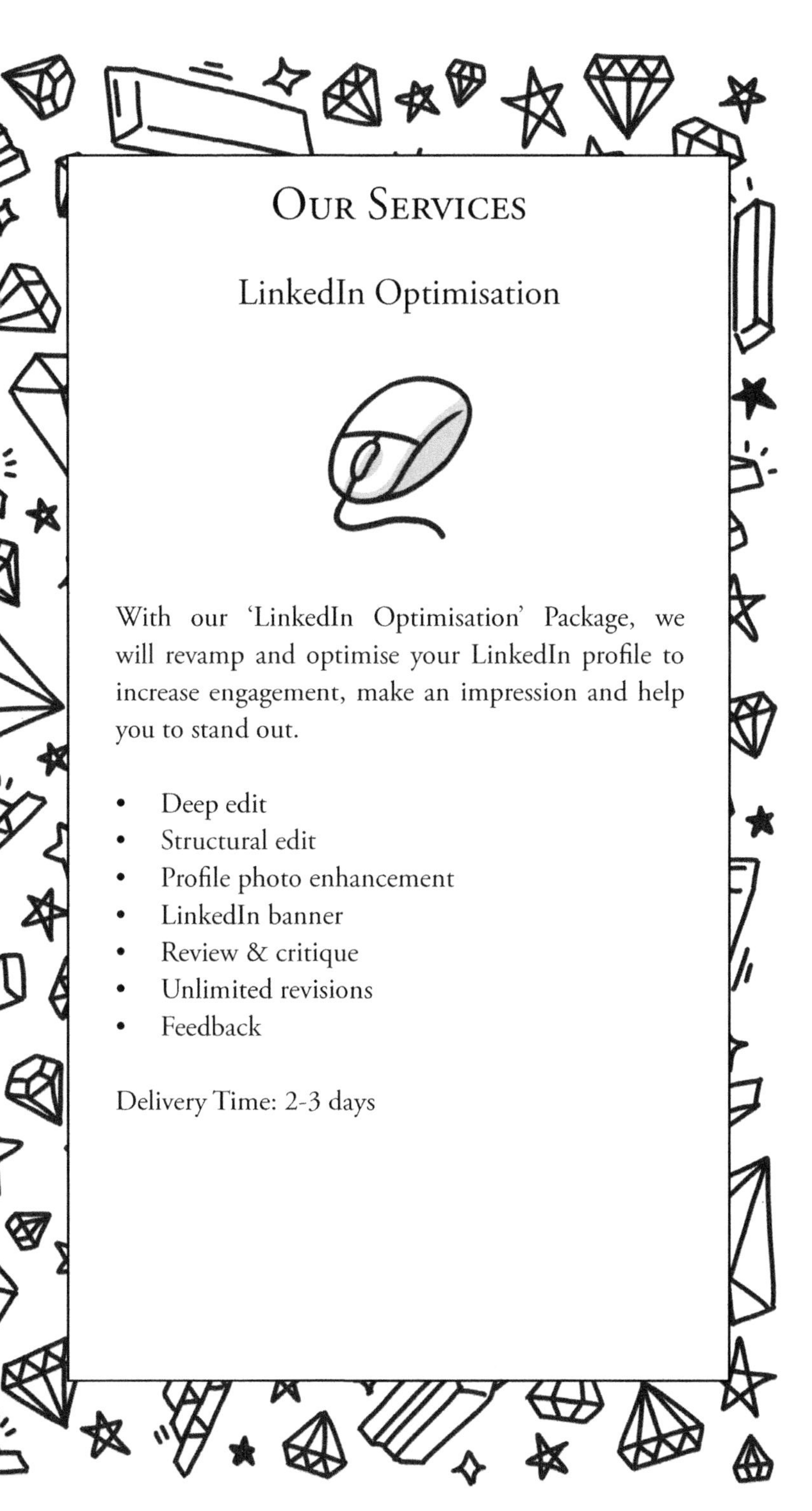

Our Services

LinkedIn Optimisation

With our 'LinkedIn Optimisation' Package, we will revamp and optimise your LinkedIn profile to increase engagement, make an impression and help you to stand out.

- Deep edit
- Structural edit
- Profile photo enhancement
- LinkedIn banner
- Review & critique
- Unlimited revisions
- Feedback

Delivery Time: 2-3 days

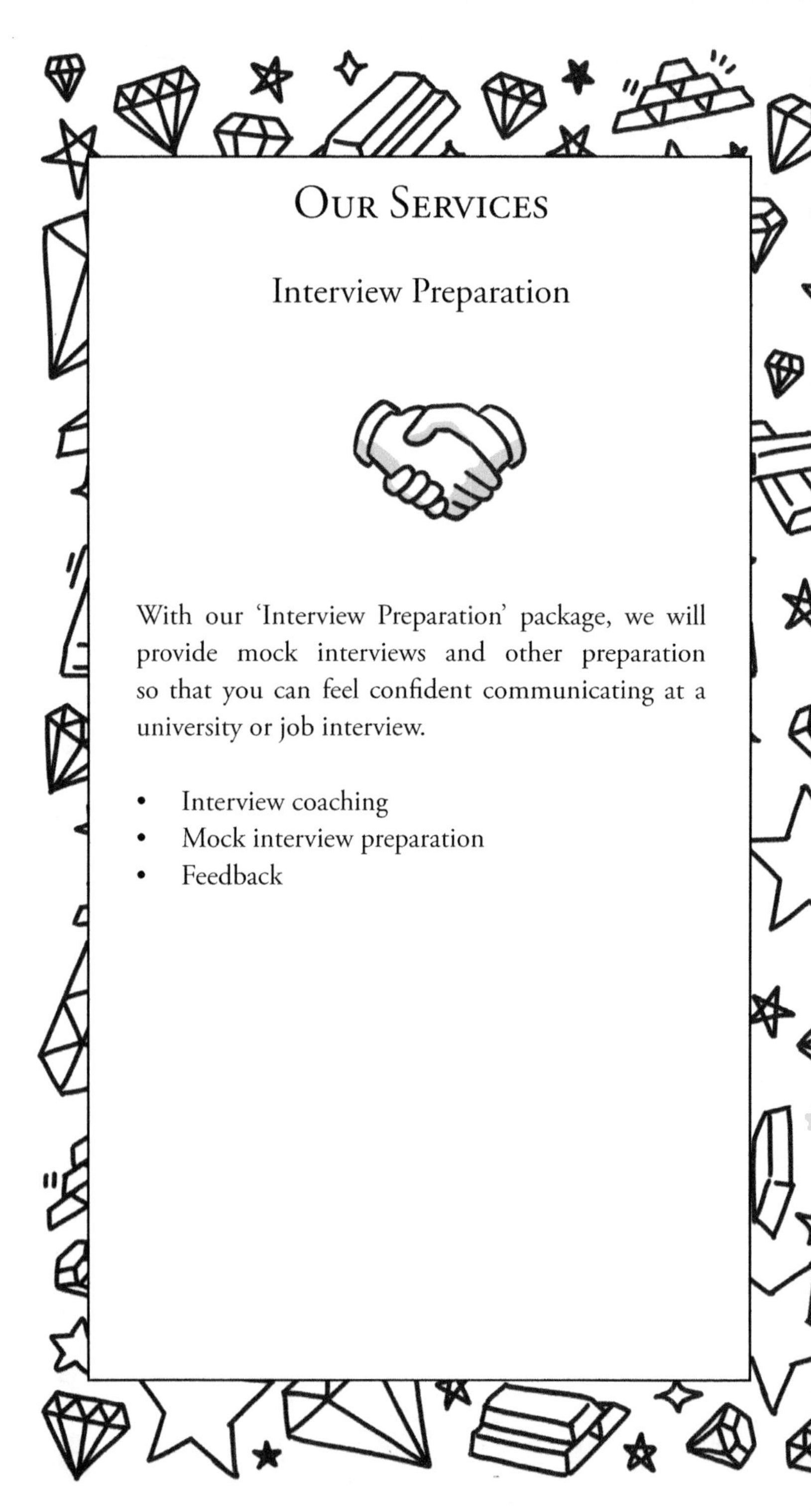

Our Services

Interview Preparation

With our 'Interview Preparation' package, we will provide mock interviews and other preparation so that you can feel confident communicating at a university or job interview.

- Interview coaching
- Mock interview preparation
- Feedback

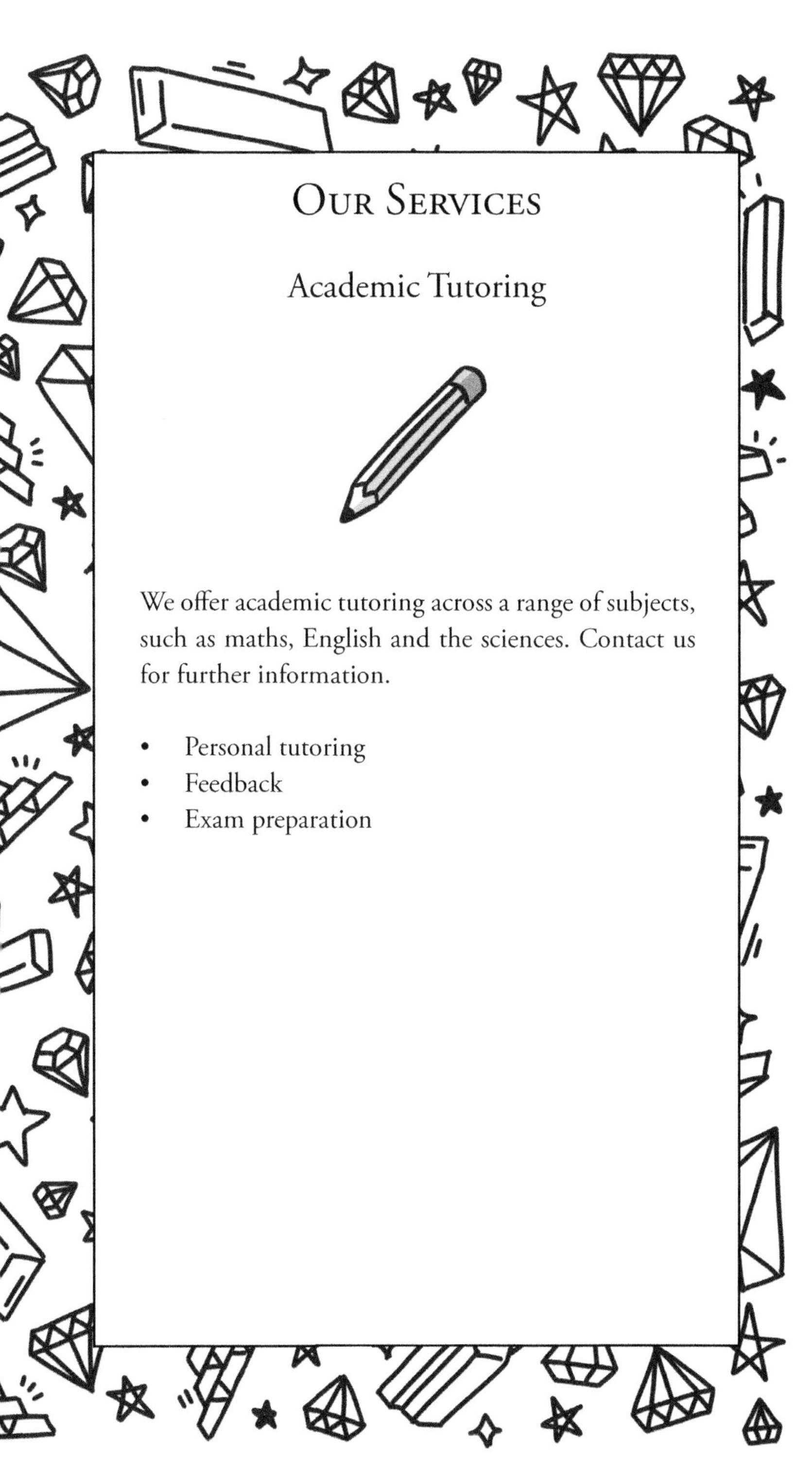

Our Services

Academic Tutoring

We offer academic tutoring across a range of subjects, such as maths, English and the sciences. Contact us for further information.

- Personal tutoring
- Feedback
- Exam preparation

Reviews for PlaceCoach

"Just received my offer from a prestigious university. PlaceCoach is the real deal. They took my personal statement and CV and gave them the polish they needed to shine. If you're reading this, stop reading and order now. You won't regret it."

*

"PlaceCoach has been an excellent resource in my MBA applications. They helped me to completely transform my statement of purpose. My mentor had the empathy and intelligence to understand my story and give it an incredible facelift. I highly recommend using their services because they're highly considerate, flexible, and polite. They will work with you until you're delighted with the results."

*

"PlaceCoach has gotten me to a point where I am competing in admissions in a T40 law school. Not only was my work proofread and edited very quickly, it was done with care and professionalism to the highest degree I've ever seen. I will always refer back to PlaceCoach from here on out, and highly recommend anyone who is keen on having a strong admissions application to seek PlaceCoach. Thank you very much. Looking forward to seeing you again soon."

Reviews for PlaceCoach

"Simply amazing. PlaceCoach edited and revised my law school personal statement to absolute perfection. This is Ivy League tier work. Not only did PlaceCoach proofread, edit, and revise my personal statement, they also filled in the missing gaps that made my personal statement fall short from being A-tier work. Thank you so much! Because of your help I can feel confident with my personal statement. I highly recommend them to anyone who feels that their personal statement, while good, can use that extra push to make their personal statement shine. I have majored in English, and I am applying for law school, but this edit has made my jaw drop."

*

"PlaceCoach went above and beyond to help with the application process! They went out of their way to help with some aspects that were not included in the original package. I am truly grateful for their collaboration, and would definitely recommend them!"

*

"Great writing skills and easy to communicate with. They catered to my needs and followed specific instructions. I wish I could write like my mentor. You will be relieved and assured when you receive the delivery."

Reviews for PlaceCoach

"Simply the best. My mentor has a talent and it is always an honor to get the chance of working with them. Exceeds expectations every time!!"

*

"I worked with PlaceCoach to modify my document and I must say, it was professional. They took the time to understand my needs and then modified the document carefully. I appreciated the level of personalisation provided, which made a difference in the final product. I would highly recommend PlaceCoach for all your modification needs."

*

"PlaceCoach was very accommodating and communicative! I very much appreciated their insight and felt that the quality of writing improved what I was trying to convey. I highly recommend this service and will use them again in the future should I need something reviewed, or help in organizing my thoughts. Thanks PlaceCoach!"

*

"The favorite writer. I will recommend the service to anyone who needs perfect and quality personal statements."

Reviews for PlaceCoach

"Definitely worth it! PlaceCoach's edit was pretty much a surprise for me. The vocabulary and sentences are enhanced. The paragraphs are restructured. And so much more. I love it!"

*

"I had a great experience working with PlaceCoach. They proofread my CV, gave me valuable feedback and advice, and were always willing to help me with the improvements. I highly recommend their services."

*

"PlaceCoach helped me improve my personal statement to apply for a master's course. My mentor was very easy-going and easy to work with. Additionally, PlaceCoach is highly dedicated to making sure you get the best value from their service! I highly recommend PlaceCoach!"

*

"Attentive and clear communication during the whole transaction. With a knack for writing, PlaceCoach will help you drastically improve your statement of purpose. I could not recommend them enough for college applicants!"

Reviews for PlaceCoach

"My mentor is an outstanding writer and really improved the flow of my personal statement. They had some experience in my area of study and knew exactly what to add. Would definitely recommend for personal statements at U.S. institutions!"

*

"Pure perfection and exactly what I was looking for. I wanted a unique voice and an improved and more convincing text, and couldn't have asked for more. Thank you, and I will definitely be returning in the future!"

*

"PlaceCoach is such a life saver. The writing is outstanding and they understood what I wanted to express, and did it in a way that I could never exceed. 100% recommend!"

*

"My PlaceCoach Mentor was very friendly and approachable, and I enjoyed communicating with him. The style of editing was natural, beautiful, and convincing. The language was also beautifully polished, which surprised me. The revision was incredibly detailed, with many structural adjustments. Thank you very much indeed."

Reviews for PlaceCoach

"This is the second time in less than a month that I have chosen PlaceCoach and I have complete trust in their delivery. Everything has been satisfactory and hopefully, with their help I will receive the offer of my choice!"

*

"I am truly thankful for all the comments and thorough feedback. They were far more helpful and encouraging than what I expected. I am fully satisfied with my introduction now. I wish that I worked with you from the start before using all my proofreading budget on other sites. I will ask for your services in the future."

*

"PlaceCoach consistently surpasses my expectations! I will never look to another editing service."

*

"For the millionth time, PlacecCach went above and beyond. Even at the peak of deadline season, PlaceCoach delivered superb work. You will not regret paying for these services. My deepest gratitude."

Reviews for PlaceCoach

"My mentor knew exactly how to write a personal statement or a statement of purpose! The language used in the edit is something I can not mimic. The structure overall was edited flawlessly, and helped me a lot with my final draft. Now I am ready to submit applications."

*

"Amazing essay editing with a keen eye for organization and vocabulary use. Very easy to communicate with and responsive, with equally as good unlimited revisions after the fact. Could not be happier with how this essay turned out. Glad I took the time to choose this service."

*

"Working with PlaceCoach was amazing! It felt like we built a friendship over the past 11 days! Very patient and reassuring especially when I felt overwhelmed with the process. I would definitely recommend and use their services again!"

*

"My mentor is a wonderful writer, and has a friendly attitude with fabulous work! I never thought that my personal statement could be written in this way. If you want a good response, choose PlaceCoach!"

Reviews for PlaceCoach

**"Do not hesitate to place your order! I was feeling all sorts of grad school application anxiety, but using PlaceCoach has placed me greatly at ease! My essay was a mess before PlaceCoach came and made it into an essay I want to read over and over! You will not regret it."*

*

"I would 100% recommend PlaceCoach to anybody who's looking for a holistic rewriting and editing service."

*

"Exceptional service. The rewriting was precisely what I needed. PlaceCoach took my work, edited it, and added more punch, improving my delivery immensely. Thank you."

*

"I'm from Indonesia and I'm glad to have used PlaceCoach's services for my scholarship essay. My mentor is a really talented writer! They fixed and perfected every aspect of my draft. They were so invested in my essay and tried to create additional value in my writing. Besides their writing, they were really communicative with me! So don't hesitate to request or ask for any queries. You will be helped a lot through their service and it will be worth every penny."

Reviews for PlaceCoach

"PlaceCoach is SUPERB, just as many other reviewers mentioned. I've tried other similar services, but PlaceCoach is the best. You have got nothing to lose, but everything to gain."

*

"Phenomenal help with an amazingly positive vibe! Would recommend PlaceCoach to everyone! The support and positivity coming from them makes the statement writing even better and less of a dread! 100% recommend ."

*

"PlaceCoach has a special gift! I can't begin to express how much they go above and beyond to complete the task! Truly gifted! I wholeheartedly endorse!"

*

"PlaceCoach were friendly, personable and beyond accommodating! Even when I went MIA because of school, they always made sure to reach out and check on me! Their policy of unlimited edits makes a huge difference and gave me the confidence that they wouldn't stop until I was satisfied! I can say that I am really happy with what they have provided me and can't wait to use them in the future! Thank you again PlaceCoach! You made my life simpler and filled with less anxiety!"

Reviews for PlaceCoach

"There's no way you can bump the quality of your personal statement like PlaceCoach does. Seriously, they turned my poor essay into a wonderful one. Do not expect only minor vocab modification — expect more! They literally restructured my essay when necessary, meaning that they fully understood my idea and points. I'm definitely going to reach out to them for my other university applications."

*

"Perfection at your fingertips! If you're looking for someone to perfect your work, look no further. PlaceCoach went above and beyond with my order. My jaw literally dropped as I read my essay. I turned in something jumbled and wordy and he turned it into a masterpiece. They created imagery that took my paper from blah to something I can brag about!!!"

*

"They are the best of the best, and worthy of the price, even over. My mentor was so professional and productive. I will definitely recommend them to my friends."

*

"PlaceCoach did an amazing job. They will make your paper flow in a cohesive and organized way. Trust me, you won't regret their work."

Reviews for PlaceCoach

"PlaceCoach is a wonderful service. They absolutely deserve this review, as they are the best for writing. My mentor was like a friend, always available to answer my questions, and professional and friendly. I will surely choose them again if I need another order."

*

"PlaceCoach did it again! You can tell by their work that they throughly enjoy their craft. This is my second time using PlaceCoach and I'll be back again. They show great detail that takes an 'ok' essay and brings it to life! Look no further, this is the service for you!"

*

"This was the second time I worked with PlaceCoach as my paperwork covered three different research areas, and they were very patient in reviewing it and gave a lot of useful advice. Thank you very much for your guidance."

*

"Wow! That was a great modification, PlaceCoach! After his deep revision, the PS became more incredibly convincing and sincere. He could not have been more supportive during my anxious application season. I'm genuinely grateful for his help and hope to receive my dream offer."

Reviews for PlaceCoach

"PlaceCoach provided me with different versions and very simple clarifications that helped me to improve my first steps of building my resume for future career opportunities. They were punctual, very detailed, and delivered before the expected date."

*

"This was very well done. I had ordered for only a review of my UCAS personal statement, but I also got the grammatical errors and spelling mistakes corrected. The positive feedback also made me feel more confident for my application, as I am an Oxford applicant. Overall, it was quite the service I needed for my personal statement."

*

"PlaceCoach is highly competent. Not only did my mentor have outstanding writing skills, but what's truly remarkable is how he thinks ahead of me by bringing significant additions to my personal statement. I really appreciate the thought, the time and the effort that he put into helping my personal pursuit. I will definitely recommend PlaceCoach to others."

Reviews for PlaceCoach

"PlaceCoach's revision startled me, the paraphrasing and restructuring of the whole document not only fit my purpose very well, but also led me to focus on points that can really help my statement stand out, and avoid redundancy. Great experience!"

*

"My PlaceCoach Mentor was like a friend — very communicative and amazing at his work. I had a great time talking with him and working on my project. He never said no to any of my requests and I provided him with a lot of suggestions/information, and he incorporated them very well, and took into consideration each one of them. He is very sweet and hard working. Available for you all the time. He is a good human. The work is very professional and beautiful. I was blown away by the words he used in my essays. They were very good. I bugged him with a lot of queries too and he always answered them without getting frustrated. So if anyone wants an excellent service, reach out to PlaceCoach!"

*

"PlaceCoach helped me to edit and proofread my recommendation letters. They really did a great job and delivered them before the deadline. They also helped me to modify the format to make the letter look more formal. I really like their work! Thank you!"

Reviews for PlaceCoach

"The perfect edit!!! This is exactly what I wanted and PlaceCoach accomplished it so well. They really paid careful attention to the content and made it better. And they really understood what I was trying to say and rewrote it in an excellent way. Thanks so much for your help, and I think I will contact you again if I have a similar need."

*

"It has been amazing to work with PlaceCoach. They have been trustful, very dedicated and professional, and willing to help me in the different parts of my application. I love to work with such a great person and professional. They supported me in finishing the essay, and they care about the delivery of the best possible work, no matter the number of revisions. We reviewed the document so many times until it was made perfect. That was great along with their patience and care of the documents. Thank you so much, PlaceCoach. You are the best!!"

*

"As an American, I had no idea how much weight personal statements carry for UK university admissions. I didn't want to risk my one shot. PlaceCoach had me covered. I'm so happy with the final result. Definitely worth it, as I received an unconditional offer."

Reviews for PlaceCoach

"This editor is wonderful! They were able to edit a statement in a professional matter that flows perfectly. Besides edits, you can ask questions about certain parts of the essay and what works well and what doesn't. They have great insights and catch all the minute details that go into editing. They are also very understanding and will help you with any time constraints you have. I am very grateful for choosing PlaceCoach and I am excited to work with them again if the time ever comes!"

*

"PlaceCoach turned my fairly average personal statement into something so professional and mesmerising to read . Truly incredible work! I would highly recommend them to anyone out there who is looking to enhance their personal statement. They were very easy to work with and made things so simple for me, and they were so friendly and on time with the delivery. Again, I would highly recommend this service to anyone."

*

"Incredible work! PlaceCoach truly brought my vision to life. Thank you so much. I would highly recommend working with them. I wish I contacted place coach much earlier on!"

Reviews for PlaceCoach

"What distinguishes PlaceCoach from others is that PlaceCoach actually goes the extra mile to do research about the programme that you are applying to. This was a pleasant surprise to me. They incorporated new information in my statement of purpose to make it sound more developed. They also responded very quickly and did revisions based on my comments. I highly recommend PlaceCoach!"

*

"Placecoach is the best in the business. I know from experience how hard it is to find reliable and qualified writing help. Traditional proofreaders and literature writers are no longer enough when you need academic prose and familiarity with other disciplines like law. Now I rely on PlaceCoach whenever I want to submit work I can be proud of. Their skills extend beyond spelling and punctuation corrections to improving layout, structuring, and clarifying viewpoints, improving language and constructing arguments tailored to you. My experience with PlaceCoach has been very positive. They were highly responsive and produced high quality work. I would recommend him without hesitation."

*

"PlaceCoach is the best. If you get the chance to work with him, do not throw the opportunity away; you will definitely regret it."

Reviews for PlaceCoach

"After working on my personal statement essay for days on end, it was definitely worth the money to have someone proofread and revise my essay from a completely objective unbiased perspective. I feel so much more confident in my essay now, and that reassurance and peace of mind is, in my opinion, absolutely invaluable. I will highly recommend PlaceCoach to anyone it may be of value to from here on out."

*

"PlaceCoach was absolutely amazing!! They were really communicative, friendly and knew how to rewrite the essay, thereby making it 100 times better. They also listened to my concerns and were fast to address them. I would highly recommend them, as they have exceeded my expectations! Thank you PlaceCoach!"

*

"In the revision of my personal statement, PlaceCoach not only helped me to point out and correct deficiencies in my wording and logic, but also helped me to make extensive rewrites (including additions and deletions). The opening paragraph was perfect. And, as always, PlaceCoach was excellent in revising my recommendation letter view, and was very professional."

Reviews for PlaceCoach

"You get what you pay for. Quality work, punctual delivery and great communication. Writing a statement of purpose could be a nightmare, because it is one of the prominent documents that can make or break your admission chances. I am sure that PlaceCoach will help you out, and with unlimited revisions!!! You can't go wrong."

*

"PlaceCoach was an amazing help with revamping and developing my personal statement. With their expertise, they helped with transforming my personal statement to be better suited for admissions. Thank you very much for your help. It was great to work wiht you."

*

"PlaceCoach did an amazing job at clarifying sentences in my personal statement that might have sounded confusing. They will make your personal statement flow in a cohesive and organized way. Trust me, you won't regret their work."

*

"My PlaceCoach Mentor was very patient and helped me. Working with them made me feel at ease during the application process. They are very professional and meticulous in polishing the documents. I hope to have the opportunity to cooperate with them in the future!"

Reviews for PlaceCoach

"This guy is a boss! You can be sure that when you ask him to do a task, he will do it perfectly and really quick!"

*

"PlaceCoach is easily one of the best editors you can find for personal statements. They give a whole new perspective and structure to your essay and are also very kind in accepting all your suggestions for improving your writing."

*

"Thank you very much for your work. It is amazing, and I cannot find a fault in this. I appreciate everything. All the best, and I will connect with you in the future."

*

"I wanna say thank you! The beginning of my personal statement is edited just like a novel! I feel so surprised! Based on my draft, there are so many advanced vocabularies used in the edition! Looking forward to the next cooperation!"

*

"You're going to adore the services PlaceCoach offers. The way to handle and talk with customers is another thing I want to mention about this service. Thanks a lot!"

Reviews for PlaceCoach

"Hello all! You don't need to go anywhere else for help, Placecoach is unbelievable and I don't exaggerate. Their revisions and total revamping of a letter of recommendation I needed to make, was perfect and exactly as I requested! They understood what I needed right away and I cannot recommend them enough!"

*

"PlaceCoach really did an amazing job! They not only proofread my order, but also looked through everything and made sure it was outstanding for personal statement. Definitely worth every penny that I've spent."

*

"PlaceCoach is the best editing service I have ever had. They helped me to convey my ideas in the most perfect way, and they also helped me to reorganize my thoughts and make my paper more organized. I highly recommend PlaceCoach."

*

"The highest quality service at the most affordable price. If you need your personal statement edited, you should definitely use PlaceCoach! They edited my personal statement in great detail. The response was also very timely, and the revision after the delivery of services also fulfilled my needs! I'm sure they won't let you down!"

Reviews for PlaceCoach

"PlaceCoach has transformed my piece of writing from a mediocre one to a professional, yet genuine one. They also did some extra research for me to put in my statement, so it is more well-rounded and sincere. I am more confident that my statement of interest can get me into the university that I want!"

*

"Love this guy. His work is amazing. I actually ended up approving the very first work delivery — everything was that good. Also he is a very kind and understanding fellow. He made me sound so intelligent :). I feel lucky that I found him."

*

"I recommend PlaceCoach when you need to edit your documents, such as your resume and cover letter. They will communicate well and do an excellent job. They helped me when I needed to submit my application within a day. I very much appreciate their willingness to help. Thank you."

*

"Great work! Really helped my SOP go to the next level. Great writer, I appreciate the writing skills PlaceCoach put into making my MBA SOP sound professional and inspiring."

Reviews for PlaceCoach

"Do not hesitate to choose PlaceCoach. They have an attention to detail and the writing is energetic, clear, and vivid. They are professional and finish the work at the agreed time. Thank you very much PlaceCoach for my personal statement."

*

"I highly recommend PlaceCoach's editing services. Their services allowed me to take my personal statement to the next level. As medical and dental applications cost so much to submit, it is well worth the additional money to have PlaceCoach give your statement a second look over so that your application is as pristine as can be! Money well spent. Thank you PlaceCoach for the affordable and fast service!"

*

"It was like they appeared in the moment when I needed them the most. They are the best admission consultant I have ever had. They really supported me in the process to make this document shine. They made the relevant corrections and revisions to the document with great accuracy and understanding, even when the topics were quite technical. They are patient, understanding and very responsive. My PlaceCoach Mentor was great at this job and as a person too! Thank you so much for all your support! You are the Best!"

Reviews for PlaceCoach

"PlaceCoach is an amazing editing service. They did an amazing job with my secondary essays and I feel fully confident in submitting these essays edited by PlaceCoach to my dream schools. I will continue to use this service with my other secondaries as well. Thank you!"

*

"PlaceCoach was a tremendous help in getting my personal statement to sound professional! My essay was all over the place and did not flow. They made all the difference in the world by communicating my points more clearly, tightening it, and enhancing it in areas that were necessary. Thank you so much, PlaceCoach!"

*

"PlaceCoach has been an excellent resource in my MBA applications journey. They helped me completely transform my statement of purpose within 24 hours. My PlaceCoach Mentor had the empathy and intelligence to understand my story and give it an incredible facelift. I highly recommend using their services because they're highly considerate, flexible, and polite. They will work with you until you're delighted with the results."

Reviews for PlaceCoach

"PlaceCoach truly helped to convey my message within my personal statement clearly. I had been struggling for days with how I wanted to approach my statement and their help truly made a world of a difference. The feedback was very timely and they still plan to help me with any further revisions. I definitely would recommend this service to others!"

*

"I can not express in words how fortunate and happy I am to find PlaceCoach! They transformed my very rough PS to a PS that I can be proud and confident in submitting. Not only were they accommodating and personable, they truly want you to succeed as an applicant. I highly recommend PlaceCoach!"

*

"Delivery of my order was prompt. It didn't feel like it was merely a business transaction for PlaceCoach. It felt like I was getting help from someone I actually know. I really appreciate the feedback they gave me. They helped me to organize my flow and structure really well. I'm now confident with the personal statement that I will use for the schools that I'm applying to."

Reviews for PlaceCoach

"PlaceCoach really did a great job. They helped modify the whole structure and content and also answered lots of application questions. They always told me no hurry and no pressure to close the order."

*

"I was facing difficulty with structuring my essay and maintaining it within the word limit. PlaceCoach has modified it really well and I was very satisfied with the final outcome of my SOP. Would definitely recommend to anybody struggling with the same issues."

*

"I took PlaceCoach's help for my law school personal statement. They were incredibly helpful and provided me with detailed feedback on my work. They also advised me on the strategies I could use to improve my personal statement. My PlaceCoach Mentor had an immense knowledge of the admission process in different countries. They replied quickly and it was an amazing experience to work with them."

*

"Went above and beyond to help with the application process! Even went out of their way to help with some aspects which were not included in the price at all. Truly grateful for the collaboration, would definitely recommend!"

Reviews for PlaceCoach

"It has been an absolute pleasure working with PlaceCoach. I will definitely come back, and would 100% recommend. They have been patient with me throughout the whole process and accepted multiple revisions. Thank you so much for all your help and hard work. All the best."

*

"This has to be the best editing service I have ever used. PlaceCoach tried at first to understand my background and my requirements to make sure that I was representing myself clearly in my statement. Always prompt in delivering work and will go out of their way to offer more than you pay for. I am very satisfied."

*

"I absolutely loved the result, PlaceCoach makes your personal statement sound really professional and creates a smooth line to read it and show your intentions. Glad I found this, really good service."

*

"PlaceCoach is totally an angel to a student tortured by the application deadlines. Great language, great style, and a considerate service! The most important to me is that they gave me advice on logic and structure, and I can see that they were dedicated to the edition with thorough thinking."

HOW TO WRITE AN EXCELLENT PERSONAL STATEMENT

An Illustrated Guide

on Writing a University or College Admissions Essay

Written by Quincy Washington

Illustrated by M. W. K. Asror

STORYBUSH BOOKS

HOW TO WRITE AN EXCELLENT PERSONAL STATEMENT

An Illustrated Guide

on Writing a University or College Admissions Essay

Printed in Great Britain
by Amazon

56067877R00300